Thanks for supporting the book!

Rising from Katrina

Kathleen Koch

Rising
from Katrina

*How My Mississippi Hometown Lost It All
and Found What Mattered*

Kathleen Koch

Foreword by CNN's Anderson Cooper

JOHN F. BLAIR
PUBLISHER
Winston-Salem, North Carolina

JOHN F. BLAIR
PUBLISHER
1406 Plaza Drive
Winston-Salem, North Carolina 27103
www.blairpub.com

Manufactured in the United States of America

JACKET IMAGES

CNN producer Janet Rodriguez and the author with the residents of the Second Street Elementary School shelter
COURTESY OF JANET RODRIGUEZ / CNN

Plaintive plea at a former Bay St. Louis homesite
PHOTOGRAPH BY JOHN WILKERSON

A portion of the proceeds from this book will be donated to Pneuma Winds of Hope and LESM Coast Recovery Camps, two nonprofit groups working on the Katrina recovery effort in Bay St. Louis.

Library of Congress Cataloging-in-Publication Data

Koch, Kathleen, 1959-
  Rising from Katrina : how my Mississippi hometown lost it all and found what mattered / by Kathleen Koch ; foreword by Anderson Cooper.
      p.   cm.
  Includes bibliographical references and index.
  ISBN 978-0-89587-383-5 (hardcover : alk. paper)—ISBN 978-0-89587-384-2 (pbk. : alk. paper)—ISBN 978-0-89587-390-3 1. Bay Saint Louis (Miss.)—History—21st century. 2. Bay Saint Louis (Miss.)—Social conditions—21st century. 3. Bay Saint Louis (Miss.)—Social live and customs—21st century. 4. Hurricane Katrina, 2005—Social aspects—Mississippi—Bay Saint Louis. 5. Disaster relief—Mississippi—Bay Saint Louis. 6. Koch, Kathleen, 1959- 7. Bay Saint Louis (Miss.)—Biography. 8. Women journalists—United States—Biography. I. Title.
  F349.B39K63 2010
  976.2'14—dc22
                            2010015462

DESIGN BY DEBRA LONG HAMPTON
MAP BY MIKE MARTIN

To Mom and Dad,

who taught me anything is possible if I put my mind to it

Contents

Foreword

THOSE FIRST FEW DAYS AFTER KATRINA came ashore, I was in Mississippi on the Gulf Coast. I'd been in Baton Rouge, Louisiana, when the storm hit, and had followed it to Meridian, Mississippi, later that night. By the next morning, the hurricane had passed. While searching for gas, I met a woman who said I should go to Waveland. "It's a small town," she told me, "and I haven't heard any news about it." Small towns often get passed over on big stories, but of course a hurricane doesn't make such narrow-minded judgments. I took the woman's advice and headed for the coast. When I got to Waveland, a FEMA search-and-rescue squad was just beginning its work. It was searching for the dead, and it found plenty.

I stayed in Waveland for several days before heading to New Orleans. I will never forget what I saw there, and in Bay St. Louis, and in Gulfport, and all along the Mississippi Gulf Coast. I'd spend the day driving around, talking to survivors, shooting stories. At night on the air, broadcasting for CNN, I'd hear politicians thank one another, talking about the tremendous relief effort that was under way and what an unprecedented, unpredictable disaster this was. It was stunning. Katrina may have been unprecedented, but it certainly wasn't unpredicted.

In Mississippi in the days after the storm, the silence was shocking. There was little heavy earthmoving equipment, few trucks with aid rumbling past. I'd stand in a field of timber that once was a street and hear the wind blow through the remains of people's lives—a sheet of plastic caught in a tree would rustle in the breeze, flies would buzz over the corpse of a dog. A few seconds' intrusion, then silence once again.

Katrina touched all of us in different ways. My dad was from Mississippi, and we'd visited the Gulf Coast together when I was little. Those of us with ties to Mississippi found it impossible not to see the past in the present. Kathleen Koch saw it all around her as she reported from Mississippi. She'd lived in Bay St. Louis. She had memories there—friends, too.

People would come up to reporters in those dark, difficult days and say, "Don't let them forget about us." It always made me incredibly sad. The idea that our fellow citizens had to ask not to be forgotten.

It's been five years now, and much of what happened along the Mississippi Gulf Coast threatens to be forgotten. There have been other disasters since, other headlines that have captured the nation's attention. But for the people along the coast, the storm winds still blow. There has been rebuilding and rebirth, but there is still much to be done.

Kathleen Koch saw it all firsthand and made sure the world saw what was happening to the town and the people she knew so well. It's been five years, but Kathleen has continued to follow what's happened in that town, and to those people. In these pages, she tells their story and her own deeply personal one. A story of survival and resilience, courage and compassion. It is a story none of us should ever forget.

Anderson Cooper, anchor of CNN's *AC360°*

Rising from Katrina

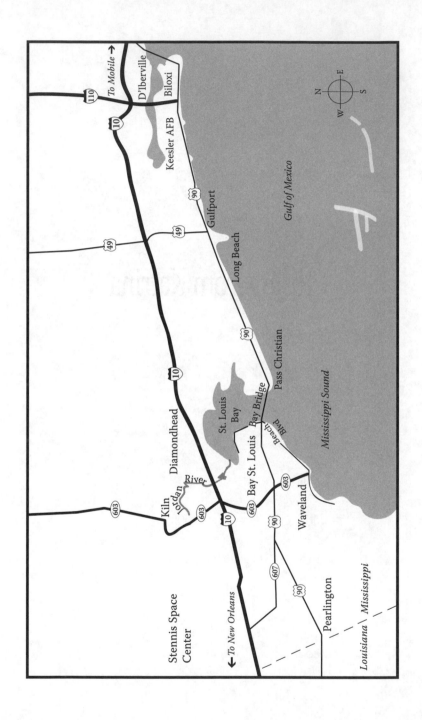

~PROLOGUE~

Moving In

THE AFTERNOON SUN STREAMED in the rear window of our white '71 station wagon. I yawned, stretched, and uncrossed my stiff legs. My sister Gerri leaned her head against the red vinyl interior and wiped the bead of sweat that ran down her neck.

"When will we be there?"

It was the dreaded road-trip question my mother had fielded at least a dozen times that day.

"Soon," she assured us with a sigh.

We'd left before dawn. My parents' routine on long drives was to pile my younger siblings, Mark, Laurie, and Krissy, into the car while they were still asleep and get a few blessed hours of quiet. Gerri and I would climb in the coveted rear-facing seat to read and talk as the miles went by. It was nearly seven hours from Huntsville, Alabama, to the Mississippi Gulf Coast. We were used to long drives—and moving. Dad worked in the aerospace industry. And at Martin Marietta, if he wanted to move up, he moved around. Bay St. Louis would be home number seven. We were always the new kids in school, peppered with the inevitable question: Where are you from? I hated it because I never knew how to answer. Should I tell them where I was born, where I'd lived the longest, or where I'd just left?

For us, home was portable, not permanent. Friends were people we knew for a while and then left behind. We kept on moving and never looked back. It was the only reality we knew.

"Hey, kids, we're almost at the water!"

My dad's excited voice was like a wake-up call. The scenery had changed. For hours, it had been a blur of tall southern pines broken only by gas stations and ragged roadside restaurants. Now, we saw beach souvenir shops. A bakery. A hardware store.

As we turned off Highway 90 and down a two-lane road into a residential area, we rolled down the windows to see if we could smell the salt water. A wave of humidity rushed into the car.

"We're coming up to some tracks. Look both ways," said my mother.

The railroad tracks sat elevated on a ten-foot hill. When we came down the other side, I caught my breath. The street ahead was lined with enormous live oaks, their branches heavy with Spanish moss intertwined like giant arms across the street, creating a shaded haven from the sweltering heat. And at the end of the allée sparkled the water.

Excited squeals filled the station wagon. The dogs leaped up from the floor to see what was going on. Ahead of us stretched yards of white, sandy beach.

"Dad, where are the waves?" asked Mark. "You sure can't body-surf in that."

"The barrier islands out in the gulf block the surf," explained my father. "But there's plenty of good fishing!"

We turned left down the beach road. Grand southern homes and quaint Acadian cottages surrounded by lush tropical plantings stood next to new houses, some perched high on pillars. Unlike the homogenous suburbs we'd left, these houses had cupolas, gabled dormers, Palladian windows, balustrades, and a distinct charm and grace. Porch swings hung on spacious verandas overflowing with ferns and potted bougainvilleas. Long, green manicured lawns stretched down to the road. The live oaks, strong and majestic, stood in yard after yard like stately guardians looking out over the calm water.

Then we passed what looked like a vacant lot. Then another.

And another. Though devoid of structures, they had steps leading up to the overgrown properties. On one, a set of rusted iron railings remained, waiting to steady an invisible owner's hand. Insistent clumps of weeds pushed their way through cracks in the long, curving driveways. The lots stood out like ugly scars on the otherwise pristine coastline.

"Mom and Dad, what are those?" I asked.

My mother took a deep breath, turned, and looked back. "They were destroyed by the hurricane. You remember. The one we told you about—Camille."

I was in elementary school when Hurricane Camille hit the Mississippi Gulf Coast on August 17, 1969. A monster Category 5 with two-hundred-miles-per-hour winds that pushed ashore a twenty-four-foot wall of water called a storm surge, Camille was the strongest hurricane to strike the United States in modern history. It left 131 dead and 41 missing on the Gulf Coast alone.

But three years later when our parents told us we'd be moving to Bay St. Louis, Mississippi, into a beachfront house rebuilt after the hurricane, I'd assumed everything else had been rebuilt, too. I was wrong.

I studied the abandoned, weed-covered lots as we drove by. They were an unsettling contrast to the well-tended homes around them. I wondered what had happened to the people who lived there. Had entire families died on these very spots in the storm? Or had they lost everything they owned and couldn't afford to start over? Or could they not bear to risk losing it all again and just walked away? It was a mystery that would haunt me every time we passed the empty slabs.

"Here we are!"

We turned left where a set of tree-lined white retaining walls opened onto a circular shell driveway. At the end was a sturdy, two-story red-brick Colonial with white columns and a carport.

We five kids tumbled out of the car, laughing and jockeying to be the first one in the house.

"I want to pick our room!" Laurie shouted to Krissy.

"It's upstairs on the right!" yelled Mom to the crush of backs rushing up the front stairs.

~THE KOCH FAMILY HOME ON SOUTH BEACH BOULEVARD IN BAY ST. LOUIS,
MISSISSIPPI
Photo by Mary Lou Koch

Gerri and I got the bedroom on the west side. It ran the width of
the house and had windows overlooking the beach, the neighbors'
home, and the backyard and pecan grove beyond.

We dashed downstairs to see the rest of the house.

"Why is there a phone pole in the kitchen?" asked Mark. Rising from the yellow linoleum floor into the ceiling just to the right
of the central staircase was what appeared to be the lower half of a
telephone pole.

"Well, this is a hurricane-proof house," explained my father.
He pointed to the paneled walls around us. "You see those sections
every six feet where the paneling juts out? Telephone poles are in
there to reinforce the structure."

Around the perimeter of our house and smack in the middle,
the builder had sunk telephone poles ten feet deep. Apparently, the
owners who'd lost their home to Camille had been persuaded this
architectural innovation would save the structure if a killer hurricane ever threatened again.

~Historic live oak behind the Koch house
Photo by Mary Lou Koch

We raced out to explore the backyard. We had our own immense live oak with a gigantic branch that formed a canopy over a generous square concrete patio. Next to its trunk sat a pile of bricks. I noticed that the color and texture were different from the bricks in the house.

"Mom, what's this? Were they going to add on?" I asked, poking at the stack with my tennis shoe.

My mother, an avid gardener, was already making her way back to examine the pecan trees that filled the rear half of the yard. "No, honey," she offered over her shoulder. "That's all that's left of the house that was here before Camille."

~

At first, I wasn't sure what to make of the little town of just over six thousand nestled on a peninsula between St. Louis Bay and the Mississippi Sound. It boasted just three traffic lights. In a short bike ride, I could cover the entire length of Beach Boulevard, the five-mile-long road that hugged the town's perimeter, separating homes and businesses from the water.

~Mark, Kathleen, Kris, Laurie, and Gerri Koch
canoeing in Bay St. Louis
Photo by Mary Lou Koch

The water was the focus of life here. Some residents were fishermen. Others worked the oil rigs out in the gulf or crafted massive vessels at Ingalls Shipbuilding fifty miles to the east in Pascagoula. Many catered to tourists who came to enjoy the beach. And even the small business owners and aerospace workers employed at one of two nearby NASA facilities had homes overlooking the bay or plied its placid waters evenings and weekends in fishing skiffs or sailboats.

Growing up a corporate vagabond in suburbs with other transferees, I'd never known people so rooted to a place. In Bay St. Louis, families often lived in the same homes for generations. Eventually, like grooves worn in a staircase by thousands of footsteps, the families' names became imprinted on the houses themselves. The Breath home. The Haas home. The De Montluzin home. I loved that sense of history and permanence and relished the fact that my parents had decided this was the place we would finally stay.

The homes had their own character, like living things. The old-

~KATHLEEN, LAURIE, RAY, KRIS, MARK, MARY LOU AND GERRI
KOCH IN FRONT OF THEIR BAY ST. LOUIS HOME
Courtesy of Mary Lou Koch

est, built before air conditioning, had twelve-foot ceilings and thick glass windows speckled with tiny bubbles that caught the light. The traditional southern design with a long central hallway meant that by merely opening the front and rear screen doors, residents could allow the breezes off the water to flow through, cooling every room.

Bay St. Louis was sixty miles east of New Orleans. Over the years, residents of that city who came for the beaches ended up building summer homes here. So the architecture echoed that in the Big Easy—Victorian, Greek Revival, Queen Anne, shotgun houses, Creole cottages. But the demographics of Bay St. Louis were vastly different. Like the rest of the Mississippi Gulf Coast, it was mostly white, while New Orleans was predominantly African American.

In Bay St. Louis, not only did everyone know everyone, they looked out for one another. It wasn't just what was taught in church, though faith ran deep in the six-square-mile town that boasted fourteen houses of worship. Rather, the town had a special inter-connectedness. From day one, we were greeted as though we'd lived there since birth. At school and at Our Lady of the Gulf, the historic church on the water we attended, we were welcomed into clubs and activities like chorus and the Catholic Youth Organization (CYO). We performed in plays at the Bay St. Louis Little Theatre. My mother, Mary Lou, taught at two local schools, Our Lady Academy and Bay High.

My dad, Ray, and my brother, Mark, ardent fishermen, were in heaven. In the evening, they would trek to the middle of the two-mile-long bridge connecting Bay St. Louis to the rest of the Mississippi Gulf Coast and haul in hungry speckled trout that lurked and fed under the glow of the lights. Come flounder season, Mark tried to school us in the fine art of gigging the flat bottom feeders. But at night, as we shuffled behind him through the brackish water to avoid stepping on stingrays, our giggles and chatter sent the fish fleeing. I was amazed at my brother's patience—and that, under the wildly swinging kerosene lantern, none of us impaled our feet.

We had better luck with the pecans that ripened and dropped by the hundreds every fall from the trees in the backyard. We harvested, bagged, and sold them at a folding table at the end of the driveway. We had a heavy incentive to succeed, since what we didn't sell we had to shell by hand. Though we hated the tedious process, we reaped a consolation prize—the intoxicatingly sweet, buttery smell that filled the house as my mother's pecan pies baked to crispy perfection.

Without realizing it, we slipped into the gentle, quiet rhythm of life in Bay St. Louis. The time between when the sun sent its first rays to paint the bay a warm shade of peach and when it set like a gleaming red ball behind the live oaks stretched out languorously. We joined the local kids in their nimble Sunfish and learned how to sail. On weekends, we stacked driftwood and fallen branches into massive piles and had bonfires out front on the beach. We still stood out when we paddled our red fiberglass canoe into the bay. And residents shook their heads when my parents decided to turn an old pool hall downtown into an ice-cream parlor. Fixing it up was a challenge. But my parents always taught us we could do anything if we put our minds to it. Soon, we were scooping out thirty-two flavors and learning the responsibilities of running a business.

The ice-cream parlor was perched on a picturesque bluff overlooking the bay. At thirty-one feet in elevation, downtown Bay St. Louis was the highest point in the United States on the Gulf of Mexico—perhaps one reason early French explorers had built a fort here in 1699, twenty years before New Orleans was founded. So our town had no levees, unlike the fragile network that stretched around most of southeastern Louisiana.

Hurricane Camille was long gone, but it had made a permanent imprint on Bay St. Louis. As newcomers, we were at turns fascinated and frightened by the stories of its ferocity.

CYO president David Treutel described how his entire family had to scramble into the attic of its single-story home on St. Charles Street during the hurricane. "Here you are in water. You're in pitch darkness. The younger kids are crying." His voice was low, his eyes big. He leaned toward me. "There were whitecaps on the water. You'd hear what sounded like trains in the distance—tornadoes! In the flashes of lightning, you could see broken power lines whipping around like electric eels. Once we were in the attic, my dad had to break through the roof in case the water kept rising, or all eight of us might have drowned."

Others talked of how some profited from the storm. "I know someone who bought up all the chain saws at the local hardware store days before the hurricane hit," said Kenny Murray, a classmate at Bay High School. "He cleaned up afterwards renting them out to everyone."

Before long, we had our own storm stories to tell. Every few years, the Mississippi coast found itself under a hurricane watch. And after what we'd seen and heard, we didn't question evacuation orders.

When the first storm approached, Dad carefully cut plywood to fit each window in the house and numbered the boards so we knew which went where. But the process of hauling them around, dragging them up a ladder, and pushing them into place took longer than we expected. By the time we finished, the whipping winds had turned the sheets into sails that threatened to pull Dad off the ladder. Police officers were driving up and down the beach through the pouring rain, pounding on doors and warning residents to leave while they still had time.

"Come on!" shouted Mom as she tried to herd us into the car. "Grab your things. We've got to go!" My parents had told us to choose whatever was most important to us in this world—whatever we couldn't live without—and bring it with us. With seven of us, plus two dogs, we didn't have room for much.

Wet and breathless, we piled into the station wagon, clutching our treasures. As we pulled out of the driveway, I gazed back at the house until it was out of sight, trying to memorize every detail. It would become my evacuation ritual. Because it wasn't just a house anymore. It was home—the Koch home. And I knew that mental picture might be all I would have left. I realized that we could come back to nothing but a pile of bricks and stairs and a driveway to nowhere.

~1~

The Assignment

THE CHEERFUL E-MAIL FROM THE CNN assignment desk came Thursday just after noon.

> Subject: Katrina
>
> good news. assume you're going. will confirm shortly (we want to see your hurricane curly hair get blown around!).

I'd been following the hourly weather bulletins on Tropical Storm Katrina for days. Forecasters were saying it could strengthen into a Category 1 hurricane before it crossed Florida's coastline.

Reporting on hurricanes was a relatively new assignment for me. As a Washington correspondent for CNN, I covered beats like the Pentagon, the White House, and Capitol Hill. My wardrobe was dress suits, not slickers.

But in 2003 when Hurricane Isabel threatened Virginia Beach just four hours away, I had been thrown into the mix. When I reported the deteriorating conditions, I made it clear this was not fun and games. Hurricanes could kill. Evacuating was serious business. I knew it firsthand.

Even a storm as relatively small as Isabel had its surprises. One minute, I stood in the driving rain clinging to a massive cement planter while reporting how the hurricane's winds had strengthened to seventy-five miles per hour. Off the air just five minutes later, I heard a loud boom and looked up to see the roof of the hotel next door flying off in pieces. I called my cameraman out to shoot it, eyeing the chunks as they landed and calculating that even if they had hit one of us during the live shot, we probably wouldn't have been killed. I did a live report by phone detailing the new damage and headed inside.

I was drying off when my cell phone rang. I was mortified to hear the frightened voices of my nine- and twelve-year-old daughters, Kara and Kaitlyn. "Mommy, come in out of the hurricane!" they pleaded, on the verge of tears. "You're going to get hurt! Tell CNN you won't go outside anymore."

The effects of Hurricane Isabel reached all the way to Maryland, where school was canceled for the day. The girls and my husband, Rick, had been watching our coverage.

"Sweeties, don't worry," I assured them. "Mommy's moving to report in a safer place. I'll be fine."

"But roofs are coming off buildings!" protested Kaitlyn.

"Just small pieces. And they didn't fall anywhere near us," I insisted.

I didn't realize until the next day that the noise I'd heard was actually a fifteen-square-foot section crashing through the corrugated fiberglass roof of the pool enclosure just fifteen feet from where we'd been doing our live shots.

I was rattled by our close call. But it was nothing compared to my dismay when my planter-hugging hurricane debut ended up in a montage on *The Tonight Show with Jay Leno*. There I was in my yellow slicker, along with a correspondent losing his pants in the wind and *NBC Nightly News* anchor Brian Williams being swept off his feet by Isabel's force. "Why do reporters feel they have to cover hurricanes?" quipped Leno. "You can't cover hurricanes!"

Nothing was funny about the track Katrina was taking in the

gulf and the strength that was building. The Florida Panhandle and much of the state's western coast were under a hurricane warning or watch. Forecasters were talking about a possible Category 4. My assignment was Panama City.

Every time before I deployed to cover a hurricane, I did my homework, including checking to see which other storms had followed the same early path and where they had ended up. I logged onto wunderground.com and clicked on *Katrina* to see if the past would in any way be a predictor of the future.

The sweeping color-coded tracks of five hurricanes displayed, but one name leaped off the screen—Camille. My heart started to pound, and the color drained from my face. I realized Bay St. Louis could again be at the bull's-eye of a killer storm. By Friday afternoon, the National Hurricane Center shifted Katrina's likely landfall to the Louisiana/Mississippi Gulf Coast.

I'd be working with a new team. Janet Rodriguez, one of our top-notch D.C. live producers, would be my field producer. Beautiful, with raven hair and flawless olive skin, Janet was a woman of few words and cool temperament under pressure. She'd never covered a hurricane before, so I walked her through a supply list over the phone. Hat, sturdy rain jacket and pants, rain boots at least up to the knees, flashlight, lots of batteries. Ziploc bags for keeping notepads, phones, BlackBerries, etc., dry in the driving rain. And a rechargeable AM/FM radio lantern fan.

"Why do I need that?" asked Janet.

"Well, it's got a fluorescent lamp to work by, and a spotlight. Once the power goes out, we'll have the radio to get weather and damage reports and the fan to keep us cool," I explained. "Two really handy features are the siren and blinking light. We can use them to guide rescue crews if a roof or wall collapses on us and we're trapped."

The phone was silent.

"Well," said Janet, taking a deep breath. "Guess I'd better go find one of those."

Sunday morning, I said my goodbyes to my family. Though I traveled frequently covering breaking news, hurricanes were different. My husband, Rick, trusted I wouldn't take any chances. My daughters weren't so sure.

"Be careful, Mom," warned Kaitlyn, now fourteen. "Don't do anything stupid."

"Mommy, you're going to miss my first day of middle school!" protested Kara, painfully aware of the difficult transition that would begin for her the next day.

"I know, baby. And I'm so sorry." I hugged them both tightly, kissing Kara on the forehead. "I'll be back as soon as I can, okay? Promise."

I met Janet at the airport, and we boarded a flight to Atlanta. We were now to be positioned in Alabama on the eastern edge of the storm to keep the network on the air when the winds got so bad to the west that they knocked out all the other crews' signals.

As we awaited our connecting flight to Mobile, a news bulletin flashed across a television overhead. Katrina's barometric pressure was now 902 millibars, lower than Camille's. And when it comes to hurricanes, the lower the barometric pressure, the deadlier. The knot in my stomach grew tighter.

Then the e-mails from home started coming.

Subject: Chasing Katrina

We went north last night to Laurel MS. I think this is the mother of all storms. I fully expect to lose *Tranquility* and our new home. I am ok with that. I just wish the best for the folks that can't get out.

Please be safe. Your girls depend on you.

I will try to reach you later.

Kenny

It was Kenny Murray from high school. He was now a successful businessman in New Orleans, married, with two beautiful young daughters.

I responded, mustering some false optimism.

We arrived midafternoon Sunday on one of the last flights into
Mobile. Luckily, our New York crew, Emmanuel Tambekakis and
Gil De La Rosa, had made it there earlier, picked up our two SUVs,
and stocked them with food, supplies, and extra gasoline.

Hotels, restaurants, stores, and other businesses throughout
the city were closing fast. Our hotel, the Riverview Plaza on Water
Street was no exception. As the name suggested, it was probably not
the best spot to ride out a hurricane. So after a last-minute scramble, we found one of the few still taking guests—the Lafayette Plaza
Hotel.

"Four rooms on the twelfth floor!" Janet shouted, waving the
room keys victoriously.

"Janet," I smiled, shaking my head. "The power's going to go out.
We're going to get a hell of a workout running up and down twelve
flights of stairs."

We were plotting locations for our live reports when I received
an ominous e-mail.

Kenny didn't have to say anything more. We both knew what he
meant. If the hurricane hit New Orleans head on, thousands would

die. We had to pray it went east—right into Bay St. Louis.
    I answered.

        Subject: Turning

        I hope you're right.

~2~

Getting Ready

In Bay St. Louis, the afternoon CSX train sounded its whistle as it did every day, riding the tracks parallel to the beach before jogging east and across the long bridge over the bay. Businesses were closing early. There was a buzz of activity but no panic. All around town, people were making what they didn't realize at the time were life-and-death decisions.

Mayor Eddie Favre, distant cousin of NFL quarterback Brett Favre, was going down his standard hurricane checklist. He'd been in office since 1989 and knew the list like the back of his hand. Test backup generators on water wells. Test backup generator on the sewage lift station. Fuel up public-works and emergency vehicles. In the past, those preparations had always been sufficient.

Eddie, whose girth was as generous as his spirit, was known for his culinary skills. So Sunday morning after covering his city duties, he loaded his pots, pans, burners, and other cooking equipment into his old Crown Victoria to store at his brother's home downtown on Main Street, just in case. His mother, nephew, two sons, daughter-in-law, and one-year-old granddaughter would all be staying there on some of the highest ground in town. It seemed wise to bring necessities as a precaution.

As the forecast worsened, Eddie made more trips to his home on vulnerable North Beach Boulevard. He loaded up the

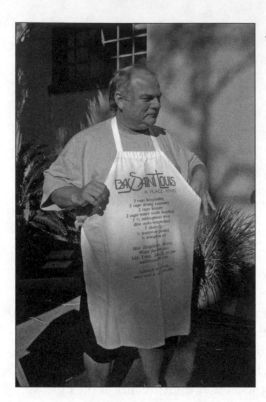

~Bay St. Louis mayor
Eddie Favre
Photo by Gerri Koch

computer, copy machine, printer, TV, stereo, clothing—anything he could carry. He was calm on the outside. But as he pulled away and headed to the police station for the night, a feeling of foreboding swept over him unlike anything he'd experienced before. It was as though someone were reaching inside and twisting him. *This is the last time I'm going to see this*, Eddie thought. *It's all going to be gone.*

Firefighter Monte Strong reported to work Sunday along with other Bay St. Louis first responders. They stockpiled three days' worth of water and canned goods in the firehouse and brought along a few changes of clothes. *We're going to be here two or three days*, thought Strong. *And then, you know, everything will be fine.*

Back at home, his wife, Danielle, and their three children were equally upbeat. "Hurricanes have never bothered me," Danielle insisted, leveling her blue eyes resolutely at anyone who asked. "I've always stayed."

She was still stinging from two previous evacuations that had

~Bay St. Louis firefighter Monte Strong
at work
Photo by Kathleen Koch

backfired—one in 1998 for Hurricane George and the other in 2004 when Hurricane Ivan threatened the Gulf Coast. For George, Danielle fled seventy-eight miles north to her brother's house in Hatties-burg, Mississippi. For Ivan, the family sought refuge at her mother-in-law's home in a high section of Bay St. Louis. In each case, she ended up stuck without power for days while her own neighbor-hood was unaffected.

"Well, I'm not leaving my house next time," vowed Danielle. "I'm staying here."

But Sunday morning, neighbors who had been planning to ride out the storm with the Strongs stopped by to say they were evacuating. And then her mother called. A longtime coastal resident, Joan Garcia always stayed put. "Well, where are you going?" she asked.

"Nowhere," replied Danielle matter-of-factly. "I'm not leaving."

"Honey, this is going to be really bad," warned Joan, her voice trembling. "I mean it. You've *got* to go! I am."

That was enough to scare even a diehard like Danielle. She re-luctantly locked the family's golden retriever, Chance, and yellow Lab, Holly, in the dog yard. Then she and the kids joined the long line of traffic snaking east toward Panama City, Florida, to wait it out.

David Treutel, my CYO friend, drove downtown to make sure the storm shutters were closed on his insurance office one block from the water. Selling insurance wasn't his dream job. In fact, in high school, David had sworn he would never work at the independent agency his grandfather had founded back in 1925. To a teenager, it reeked of tedium. David never forgot how, after Hurricane Camille, his job as an eleven-year-old every day after school had been to file away a seemingly endless stack of claims. But his dad, gentle yet persistent, wore him down, and he'd joined the family business, helping townspeople put together the right combination of insurance policies from a variety of providers. Still, the company carried no flood insurance on the building. "There's never before in recorded history been water in this part of town," David reasoned.

David collected some papers and drove to his one-story home to ride out the storm with his teenage son, Alex. But at seven-thirty, the phone rang. It was his wife, Angelyn, out of town on business and frantic that her seventy-two-year-old father wouldn't evacuate his home across the bay in Pass Christian. His neighborhood was surrounded on three sides by water. "Would you go talk to him?" she begged.

"Well, I don't know if he'll listen to me," David responded.

"Well, go talk to him," said Angelyn. "Just try."

So David and Alex headed east across the two-mile-long bridge that linked the little towns on either side of St. Louis Bay.

A. J. Scardino had been a sheriff's deputy in his youth and had ridden out numerous storms. He was adamant. "I've moved my car to high ground. And if the windows blow out, I want to be here to protect my home and my property."

After an hour of cajoling, David finally tried humor. "Look, A. J., not only will you be much safer if you evacuate, but all your daughters and your wife keep calling me." David smiled the infectious grin that few could resist. "So do me a favor and come with me so they'll quit."

Five minutes later, the three were on their way to NASA's Stennis Space Center, the biggest employer in the area and a safe evacu-

~Independent insurance agent David Treutel in front of his home
Photo by Kathleen Koch

ation site far from the water. David and Alex dropped off A. J. But as the two tried to leave, the security guard at the gate warned them that many local roads were already covered in water, and that they might not be able to make it home. So David and Alex reluctantly joined the hundreds of other residents hunkered down at Stennis.

Diane Frederick had been a housekeeper for David's family when he was young. The cheerful middle-aged woman now owned a cleaning service and drove a school bus as well to help her family make ends meet. Diane's husband, Allan, was in the hospital in nearby Gulfport, so she handled preparations alone with the help of their sixteen-year-old daughter, Cookie.

"Baby, run some water in the tub," she told the teenager as she packed a small overnight bag, tucking in three days' worth of clothing, Vienna sausages, a flashlight, and an all-weather radio. "I want to make sure we have water when we get back."

They lived in Bay St. Louis's Third Ward, a largely African American community of simple homes well inland from the water. "Our little home is ours," Diane liked to say. "We're friendly, God-fearing. Just a nice bunch of people." Diane was going to ride out the storm

~Housekeeper Diane Frederick outside her Bay St. Louis home
Photo by Kathleen Koch

with Allan at the hospital while Cookie stayed in Bay St. Louis with
a friend in a two-story apartment.

On the western edge of the ward, home health care aide Shannon Evans sat anxiously with her four daughters in the tiny white
clapboard home they rented on Washington Street. Backing into
her driveway Saturday, her car had slipped into the ditch and broken three of the five bolts on one wheel. It wasn't safe to drive. Shannon had no choice but to stay.

Another former classmate of mine, Pat Kergosien, had stocked
plenty of food and water. He and his wife, Hope, were expecting
seventeen members of Pat's family to ride out the storm with them
at their home on Carroll Avenue. Though just six hundred feet from
the water, it was located at one of the highest points in town. Pat
knew that if he, Hope, and the kids evacuated, his relatives would
go back to their homes, which were all in lower spots. *If I leave, they
could all die*, thought Pat, betting his family's lives that everyone
would be safe at his home.

Still, he had a nagging feeling as Katrina grew stronger out in
the gulf. "Erin, why don't you take the video camera and go out

~The Kergosien family at their home on Carroll Avenue.
From back to front are Pat, Jaynie, Erin, Hope, Kristin, and Pierce.
Photo by Carolyn Kergosien

and get some shots of the town?" he asked his sixteen-year-old daughter.

So Saturday and Sunday, Erin and a friend drove up and down Beach Boulevard—a bit too fast, music blaring, as teenagers do—recording what no one knew would be the last video of the city intact.

Nikki Cleveland and her husband, Patrick, a local veterinarian, lived in a home raised on pillars in a small community on a series of canals off the Jordan River, which flows into St. Louis Bay. The young newlyweds knew it wouldn't be wise to stay there. On Sunday afternoon, the tall, handsome, dark-haired vet and his petite blond wife boarded the windows and made what might seem an irrational decision—they evacuated to her parents' home on the beach. To the casual passerby, it looked like a contemporary white two-story stucco house. But inside, it was a fortress. Fourteen-inch-thick cement walls covered welded steel rebar. It would take dynamite to bring the home down.

Ralph and JoAnna Dagnall had moved to Bay St. Louis in 1969 the day before Hurricane Camille hit, just in time to witness its devastation firsthand. So Ralph, whose construction battalion in the army had built bridges, was determined to design a house to protect his family.

~Ralph and JoAnna Dagnall's hurricane-proof home on South Beach Boulevard
Photo by John Wilkerson

"Growing up, it was always hurricane-proof. And that's what we all believed," said Nikki, reasoning that it would be the safest place in town to weather the storm.

Next door in the town of Waveland, Mayor Tommy Longo and his staff went door to door on the streets near the water warning residents to get out. Tommy knew the drill well. Thirty-six years earlier, his father had been mayor of Waveland during Hurricane Camille.

Officials up and down the Mississippi Gulf Coast were making the same argument and often getting the same response. Some residents couldn't afford to leave or had nowhere to go. But many more simply refused. And it wasn't because they weren't educated or intelligent. I dubbed it "Camille survivor syndrome."

While covering Hurricane Ivan in 2004, I had interviewed Mayor A. J. Holloway of Biloxi, Mississippi, about the evacuation orders going into effect for that storm. A short, balding man with an ever-present smile, he'd lived on the coast his entire life.

"What are your plans?" I asked.

"Well, I'll be at home," said Holloway matter-of-factly.

"You're staying in your house a block and a half from the beach?"

I was incredulous. "Is that wise, when you're advising residents to evacuate?"

"Well, I was there during Camille. My wife wouldn't leave," he responded with a chuckle, shaking his head. "A lot of people are not going to leave. They just won't. And what can I say? I won't leave either, so . . ."

Red Cross worker Jana Zehner, organizing shelter for Mississippi evacuees fleeing Ivan, heard the same from many local residents. "That they've seen it. That they've been through everything. That they're prepared to handle anything," she explained. "In a storm like this, of course, it can be gambling with their lives."

For Mississippians, Camille was the mother of all hurricanes, the benchmark against which they gauged all other storms. So if they'd ridden out Camille in a home or building, in their minds it was hurricane-proof, just as they themselves were hurricane-proof.

The reality? They had been damn lucky once. They wouldn't be damn lucky twice.

~3~

The Storm

THE DRENCHING DOWNPOUR from Katrina's outer bands began slapping Mobile just before five in the afternoon on Sunday. The weather bulletins forwarded from CNN got more specific: "Landfall expected tomorrow morning between New Orleans and Biloxi." Even as far east as our Mobile location, we were under a flash flood watch and a tornado watch/warning. Winds were already gusting twenty to forty-five miles per hour. On Monday, they were expected to hit forty to eighty-five miles per hour, increasing to fifty to one hundred in the afternoon.

A weather service online editor, Greg Hernandez, warned my producer.

Subject: NOAA Katrina Satellite Images

Janet,

You are in the bull's eye zone. Be careful.

We set up on the hotel balcony with the city skyline behind me, doing live shots into the night. I was the first in a long line of CNN reporters stretching west through Mississippi into Louisiana, laying out what each city was doing to prepare. But as I watched the monster storm just offshore surging in size with each update, I wondered how many of those efforts would be futile.

Perhaps that's why, in one live report, this no-nonsense, just-the-facts journalist did something I'd never done before and haven't done since. I mentioned the need to pray for the people of the Gulf Coast. It seemed to make sense. No one noted it. No one repeated it. I just felt it needed to be said.

And all the while, I was aching, both journalistically and emotionally, to be in Mississippi. I knew the Gulf Coast—the lay of the land, the officials. My first job in television had been at WLOX in Biloxi. But more importantly, I knew the people and why they clung to this humid, sometimes inhospitable but strikingly beautiful eighty-mile sliver of coastline. Instead, I was stuck in Mobile, a city I'd never set foot in.

"Dammit! I should be in Bay St. Louis, not here," I told Janet. "We could be set up at the Coast Inn, right at the corner of Highway 90 and Route 603. It's just a few miles south of I-10. We could jump up there and chase the storm east or west, depending on where the eye goes."

"Kathleen, everything happens for a reason," Janet replied, trying to calm me down. "There's a reason we're here and not there."

Wise words. But they gave me no comfort.

We got to bed just before midnight and were up again at four in the morning. The wind and rain had strengthened. But I still knew it was nothing compared to what was happening to the west.

Ninety-two miles away on South Beach Boulevard in Bay St. Louis, Nikki Cleveland was awakened at the same time by the relentless, howling wind. When she went outside to check conditions, she found trees bent sideways, nearly touching the ground. Sheets of rain pelted down, and the sky had an eerie glow. Nikki leaned her hundred-pound frame into gusts that threatened to knock her off her feet and worked her way with a flashlight to the end of the driveway to see if the water was coming up. She was stunned because it hadn't risen. It had disappeared. Katrina's winds had pushed the bay waters out into the Mississippi Sound. As far as the eye could see was nothing but sand, just like a shoreline before a tsunami strikes.

Nikki stumbled back inside, where her parents were now awake and waiting for her. "Mom, Dad, we've got to go," she insisted. "The bay is gone! There's no water. I don't know what that means, but I'm scared."

"Baby, we'll be fine," said Ralph. "This house is built above the twenty-four-foot Camille surge line. It's not going anywhere."

"But Dad, we can get out now. There's no water in the streets. We've got to go before it gets bad!"

"Sugar," JoAnna said, smiling calmly. "We're staying. Go back to sleep now."

Angry and frightened, Nikki went to the upstairs bedroom to find her husband. "Patrick, there's no water on the beach. This is bad! I want to go. But Mom and Dad won't leave."

"Well, we could head north," said Patrick. "Are you okay with leaving them behind?"

Despite her concerns, Nikki knew she'd never forgive herself if they left and something happened to her parents. So they lay down and tried to go back to sleep.

At seven-thirty that morning, sewage started backing up in the basement. Ralph and Patrick plugged the faucets and toilet, cleaned up the mess, and waited.

By eight o'clock, the wind intensified, whipping like a blender the water rushing back into the bay. Behind it was a towering thirty-plus-foot storm surge that had been building as Katrina roared across the gulf. It smashed into the house, ripping off part of the roof and sending a flood of water cascading into the back bedroom, where Patrick, Nikki, and her parents sat talking. They could hear windows shattering. The door burst open to reveal that the entire front of the house was missing.

"Oh, my God!" screamed Nikki.

Eight-foot waves began battering apart the rest of the roof and then the walls, each blow breaking off more and more chunks. Nikki, Patrick, Ralph, and JoAnna grabbed hold of what structure was left as the walls collapsed and the sheetrock began tearing off the studs. Wave after wave slammed into them, knocking them off their feet. Each time, they scrambled back up and braced themselves for the next onslaught.

"Hang on!" screamed Patrick. "We have to stay in the house."

JoAnna was near exhaustion, so Nikki and Patrick positioned themselves on either side of the sixty-eight-year-old, holding her up with each wave.

"You got to get up, Mom," insisted Nikki. "Come on. You got to hold on!"

Across a hallway from the other three, Ralph clung to plumbing pipes protruding from the floor. He eyed the situation like an engineer, calculating how long the house could withstand the punishing surge and when the water might subside. Nikki's father had faith in the hurricane-proof home he'd designed, stubbornly refusing to acknowledge their lives were in danger.

He yelled his calculations over the wind: "It's going to be high tide at nine-fifteen! If we can make it another twenty minutes, everything will start going down."

But around nine o'clock, a massive wave crashed down, ripping their hands from the studs and washing them to the edge of the house. Before they could catch their breath, another wave swept Nikki and Patrick out.

Nikki was washed under a section of the floating roof. Realizing she was trapped, she vowed to herself that this was not how she was going to die. She freed one leg and began kicking until she made a hole and dragged herself out. But now she was back in the churning water, continually being pulled under. Everything was the same taupe color, and it was hard to tell which way was up. Survival skills kicked in again. Nikki remembered what she'd learned as a lifeguard. She followed her air bubbles to the surface and popped up, gasping for breath. Her strategy now was to stop fighting, conserve energy, and just float, keeping her feet and head out of the current and letting the water take her.

Patrick was still reeling from the wave that had smacked him like a punch in the face. For a minute, he couldn't see. Then the water slammed his head into a rafter on the back porch. He ducked under, and the swirling current pulled him out. Patrick felt his shoes rip off, then his shorts. Wearing just a T-shirt, he began grabbing at trees as the surge carried him along. Though he was muscular from his work as a large animal vet treating horses and cattle, exhaustion was setting in. He caught hold of a tree but found himself facing the roaring surf and was quickly swept off. Patrick grabbed a small limb and perched on it for a few minutes. But Katrina's relentless waves and flying debris knocked him from safety there as well. Finally, after being torn from nearly a dozen trees, Patrick managed to position himself on a huge live oak. He was naked now. Shivering, he breathed fast and shallow from having inhaled so much water. He wrapped his arms, scraped and raw, around the trunk and hung on for dear life.

Patrick began to consider the others. He assumed the worst. *I'm the strongest of the group*, he thought. *If it took everything I had to make it, how could they?*

Nikki, too, sought refuge in a tree, hundreds of yards away, where she was being pummeled by boards, shingles, furniture, and other wreckage swept along by the churning current. One four-by-eight-foot sheet of plywood covered with nails was particularly menacing, striking her on the head over and over. As she reached up to push it aside, Nikki noticed something shiny dangling from one of the nails. It was Patrick's wedding ring. She gasped, plucked it off, and slipped it on her finger before shoving the board away. A few minutes later, Nikki saw Patrick's shorts hanging on the branch of a nearby tree. *He's dead*, she thought.

A mile and a half up the beach, Pat Kergosien stood transfixed at the sight of the brown bay waters surging past his house on Carroll Avenue. Just like the old downtown, it sat on a thirty-foot bluff. Never before in the history of Bay St. Louis had water crested the sea wall and spilled onto his street.

Katrina's winds had been roaring at 125 miles per hour all morning. Gusts as high as 145 miles per hour strafed the city, ripping off roofs and tipping over trees like toothpicks. Power had gone out all over town around five-thirty that morning. From his vantage point on the front porch, Pat had watched the window and porch awnings on the neighbor's house across the street peel off and blow away. The trees that were still standing were bent nearly horizontal. He could hear sharp popping sounds but wasn't sure if they were power lines snapping or boards and shingles being pried off houses and going airborne.

Pat grabbed his camera and started videotaping the giant waves that crashed at the bay end of the street, sending a raging torrent inland to engulf the town. The house had become a fragile island, shaking from the force of the water rushing underneath. His wife, Hope, ushered the children into a bedroom while other adults shoved towels beneath the doors in a frantic attempt to keep the water out.

Sixteen-year-old Erin, who the day before had casually driven around videotaping the town, now stood petrified as the city's emergency siren began to wail. "Mom, I don't want to die," she whispered as the younger children sat on the bed praying and crying.

Hope looked into her oldest daughter's eyes. "Honey, at least we're all together," she replied.

For Pat, the new threat simply required a new plan. If things got worse and the house was about to wash off its foundation, they would all seek shelter in the small apartment over the garage behind the house. He made his way outside to see if the waist-deep water was still rising. As he peered down the street through the blinding rain, Pat suddenly realized that all of Bay St. Louis was underwater. It sent a shiver down his spine to think that friends and neighbors were likely out there in the churning water, fighting to stay alive.

A mile or so inland, Shannon Evans and her daughters were terrified. The water had begun to rise around their small clapboard house. With each gust, the wind rocked the structure, every joint creaking and groaning as though it was about to go. As they huddled together on her bed, she watched a crack start in the wall by the window. It grew as the storm raged, snaking like a living thing across the room to the roof.

"Get up. Quick!" commanded Shannon. "We're going to sit in the hall for a bit."

They'd been there barely a minute when suddenly the ceiling over Shannon's bed caved in and they could see through to the sky. Part of the roof had been ripped off. Rain began pouring in.

"Mama!" screamed her youngest, two-year-old Mariah.

"I want to get out of here," begged fourteen-year-old Shanell, her eyes wide with fear. "We can go across the street to the neighbors."

Shannon regarded her daughter's pregnant belly and the swelling water in the street outside. "Baby, you see that water?" she said, pointing. "And feel that wind. If you try to cross, that wind will take you and we'll never find you. It's too late."

Shannon had one last hope. She reached for the phone. It still had a dial tone! Punching 911, she held her breath. *Busy. Damn!* They were on their own.

Less than a half-mile away at the police and fire station, the phone had been ringing nonstop since eight o'clock. The first panicked calls came from the beach, then from the Cedar Point area on the bay. They were chillingly similar. The home was filling with water. The cars were all swamped or blocked in by fallen trees. The callers couldn't swim. They needed help or they would die.

"We're in our second-story window and the water's steadily rising!" screamed one person over Katrina's roaring winds. "We want you to have our names so you can link us to this address if you find us later. We're going to jump!"

The 911 operators took down the names and addresses, and Monte Strong and the other first responders tried to go out on the calls. The engines, sirens blaring, sped out of the station. But they didn't get far. The roads not blocked by trees, telephone poles, and other debris were completely submerged.

So was the low-income housing project across the street. Many elderly people there hadn't evacuated. Water was already halfway up the windows of the modest one-story brick homes. Monte and half a dozen firefighters donned their foul-weather gear, waded over, and began pulling residents out of the houses. They worked with their clear face shields down, the pelting rain ripping at any exposed skin like buckshot.

"Hey, look!" shouted one firefighter, pointing behind a house. A flat-bottomed aluminum skiff was bouncing on the storm surge. They grabbed it and for hours used it to shuttle wet, frightened seniors and families to higher ground at the station.

All the while, Katrina's winds whipped debris through the air around them. Monte tried to dodge a flying shingle that caught him square on his shoulder blade. He'd been trying to stay on what he thought was the middle of the street, but the blow threw him off balance and he stepped instead into a ditch. Suddenly, Monte was underwater and felt himself being swept along in the current. He tried to scream, but his mouth filled with water. He pushed his heavy firefighter's boots in the direction of the road, dug in, threw his weight forward, and dragged himself up and out of the surge.

Wet and exhausted, the rescuers worked until the neighborhood was empty. It helped keep Monte's mind off the fact that his home was in one of the low-lying neighborhoods where the 911 calls originated.

One call came from Main Street—from Mayor Eddie Favre's son. "Daddy, Uncle Mike's got two feet of water coming in the house!"

Eddie tried to calm his son. "All I can tell you at this point is that in twenty minutes the eye's supposed to come through. Then the winds are gonna turn and it's gonna blow the water out that built up. Y'all just hang in there."

The mayor's brother, Mike, grabbed the phone. "Damn, boy! Y'all need to do somethin' about this floodin' problem we're having over here!"

Eddie sensed the anger and fear in his brother's voice. He pictured his petite eighty-year-old mother, his daughter-in-law, and his little grandbaby struggling as the fetid storm surge rose around them.

"I can't help it," he replied. "The eye's supposed to be coming, and hopefully it'll pull the water out."

Two and a half miles farther inland, the situation was deteriorating quickly at the Coast Inn. The hotel where I'd wanted to stay with my CNN crew was two stories high and had never taken on water. In fact, longtime local restaurant owner Tommy Kidd and his wife, Linda, had stayed there in 1969 during Hurricane Camille. And Tommy would never take a risk with his high-school sweetheart, a brunette with twinkling brown eyes whom he'd married shortly after they both started college. Sunday after they hung the storm shutters on their raised home on the bayou, the couple, now in their mid-sixties, followed the same game plan and squeezed into a ground-floor suite at the hotel with five family members, two Labs, a blue Doberman, and a cat.

Monday morning when water began flowing under the door of

~TOMMY KIDD IN FRONT OF HIS HOME ON
THE BAYOU
Photo by Kathleen Koch

their room, it became clear this was no safe refuge. The hurricane-force winds that had been howling nonstop for hours suddenly intensified. Before they could get out, all seven were waist-deep in brown, swirling water. Drenched and carrying their pets, they waded to the stairs and scrambled up to the second floor.

As they stood shivering on the open walkway, Tommy had an unsettling feeling. He didn't see the elderly couple from the room next door. They were in their eighties, and the husband had Alzheimer's. "We need to go back down and check on them," he said.

So Tommy and his son plunged back into the rising water. They slogged down the walkway and pressed their faces against the window of the couple's room. Tommy's fears were confirmed. Inside, they saw the woman standing helplessly with her husband almost neck-deep in the brown water as their dog floated on a mattress nearby. The men tried the door, but it was jammed shut by the force of the surge. Tommy thought about the sledgehammer in his truck, which was already underwater. They scanned the debris rushing past them and spotted a two-by-four. It was their last hope. The two gestured to the couple to stand back and began pounding the glass. Finally, it shattered, and they swam through.

"Can someone help my husband?" asked the woman in a surprisingly calm voice as she balanced on her tiptoes.

"Yes, ma'am," said Tommy, looping his arm underneath the man's and lifting him. "I got him."

The men pulled the two and their dog out of the room and up the stairs to safety.

"Thank you. Thank you so much," the drenched woman kept repeating. "I just didn't know what to do."

From the second-floor breezeway, the group peered through the blinding downpour, stunned, as the storm surge swelled higher, enveloping everything as far as the eye could see. Cars floated and smashed into one another in the parking lot. Signs, shingles, tin, flashing, and two-by-fours pried from homes and businesses became airborne projectiles, impaling whatever they hit. Powerboats appeared through the driving rain, making their way to the hotel loaded down with people plucked from trees and rooftops. The Coast Inn was one of the few two-story structures in the area. The water had stopped just short of the second floor.

Tommy worried about his daughter's restaurant, Daddy O's, just a mile down the road. If the relentless winds hadn't shredded it, then it was surely underwater.

Everyone waited for the eye to pass and give the town a respite before the winds turned and sucked the water back out. But the break never came. It felt like the hurricane that wouldn't end, an insatiable monster ripping, grinding, and battering Bay St. Louis hour after interminable hour.

Eighteen miles to the east, Diane Frederick and the patients and families sheltering at Gulfport Memorial Hospital were waiting for a respite, too. The roar of the winds outside was almost deafening. Suddenly, Diane heard what sounded like a brick being thrown through a window.

"Move the patients! Move the patients!"

Nurses came bursting into the fifth-floor critical care unit and began wheeling the beds into the hall. Diane rushed out with her husband, Allan, dragging a chair from the room with her. She pushed it against the wall next to his bed, out of the way of the nurses racing up and down in their efforts to calm the patients. Diane looked down at the plastic ID bracelets all family members had been issued, only now realizing they were for identification purposes if the hospital was destroyed.

She turned up the volume on her all-weather radio. Ham radio operators up and down the coast reported the eye was passing over. "If anyone out there has any reports from Bay St. Louis or Waveland, we want to hear from you," said one announcer. No one responded.

Diane flipped open her cell phone. No service. She got up and tried the pay phone near the elevators. No dial tone.

I'm gonna do a little adventurin', Diane thought, determined to find out how bad conditions were. She pushed open the door to the stairs and headed down. But after she passed the second floor, she stopped short. Brown, murky water filled the stairwell. *My God!* she thought. *Where is this water comin' from?*

Diane retreated back to the fifth floor.

"Our Father, who art in heaven . . ."

"Hail Mary, full of grace . . ."

The murmured prayers of patients and family members echoed down the darkened hallway. Diane sat next to her husband and joined in.

—

Back in Mobile, the rain and winds were strengthening by the minute. Police began getting calls for help. Mobile Bay was spilling over its banks and into downtown, swamping the streets with several feet of water.

Between my early live shots under the hotel awning, I got an e-mail from Kenny.

Subject: Latest

You may get some action. Looks like the Big Easy may have dodged the bullet again.

Kenny

I was relieved. At least New Orleans was safe. All I had to worry about was what had become of Bay St. Louis, now in the deadly northeast quadrant of the hurricane.

Already at our hotel a half-mile from the water, the winds were so strong they'd blown loose a steel ventilation cover on the lobby roof. Every few minutes, a strong gust would send it crashing over. From inside, it sounded like it was about to smash through the roof. Worried it would blow off onto the sidewalk below and kill some-one, hotel management sent two workers up in the swirling wind and rain to try to anchor it.

Not long afterward, our satellite truck operator, Charlie Neis-wenter, dashed in from outside, shaking the rain from his hair. "We're down. Everything's soaked. I'm going to work on it. But it could be awhile."

Damn! So much for being the network's go-to reporter in the east. Still, it gave me a chance to run upstairs, get my radio, and bring it down to the hotel dining room, where guests were congre-gating. As I opened the door to my room, I was puzzled to hear wa-ter running. But it wasn't in the bathroom. My window sill looked like a waterfall, the persistent winds forcing the rain in around the edges of the sealed windows. I grabbed towels from the bathroom, stuffed them on the sill, and dashed back downstairs. As I set up the radio in the darkened dining room, guests began to cluster around to hear the latest weather bulletins.

I was startled to hear my cell phone go off. Phones hadn't worked for hours.

"Kathie? It's Mark."

It was my brother. I'd been so focused on work that I'd shoved to the back of my mind the fact that he, his wife, and their four children were riding out the storm in Biloxi, roughly halfway between Mobile and New Orleans. They'd assumed Katrina would stick to its westward path and they would have no need to evacuate. So when the hurricane jogged to the east, Mark decided they'd leave their Ocean Springs home and seek shelter at Keesler Air Force Base Hospital, where his wife, Maureen, worked. The sturdy five-story building was just 250 yards from the water.

"Mark, are you okay? How bad is it there?"

"We're fine. We lost power hours ago," he replied. "Part of the roof of the maternity ward blew off. Maureen and the other nurses are keeping patients alive using batteries."

I shook my head as I listened. Why the hell did they go west toward the hurricane, instead of east? True, sheltering at a hospital sounded safe. But the kids were so little. Joshua and Jeremy were one and two, Amber and Emily five and nine. What if the walls didn't hold?

"What about the storm surge?" I asked, knowing that Back Bay was just a stone's throw away.

"Well, the water's rising. It's already flooded the basement, where the generators are." Mark kept his voice low so he wouldn't scare the children. "We're upstairs. But the wind is so strong the window in the room is starting to crack. Kathie, I just don't know—"

The line went dead. The last cell tower that had somehow withstood Katrina's winds had finally gone down.

"Mark! Mark! Can you hear me? Are you there?"

He's fine, I told myself. They were in a hospital, for God's sake. If anything happened, doctors and nurses and medical equipment were there . . . all in the dark with the water rising and the roof coming off and the windows about to blow in. *Damn!* And I could do nothing about it.

"We're back in business!" our satellite truck operator announced proudly, stomping the rain off his boots as he strode into the lobby.

We donned our hurricane gear and went back out into the storm to do live reports the rest of the afternoon. By nightfall, the American flag that had flown on the front of the hotel hung in shreds. I just wanted the day to end so we could be cleared to head to Mississippi.

But then everything changed. Though New Orleans had escaped the brunt of the storm, reports came that the levees there had broken. I could almost see the giant media spotlight swinging west to focus on the inundated Crescent City. I didn't yet realize it, but at that moment Mississippi became a footnote. To the nation, Katrina would always be known as the hurricane that hit New Orleans.

~4~

The Aftermath

THOUGH HE WAS A CONGRESSMAN, Gene Taylor knew his way around boats. The one-time boatswain's mate with the chiseled features of a young Robert Redford had served thirteen years in the Coast Guard as the skipper of a search-and-rescue vessel. And he was a "Bay rat"—a Bay St. Louis local who had grown up sailing and fishing the salty waters of St. Louis Bay, the Jordan River, and surrounding tributaries. So as soon as Katrina's winds began to drop, Gene and his seventeen-year-old son, Gary, hauled his thirty-year-old Boston Whaler to the nearest body of water—Route 603, which had disappeared underneath six feet of storm surge.

As they headed south toward Bay St. Louis, the contents of people's homes drifted by. Gary spotted a pool table, the balls still neatly racked in the center, as though waiting for a couple of players to pop out of the water and start taking shots. "Dad, can we keep it?"

"No," said Gene. "Whoever owns this is going to want it back."

He steered the boat onto the Jordan River, which was fifteen to twenty feet higher than normal. They cruised past waterfront

~THE VIEW FROM I-10 LOOKING NORTH ON ROUTE 603 TOWARD
KILN, MISSISSIPPI, ON AUGUST 29, 2005
Photo by John Wilkerson

~THE VIEW FROM I-10 LOOKING SOUTH ON ROUTE 603 TOWARD BAY ST. LOUIS,
ON AUGUST 29, 2005
Photo by John Wilkerson

homes, peering into the second- and third-story windows. Thirty- and forty-foot boats perched in the trees. Finally, it dawned on Gene that he had no need to follow the river. Everything was underwater. *There's no Bay St. Louis*, he thought. As far as he could see, any area that had once been land was now part of the Gulf of Mexico.

They set a course for the two-mile-long Bay Bridge. Gene was careful to dodge the roofs and treetops that poked out of the water around them. As they neared the mouth of the bay, they found themselves following a bizarre flotilla of debris being sucked slowly out to sea. Cars, boats, couches, refrigerators, and all manner of refuse flowed south at a good six knots. Gene worried that it would all dam up at the bridge.

The massive four-lane Highway 90 bridge that connected Bay St. Louis to the rest of the Mississippi Gulf Coast had its spans toppled by Hurricane Camille in 1969. Now, Gene was astonished to see that every inch of the roadway was gone, as was the CSX train bridge beyond. Only the drawbridge and the supporting piers jutted from the water as the wreckage floated by unimpeded.

Gene brought the boat around and began scanning the shoreline for damage, cruising parallel to North Beach Boulevard, where the homes of friends and family had stood for decades. He and his wife had raised their three children there in a charming three-bedroom shotgun, where they'd lived since 1978.

The previous day, the congressman and his son had carefully fastened new storm shutters made of plasticized decking to the windows. They were guaranteed for life. "This is the last pair of shutters we'll have to put on this house," Gene had declared as they finished the job. Glancing up, he'd noticed a bit of paint peeling under an awning. "I am going to have to paint this house pretty damn soon."

Now, nothing was left on the street where he'd lived for nearly thirty years. Not a dock. Not a wall. Not a shed. Not a porch. Nothing. Gene's gaze moved from left to right. The Tanner house was gone. The Kennedy house. The whole Eagan compound. The Chamberlain house was gone. Only a crumpled dumpster stood at Gene's childhood home, which his brother had recently bought from their parents and remodeled. Gone, too, was the little shotgun home where Gene and his wife, Margaret, had lived since they were

~Representative Gene Taylor showing Lieutenant General H. Steven Blum, chief of the National Guard Bureau, and reporters what was left of his home on North Beach Boulevard
Courtesy of National Guard Bureau

married, where their children had taken their first steps and then walked away as adults.

He felt as if someone had punched him in the stomach. Katrina had wiped the shoreline clean of every structure. The only things standing were the yacht club flagpole and the battered frame of one home situated on a slight hill overlooking the Cedar Point neighborhood.

Gene and his son sat silently. They had hoped to rescue some living being, even a dog or a cat. But they'd seen nothing alive except a few weary sea gulls. *This must be what the place looked like when the Frenchmen landed,* thought Gene as he regarded the barren landscape.

"Dad, you want to tell Mom, or do you want me to?" asked Gary.

"No, son. That's my job."

"Well, you know it's gonna get pretty dark pretty fast," said his son. "We'd better get back."

They navigated by memory as darkness fell—a blacker darkness than they'd ever seen. Not a single light was visible anywhere. Even the moon and stars were blocked by Katrina's lingering cloud bands.

Gene dreaded what lay ahead—facing the family and friends who'd congregated at his brother's farm in "the Kiln" north of Bay St. Louis, anxious for word on how their homes had fared.

By the time they returned, a gauntlet of more than twenty people waited in a narrow hallway between the garage and main farm building.

His brother saw him first and knew by the look on Gene's face. "It's gone, eh?" asked Dean.

"Yeah," responded Gene with a short nod as the group crowded around him.

"How's my house?" asked one neighbor.

"And mine, Gene," chimed in another.

"It's gone."

"You mean the roof is gone?" pressed one.

"No. It's gone," Gene repeated.

"You mean the windows are blown in?"

Gene sighed. "No, it's . . . Nothing is there."

Margaret Hadden stepped forward. "How's my house, Gene?" She'd lost her home in Camille and rebuilt a taller hurricane-proof home on pilings.

"Well, it's gone," he replied.

"But you can't see my house because Corky's house is in the way," Margaret insisted.

"Corky's house is gone."

"No. It's a hurricane-proof house," she maintained, her voice quavering. "That's impossible."

"Margaret, your house is gone. Corky's house is gone." Gene spoke with as much finality as he could muster. "Every house that you can see from the water is gone."

For the next hour, the grim process continued as one by one they got the news. Each watched the shock and disbelief on the face of the previous person, praying that when it was their turn they would be the exception. No one was.

Gene finally turned to his wife, Margaret. Blond and with clear blue eyes the shade of the sea, she had a staunch inner strength and calm when things were at their worst. Margaret had seen the others and knew what was coming without asking.

"It's gone," he said, wrapping his arms around her and pulling her close. "Nothing is there, absolutely nothing there."

Back in town, Mayor Eddie Favre, first responders, and public-works crews got chain saws, backhoes, and heavy equipment and started clearing the streets when the winds and water finally began to subside. They worked at a feverish pace, each in the back of his mind hearing the desperation in the 911 calls. Each feared finding bodies when they finally got through.

A dump truck was the only vehicle that could maneuver around the trees and over the debris that filled the streets. Eddie and a city worker climbed in and wove their way down Highway 90, the town's main business artery. Initially, they noticed roof and water damage. As they neared the bay, buildings were missing front and back walls, their interiors swept clean by the storm surge. Then entire structures were gone.

Eddie took it in slowly, building by building. Reiman's Funeral Home, gone. Peter's Wieners, gone. Pic a Pac, gone. McDonald Realty, gone. On Phillips Street, the Kergosien Real Estate building, gone. The Dantagnan house and business, gone. Home after home, business after business. Nothing was left. The mayor was in such stunned disbelief that they drove almost the length of the highway before he was finally able to acknowledge reality. Entire sections of the town of eighty-two hundred no longer existed.

The dump truck turned off the highway and headed to the mayor's brother's house on Main Street, where he'd promised his mother and daughter-in-law they'd be safe. The front door had been kicked open. Inside, a thick sludge of mud covered the floor. A water mark ringed the room at around six feet, just above Eddie's head. Furniture was strewn about, broken and flipped upside down.

Eddie heard a tiny wail rising from one room. Sitting atop a soggy mattress propped against a sofa was his grandbaby, crying frantically. Next to her, filthy and exhausted, was his daughter-in-law, Karen. She uttered not a word but cast him a look filled at the same time with frustration and relief.

"Baby, I'm sorry," said Eddie, wrapping her in an enormous hug. "I'll never do this again."

Hanging open above their heads was the door to the attic, where

~Bay Town Inn, a historic bed-and-breakfast on North Beach
Boulevard, before and after Hurricane Katrina
Photos by John Wilkerson

she, the baby, and Eddie's mother, brother, sons, and nephew had ridden out the storm.

Eddie looked outside. The garage where he'd stuffed all the belongings he could carry from his house so they'd be safe was full of mud. The three cars had been pushed helter-skelter by the surge.

A mile and a half south, Patrick Cleveland was lowering himself from the live oak he'd clung to for the last eight hours. He'd lost not just his clothes but his glasses. Still, he managed to stumble back to the crumbled ruins of Nikki's parents' house, hoping to find someone alive. One small section of the first floor attached to the garage remained. Upstairs, only the stone fireplace was intact, jutting resolutely skyward.

"Nicole! Ralph! JoAnna! Is anybody here?" he called.

The only answer was the whistling winds of Katrina's southern bands as the hurricane churned inland.

Panting and struggling to breathe, Patrick realized how cold he was. He looked inside, but the house had been stripped bare, too. So he made his way to the back of the property, where they'd parked their cars on high ground. He hoped to crawl inside one until he was found.

~Debris field on Washington Street in Bay St. Louis
Photo by Mark Proulx

He spotted a man waving his arms. Unable to tell who it was, Patrick pointed toward a clearing in the debris where they could meet.

"Are you looking for your wife?" asked the man.

"I sure am," said Patrick, his heart racing at the possibility that Nikki may have made it through the storm.

"Well, she's right back here," the man responded.

As they picked their way through the debris, the man reached up, pulled a soggy Mexican poncho out of a tree, and handed it to Patrick. "Not much. But it's better than nothing."

Half an hour earlier, Nikki had spotted the same man and his family and dropped from her perch in the branches into the water, screaming to get their attention. They rushed over to fish her out as Nikki's legs collapsed like rubber beneath her. After eight hours clinging to the tree, she'd lost all feeling in them. It took several excruciating minutes of sharp pin-prick pain up and down both limbs before her circulation was restored.

Still, when she saw Patrick walking barefoot toward her across the field wearing the muddy poncho, Nikki jumped up and managed to sprint the last hundred feet to her husband, throwing her arms around him. "Patrick!"

"Baby, you're okay!" Patrick embraced her gently as he fought to catch his breath. "Oh, watch it. Not so hard." He pulled back to reveal his battered forearms, the flesh raw.

"You're both coming to the hospital—now," insisted the man as he directed them through the rubble toward the nearest road.

Back downtown, the fire engine carrying Monte Strong and his crew slowly followed a city bulldozer and a front-end loader as they cleared the road, first of trees, limbs, power poles, and pieces of roof. Then cars, washing machines, refrigerators, and entire houses blocked the way.

As the procession inched forward, the firefighters got out, clambered into the houses they could enter, called out, and then marked where they had searched with a spray-painted X. They then filled in each quadrant of the X with the date, search team, hazards inside, and number and condition of victims.

~Court Street Station, a Bay St. Louis antique shop,
before and after Hurricane Katrina
Photos by John Wilkerson

"Fire department! Anybody here?" called Monte as they climbed through both levels of a two-story house in the hard-hit Cedar Point neighborhood.

No answer. But something made the firefighters stay. It was the same sixth sense that often led them to panicked residents hiding during house fires. Someone spotted a trapdoor leading to a tiny attic crawlspace and pulled it open. Curled up in the corner was a man in his mid-fifties wearing shorts and a T-shirt.

"Are you okay?" they asked.

The man nodded but stayed tucked in his fetal position.

"Is anybody else in the house?"

The man slowly shook his head, his eyes shifting like those of a startled animal. He was in shock.

Monte and the firefighters loaded him into a city utility vehicle for the paramedics and moved on. The walking wounded were everywhere, bleeding and mud covered, some carrying in small buckets or bags the few possessions they'd salvaged as they scrambled out.

"We made it!" an exhausted middle-aged couple told the firefighters as they approached. "We're the ones that jumped out our window."

They were the 911 callers. Monte and the others smiled because they'd feared the worst.

"We tossed out a mattress and floated on that," explained the husband proudly. "Just as it was about to sink, a log with nice big branches almost like handles drifted by, and we grabbed onto that."

His wife shook her head. "I was so worried that when the water went out, it would take us right with it. But we're here."

As dusk fell, the firefighters got a break. Monte and a neighbor mounted all-terrain vehicles, determined to make it to their neighborhood a mile and a half away. It was like navigating a maze. Finally, they parked the ATVs and began climbing through backyards.

A woman, distraught and trembling, saw their uniforms and came out of her house. "My mother. I tried to get her in the attic, but she couldn't get up there. I tried everything. Can you let someone know?"

"Yes, ma'am. We will," said Monte, lifting his radio to let paramedics know they had not just another body but another shock victim.

They slogged through water up to their thighs until finally reaching the Strong home on Pine Drive. The front door was smashed in, and the living room was jammed with mangled, muddy furniture from every room in the house. Sitting atop the soggy pile were toys, trophies, videotapes, and other belongings that had floated from the children's rooms down the hall. The surge had flowed into the attic of the one-story home, so the sheetrock ceilings had collapsed. The air-conditioning vents and ductwork dangled from above. A wet layer of white blown-in insulation coated everything.

"Chance! Holly!" Monte clambered over the mess, calling his dogs' names. He yanked the door to the laundry room, where he'd locked the golden retriever and yellow Lab the night before, but it was jammed with debris. Monte rushed outside and around to the laundry-room window. *It's a big room with plenty of space. And they're good swimmers*, he thought hopefully. But when he reached the window, his heart sank. The smashed washer and dryer and contents of the utility shelves were piled so high it was impossible to see in. Monte knew his pets couldn't have survived.

"Man, it's gonna be okay," said his neighbor, wrapping his arm around Monte's shoulder. "Danielle and the kids are alive. You're alive."

Over the next few days, Monte made the same journey to his brother's, his sister's, his mother's, and his mother-in-law's homes. Every house was gutted or gone. Everyone had lost everything.

Pat Kergosien emerged stunned to see the destruction around him while his home survived intact. But he and his seventeen family members were stranded, every single car ruined by the floodwater. Fortunately, Pat had a four-wheeler. He began ferrying everyone around to see what was left of their homes. On a trip across the highway to the battered Cedar Point area, he spotted what looked like a mannequin's legs protruding from a ravine. The skin was white and pasty. Pat drew closer and saw what appeared to be a man's body clothed in a long nightshirt covered in mud and pine straw. He noted the location. As the evening sky darkened, he made his way downtown to let police know what he'd found.

Tuesday morning, the sun rose over the bay, casting a gentle

~DA BEACH HOUSE, A BAY ST. LOUIS CAFÉ AND BEACH RENTAL SHOP, BEFORE AND
AFTER HURRICANE KATRINA
Photos by John Wilkerson

pink glow on the body where it remained in its odd, undignified state.

A block away, Pat's older sister Mary had started to clean out her flooded home when a thin-faced man in his seventies approached her in the driveway. "Oh, Mary, we can't reach Nan," he said, leaning on his cane. "Can you go see about her? I can't go anymore."

Nancy Belle Murphy and Mary were prayer partners who attended church together every week. Miss Nancy was wheelchair-bound and had never married. She referred to herself genteelly as an "unclaimed rose." George Ladner was her brother-in-law.

Mary jumped on the bicycle she'd been using to navigate the debris-covered streets. "I'm going right now."

"Just try, honey. Just try!" George called as she pedaled around the corner.

Mary's heart was pounding. She felt the adrenaline rushing through her body as she kicked and then finally used her shoulder to force open the door to her friend's one-story home. She searched through the mishmash of wet, broken furniture but found nothing.

As Mary climbed back on her bike, a neighbor on the street flagged her down and pointed out the body in the ravine. It was still coated in a layer of pine needles, the face turned to the side, as if the person were asleep. Mary leaned down and brushed the short, gray hair back from over the eye. It was Miss Nancy.

The elderly gentleman was waiting in the driveway as Mary rode up, breathless.

"I just wish I had better news for you," she said.

"I knew it." His head sank into his hands as he began to weep. Mary tried to comfort him, but he waved her off. "No, it's okay. I'm a go. I'm a go." He picked up his cane and walked slowly toward the street.

That same morning, David Treutel and his son, Alex, left NASA's Stennis Space Center and raced back to Bay St. Louis. They were among the fortunate few whose cars had survived the storm intact. Katrina's winds had turned rocks on the facility's flat roof into buckshot that blew out the windows of dozens of cars parked in front of the building.

David was still marveling at the sea gulls he had spotted when the eye passed over Stennis the day before. The wind and rain had stopped, revealing a disk of blue sky where the sun shone brightly. Trapped inside the eye were sixty or seventy tired sea gulls that had no choice but to follow the storm as it barreled north. Fly too far in any direction and they'd be shredded by the 125-miles-per-hour winds.

During the entire drive, David wove his car around and over downed trees and debris. Once in town, he and Alex began checking family homes. His parents' house on St. Charles, where the family had ridden out Hurricane Camille in the attic—gone. His sister's and brother's homes—flooded.

Downtown, a mountain of debris blocked his family's insurance business. So David and Alex climbed around back. Huge holes had been ripped in the rear and side of the building. The entire contents of the business had been pushed into the front rooms. They picked their way through carefully, looking for anything to salvage. A familiar stench filled the air—water, oil, gas, sewage. It smelled like Camille.

"Come on, Alex," said David. "Let's go home."

As they made their way back to the car, David noticed the scores of people on foot. Most vehicles in town were wrecked, flooded, or blocked in by debris, so residents were walking through the muck and wreckage in the hundred-degree heat to check on friends, family, homes, and businesses and to try to find food and water. There was no sign yet of any help.

A lanky figure waved to David from the end of Main Street. It was eighty-one-year-old Leo Seal, the former president and CEO of Hancock Bank, the state's largest financial institution. He was wearing a dirty, wrinkled seersucker suit that looked like it had dried in the sun.

"Mr. Seal, you okay?"

"Just got back to town to check the house. My yard's full of downed trees. Couldn't see a thing when I got there at dawn," replied Seal. "And the damn storm shifted my fence. So when I jumped it to get into the yard, I ended up in the pool."

"It's rough," said David. "You've been through not one but two once-in-a-lifetime hurricanes."

"Hell, Treutel! I was here in the '47 hurricane," said Seal with a laugh. "I've been in three once-in-a-lifetime storms."

David patted the elderly gentleman on the back, and he and Alex made their way to the car. They drove down Highway 90 and parked as close to Dunbar Avenue as they could. Their street was blocked by fallen trees and wreckage, so the two began slogging through. Alex, born with a mild case of cerebral palsy, had experienced difficulty walking since birth. Yet the seventeen-year-old was determined to keep pace as they neared their white-brick one-story home. David's pulse quickened as he saw the house was still standing, but then he spotted a water line of pine needles and small branches about nine feet up, on the roof. He knew then that they, too, had lost everything.

At the same time, we were racing west from Mobile, unsure what, if anything, was left of Bay St. Louis. The main highways between Alabama and Mississippi had been shut down. I'd tracked down a man who was the last evacuee to arrive at our Mobile hotel Sunday night.

"You gotta use the back roads," he advised me as I scrawled down the directions. "It's the only way you're gonna get through."

As we headed toward the cars, a thin red-headed woman stopped me. She and her husband and teenage daughter had evacuated from Waveland, the town just west of Bay St. Louis. "I know you're busy, but could y'all let us know how Waveland is? We left our dogs behind, and we're really scared about the reports we're hearing." She pressed a scrap of paper with her phone number and address into my hand.

Mobile city crews were already out in force, using everything from backhoes to leaf blowers and push brooms to clear branches and other debris from the streets. As we drove west, trees were down. Then entire stands of forest were leaning over, toppled by the hurricane-force winds. Even supple pine trees had been snapped in half. Downed power lines draped the roadway. Roofs were missing shingles, then were just missing altogether. Highway billboards were mangled and twisted. Once we hit I-10 north of Biloxi, only the empty billboard frames remained. I peered south as we passed the exit for Keesler Air Force Base, knowing my brother and his family were there somewhere, hopefully still alive.

We passed a motorcade of tree-service trucks heading west. Next in the procession came a dozen vehicles pulling Florida Fish and Wildlife boats. Then three ambulances headed in the same direction flew past us.

With every mile, my heart sank. Still, I dutifully recorded it all in my reporter's notepad, a grim catalog of destruction. Then we turned south on Highway 49 into Gulfport, and I stopped writing. I did not have enough paper or ink.

Roofs and awnings had been ripped off more buildings than I could count. Some businesses had collapsed entirely, sending a shower of bricks into the road. Debris and smashed, overturned cars littered parking lots. Mississippi National Guard units swarmed the downtown business district. Some stood guard against looters, while others operated heavy equipment to clear the main road down to the beach.

Outside the courthouse, we spotted a thin man wearing a Harrison County coroner's hat. He sighed as we asked the inevitable question: How many had died?

"We have numerous John Does, Jane Does. Everything is being documented with addresses and GPS coordinates where the bodies are being found," explained Jason Green calmly. "And we're just asking for everyone's patience."

"And the count so far?" I asked.

"Twenty-six." He looked around as if struggling to comprehend the number he'd just uttered. "It's just total destruction. It's catastrophic. Our whole Gulf Coast is destroyed."

I asked if any bodies had been found at Keesler Air Force Base.

No, the coroner's official answered, much to my relief. Thank God! At least I knew my brother and his family had survived.

I pulled Green aside and asked how he was doing and how his house had fared.

It was gone, he said bluntly. "We're holding up the best we can. We think we're strong people. But we're being put to the test now."

Across Highway 49, we saw a blond man in a red polo shirt and jeans surveying the shattered exterior of the Hancock Bank headquarters. It was John Hairston, the chief operating officer. The entire granite wall at the entrance had been ripped off, and a melamine chair sat perched on the edge of the now-visible second floor. "Don't know where that came from," he said, pointing. "We don't even have that kind of chair in our office."

Hairston explained how the storm surge and floating debris had taken out the ground-floor walls, while the building's windows had been broken by boards and roofing that had been peeled off nearby structures by the hurricane winds. Nearly every window on the bottom eight floors of the fifteen-story headquarters was shattered.

"What about your Bay St. Louis branch? What have you heard from there?" I asked.

"Bay St. Louis did not do very well," he replied. "Some of the areas are actually still cordoned off to where we can't get to them."

"Cordoned off? Why?" I asked, not sure I wanted to hear his answer.

"They're still removing bodies."

Hoping to find a route west, we drove south to the beach road but got no farther. An enormous wall of more than fifty crumpled truck trailers from the adjoining port blocked all four lanes of Highway 90, the road I used to drive to work every day. It looked

~Hurricane-battered downtown Gulfport business district
Photo by Janet Rodriguez/CNN

like a giant toddler in a rage had dumped out his box of toy trucks. Mangled and crushed, they were too high to climb over or drive around. Several protruded from the lobby of a hotel overlooking the highway. The scene was so surreal that my mind could barely process what my eyes were seeing.

Looming over the bizarre devastation was the hulking wreckage of the 450-foot-long, pink Copa Casino barge, which had once bobbed in a berth at the nearby state docks. It now rested in a parking lot a half-mile inland, its lower walls ripped open to expose slot machines and mud-covered gaming stools.

We had heard radio reports about the looting and bedlam in New Orleans. But here, many residents wandered emotionless through the wreckage. I studied them, trying to process how they fit into the chaos in front of us. A man and his daughters walked by not seeing, not reacting to the destruction, just moving. They had a blankness in their eyes I'd never seen before. I didn't know I would see it again and again and again.

Near the trailers lay a sea lion that had washed up out of the

~Copa Casino barge sitting next to Highway 90 in downtown Gulfport
Photo by Janet Rodriguez/CNN

destroyed Marine Life Oceanarium. A small group had gathered around to pour water over the animal as it panted helplessly in the blistering heat. When one person tired, someone else would take his place. Because they could do nothing about the devastation around them, keeping the sea lion alive became a way of doing something, whether it was fighting back or refusing to quit.

Larger groups of people were scrambling through the beachfront wreckage. We weren't sure where or when we'd be in danger. Power, water, and phone service were all out, and no relief supplies had arrived yet. We were careful not to open our SUVs in plain sight and reveal the food and water we had on board. We didn't want to start a riot. And as much as we wanted to share, it was all we had. In talking with colleagues, we'd already heard how one desperate Mississippi woman tried to cut a CNN team's spare gas can off its vehicle right in front of them. So we decided to keep moving.

We headed west down Railroad Street, the only east-west artery that was passable. It paralleled the CSX railroad tracks. Just beyond the rail bed, survivors had hung handmade plywood and cardboard signs on trees with their names or addresses and short messages like "All OK" and "We got out."

Where the road ended, we turned south over the tracks, hoping to make it to the beach. But other than a narrow stretch of homes close to the raised railroad, everything was obliterated. Every street leading to the water was clogged with roofs, walls, trees, cars, boats—the mangled remains of once-beautiful beachfront neighborhoods.

We drove west on Second Street and stopped next to a large culvert where a few people had gathered. Beyond it stood the shell of a Wal-Mart. From our vantage point, we could look straight through the building's missing walls to the water.

A man in his late fifties holding a baby stood next to his adult daughter, gazing at the wreckage. The entire contents of the Wal-Mart had been swept by the wind and storm surge into the drainage ditch. Washers, TVs, plastic storage bins, soccer balls, toasters— all were intertwined with masses of wet, muddy clothing, towels, sheets, and other unrecognizable fabric.

Paul Eppert said he and his daughter Crystal had both worked

~Crushed seafood delivery truck in Pass Christian, Mississippi
Photo by Mark Proulx

at the Wal-Mart—he as a manager, she as a pharmacy tech. "Pretty bad scene," he concluded.

"I'm speechless. I don't know. I don't have a job." The young woman fought back tears. "I have a home. I'm thankful for that. But I don't know how I'm . . . I don't know."

"It'll be all right," insisted her father. "We got water and food to last us . . . probably last us this week. But after that, we don't know, if something doesn't start opening up around here."

A young security guard kept watch nearby. He explained that people had been looting tires and other usable items. He must have gathered by our stunned expressions how ludicrous it seemed that Wal-Mart would attempt to salvage anything from the muddy wreckage. "And there are five bodies in there," he added, as if to justify his presence.

I glanced down at the culvert and then quickly averted my eyes. I'd never seen a dead body before and didn't want to start today. I tried not to think about the sickly sweet smell that hung in the air.

We continued west and came upon a stocky young man in a dirty gray shirt and shorts, walking down the road with a cat and a dog. Mud encrusted his legs from the thighs down. He was from Henderson Point, a Pass Christian neighborhood that jutted into the mouth of St. Louis Bay. Jim Thompson said he'd stayed in his home during the hurricane until the water was up to his chest.

"It came up high enough I was able to—because it was so high—force Willow and the cat out the window and push them up onto the roof. And once I'd gotten them out, I did the same thing." The young man's eyes were red and welling with tears.

"What did you see when you got to the roof?" I asked.

"A lot of water. A lot of water."

Thompson described how his house had come apart into four pieces and how he, his dog, Willow, and his cat, LJ, had spent nearly four hours clinging to the roof as Katrina roared onshore. "It was weird 'cause I had actually noticed that some of the other houses in the area were floating and starting to move around me." Thompson shook his head at the unreality of what he was saying.

"How are you still here alive?" I asked after hearing his tale.

"Some would say I'm supposed to be."

"Someone upstairs likes you," I offered.

Thompson cracked a weary smile. "Somebody somewhere."

After explaining that he was trying to get to family in Gulfport, he set off east.

We drove only half a mile before finding the remainder of the road was a tangled web of debris, downed trees, broken power lines, and toppled power poles. Our cameramen, Emmanuel and Gil, decided to stay and set up for a live shot while Janet and I looked for more survivors.

While Janet drove, I walked in front of the SUV, picking up shattered glass and shoving aside nail-studded boards and wreckage that might puncture the tires. What we couldn't drive over, I walked backwards and guided the SUV around and under. I tried not to think about the fact that everything I pushed aside, everything crushed beneath the truck's tires, had once been part of someone's home. I did what we journalists always do: bottled up the emotion to deal with later. It was the only way to survive. The job came first.

Progress was slow. We saw no signs of life and realized we were

~Pass Christian hurricane
survivor Jim Thompson with
his dog, Willow, being
interviewed by the author
and Gil De La Rosa
Photo by Janet Rodriguez/CNN

probably the first journalists to reach these hard-hit areas. Finally, we came upon an intersection where some homes appeared intact.

After parking, we spotted a woman clearing fallen branches from her yard. But no sooner had we gotten out than two tall men approached us. Most residents we'd seen that day were sweaty and filthy either from the storm or their efforts to clean up its effects. These men weren't.

"Hi! Are you from around here?" I asked.

They didn't respond. Janet and I followed their gaze as it went from us to our black SUV with the red gas cans strapped to the top.

"You sure don't look like you're from around here," one of them finally said slowly.

I plunged ahead, ignoring the uncomfortable feeling that was growing by the second. "We're from CNN. We're looking for people who rode out the hurricane to interview."

The men looked at each other. One then gestured over his shoulder. "There's an old guy back there that stayed. Maybe he'll talk to you."

I looked in the direction he pointed, where a mass of toppled trees almost obscured a small house. Peering out from behind the crisscrossed trunks was a nervous, bespectacled old man. Janet and I didn't have to say a word. We both knew there was no way we were climbing back there and letting these men get between us and our vehicle.

"Actually, I think we'll check first with these folks we saw clearing debris over here," I said.

"Right," said Janet. "That crowd could have some stories to tell." Catching on to my ruse, she inflated the number of people nearby. "I'll call the guys and let them know where to meet us."

I turned and walked diagonally toward the yard the woman was clearing while Janet headed toward the SUV. The woman, not interested in talking, waved me off. When I turned back to the car, the men had disappeared.

Janet and I went another block west to Espy Street before we decided it was time to turn back and rejoin the crew. We'd become keenly aware of how vulnerable we were.

As we wrapped our live shot, a car pulled up and a burly, dark-haired man with a gray mustache got out. Richard Notter, a local alderman, offered to give us a tour of what was left of the town of Long Beach.

First, he gestured to an enormous empty slab next to us. It had been an apartment complex. "It's the same view everywhere. There was a four-story hotel at the end of this street. These were houses, both sides, all the way to the beach." He gestured with both arms toward the water. "Down on the end was two huge condominium complexes, and those are totally gone. And this is repeated every street throughout the entire city."

We got in the car. As Notter drove, he pointed to mounds of twisted walls, roofs, beams, and wreckage that had been homes that withstood Camille. He didn't know if the residents had left this time.

"I noticed that nobody is showing their emotions," I remarked.

"Well, you know, I think people are just in shock," said Notter. "I just don't think they know what to think. I mean, I know I don't."

Downtown, we got out next to the flattened First Baptist Church.

Only the sign remained. An American flag planted in the rubble fluttered gently in the evening breeze.

"Several businesses went down this way. Those are all gone. This was all businesses here on our left side. Those were destroyed all the way to the beach." Notter pointed to an empty sign, the only thing standing on the waterfront. "We had some old businesses down there. The Waffle House is gone. You can look down here and see what type of debris field . . . I mean, everything is pretty much eradicated."

"Where do you begin? Where do you start?" I asked, looking at the rubble that flowed uninterrupted to the water.

"I don't know. I don't know," he confessed. "We've been through catastrophes before, and the people of this town . . . This is a very strong group of individuals. People will pull together. People will help their neighbors, and that's what it's going to take. It's going to take the help of each of us working together. I like to think that people's community, when things are at their worst, they are at their

~Long Beach's
First Baptist Church
in ruins
Photo by Janet Rodriguez/CNN

best. We just have to work together and clean the town up and rebuild."

A sunburned man and his wife walked up and shook the alderman's hand. Mike and Taylor had fled their Long Beach home in the middle of the storm.

"Yeah, about 8 A.M., the water started rising. So we got in our truck and left and gone down the street and got blocked. So then we had to climb out of our truck and run across the tracks in probably 110-, 120-mile-an-hour winds." Mike's voice was dry and raspy.

"Why did you stay?" I asked.

"Well, I didn't think it was going to be this bad. Camille wasn't like this." Mike looked at the carnage around him. "I've never seen this much devastation. It went further inland. There's nothing left."

"What happens next?"

"Patience. Time. Just a lot of hard work." He blinked back tears as he looked down at the metal toolbox in his hand. "This is what I've got right here, my clothes and my tools."

"But you've got your lives."

"That's exactly right."

"And this is a coastline of survivors."

~REMAINS OF A WATERFRONT BUSINESS IN LONG BEACH, MISSISSIPPI
Photo by Janet Rodriguez/CNN

"Oh, we'll be back. I'll build another house. We'll be here." Mike shook my hand. "Thank you. Just send help."

I stepped back and the two men embraced, Notter patting Mike on the back. "It'll be good," he reassured his friend.

"It's not going to be good for a while."

"Yep," acknowledged Notter.

—

Thirteen miles to the west, chicken and sausage sizzled on the stove outside the third Emergency Operations Center, or EOC, set up in Bay St. Louis. The first two had flooded out. This one took on water but was at least usable.

"You want something to eat?" asked the self-appointed chef as Congressman Gene Taylor pulled up in a battered 1980 Mercedes 300D. The car had been sitting in a storage shed so long the windows wouldn't go down and the air conditioning wouldn't work. Its top speed was just thirty miles an hour. But it ran on diesel, a fuel that was easier to find than gasoline. And the congressman discovered he could get ventilation as he drove by holding the door slightly ajar with his foot.

"Where'd you get all that?" asked Gene, surveying the meat and realizing it had been awhile since he enjoyed a hot meal.

"Oh, we looted the Wal-Mart," replied the man.

Gene's mouth dropped in disbelief.

"Oh, yeah. By the way, if you want a T-shirt or somethin', we took those, too," the man added.

Eddie Favre and Tommy Longo, the mayor of nearby Waveland, were sitting on the stoop. They confirmed that they and the Hancock County Board of Supervisors had sanctioned the looting of local stores so residents would have food, water, and clothing. They had few options, since relief supplies were still nonexistent.

"Hell, it was David Yarborough who picked up a pipe, broke the window at the Spur Station, and said, 'Let's get whatever we can outta there,'" said Eddie.

Gene shook his head at the thought of a county supervisor being forced to break into local businesses.

"Gene, we finally said, 'What are they gonna do? Put us in jail?' " Eddie explained. "Get what we can out of it. There ain't nobody here gonna use it."

"The Wal-Mart, too?"

"Well, the windows were broken, so I said, 'Let's go on in,' " the mayor said. "Same at Winn-Dixie. Eckerd. We went on in and took everything we could. Then we took a school bus, started making all kinds of runs down to the high-school gym, where we set up a shelter."

Gene glanced inside the EOC at the clothing, water, soft drinks, canned goods, potato chips, and cookies the band of official looters had accumulated. "So is anybody at the stores now?"

"Gene, we're basically letting people who need stuff go in and get it," Eddie said.

"No police there?"

"They're going back and forth. I told the guys, 'Look. If people are looting for items they need to survive on, leave 'em alone.' " Eddie leaned forward. " 'But if it's not things that they need to survive, shoot the bastards.' "

At the Coast Inn, Tommy and Linda Kidd and the other guests took advantage of the edict. All their cars had been flooded. Linda's even had a gaping hole in the windshield from a boat propeller. So no one was going anywhere. But the Kmart was across the street and the Wal-Mart next door, making it an easy walk to find water, ice, and food. Someone hauled a gas grill out of one of the stores and began cooking whatever people brought.

"We're living large!" exclaimed Tommy, taking his turn at the grill. He'd spent all morning handing out ice and water at the back of the Kmart and helping keep an eye on the sanctioned looting. Though the store had been flooded with seven to eight feet of water, items on the top shelves were still dry. Most people were climbing up and pulling down necessities like diapers, medical supplies, canned goods, and pet food. Tommy had to step in only once, when a handful of young men in their early twenties tried to smash open a jewelry case.

He sauntered over and smiled up at the ringleader. "Don't do that."

"And who made you police chief, old man?" cracked one of the boys.

"Oh, no. I'm not the police chief," laughed Tommy, his eyes twinkling as he reached in his pocket and pulled out a badge. "Just deputy sheriff. Y'all move along, now."

Two miles down the road, Nikki and Patrick Cleveland wandered outside the high-school shelter trying to find help. Bruised and battered from head to toe and wearing nothing but hospital gowns, they were a bizarre sight. They'd been discharged at six that morning with a fistful of antibiotics and pain relievers, despite the fact that Patrick had been near death from aspiration pneumonia. Nikki had spent what felt like endless hours watching hospital workers pound on his back to break up the water that had pooled in his lungs.

Since it was nearly empty of cars, they decided to try the highway. They'd heard that Dr. Waddy LeBourgeois, a fellow veterinarian and Nikki's father's best friend, was looking for them. They had no money, no identification, no car, no clothing. And no one had seen Nikki's parents. Nikki hoped they were with Dr. LeBourgeois and was determined to get there.

"Stop! Help!" screamed Nikki, waving her arms at the few cars that went by. But no one would stop.

Patrick had been heavily sedated all night and was still weak and groggy. It was evening now, and the traffic was dropping off even further. When a police car approached, Nikki decided to take a chance. She ran into the road in front of it. "Help us! Please stop!"

"Miss, are you crazy?" shouted the officer as the patrol car screeched to a halt. "I could have killed you!"

"Thank you. Thank you so much," said Nikki before she blurted out their story.

"Well, y'all get in. My family's over there on Old Spanish Trail near where he is," said the officer, figuring at the very least he was getting the odd duo out of his jurisdiction. "I'll drop you off and check on them."

———

It was getting dark as my CNN crew navigated the eerily empty roads back to Gulfport. We reported late into the night in front of a gutted gas station across from the twisted stack of box trailers splayed across the highway. Morning live shots would start at five, so Janet and I scrubbed down with baby wipes, brushed our teeth in the debris-littered parking lot, and climbed into the back of the SUV to sleep. We set up our rechargeable lantern fans and cracked the windows slightly so no one could reach in. The night was hot and unbearably humid. As uncomfortable as it was, I knew tens of thousands along the Gulf Coast were enduring much worse. I folded a shirt into a makeshift pillow and slipped into a fitful sleep.

The day replayed in fast forward in my dreams, the people we'd met flowing past on a rushing tsunami of wreckage. I dreamed of my golden Labrador, Nick. Normally gentle, he morphed into a fierce beast, snarling, growling, and biting. I tried to calm him but couldn't. I wasn't strong enough. Nick, like everything else, was out of control, and I could do nothing to change it.

Wednesday morning, we were into our second hour of live shots when the silence of Gulfport's desolate, mangled waterfront was broken by the roar of engines. A motorcade of backhoes, front-end loaders, and dump trucks rolled past us and began scooping up the debris, much of it goods Katrina had strewn over the waterfront from the nearby port. On a normal day, the port hummed with traffic as products like grain, timber, and poultry were shipped out while imports from bananas to cars to lingerie were off-loaded onto trucks and trains. Now, the stench of tons of rotting chicken and pork bellies hung in the air. Huge three-ton rolls of brown paper dotted the landscape. Bags of cat and dog food were tossed everywhere, most still intact.

No one knew when stores would open again or when food for people or pets would begin arriving. So we stopped the few cars that passed and asked if those inside wanted cat or dog food, and to spread the word. One man pulled over and began loading bags into his trunk. As the backhoes approached, we tried to snatch the pet food out of the way. We kept up the crazy game of cat and mouse until we'd passed out all the bags we could. It wasn't much, but it felt good to do something to help.

~Videographer Gil De La Rosa, the author, and videographer
Emmanuel Tambekakis preparing for a live report in Gulfport
Photo by Alec Miran/CNN

In the morning light, we could see into the smashed gas station that had been our backdrop the night before. The refrigerated cases were still packed with water and drinks, and food on the shelves appeared to be salvageable.

"Guys, what do you think?" I asked Emmanuel and Gil. "Should we tell people before it goes bad? I mean, it seems a shame to just let it rot."

I knew in asking the question that I was wandering into territory that was off-limits. Journalists are supposed to be neutral observers, not active participants, even in war zones. Otherwise, they could impact the outcome of a story and bias their own reporting.

But no one had ever talked about how to respond when ground zero was your hometown.

"I don't know," responded Gil with a shrug. "Better leave it."

I was frustrated. Would that really be looting, or just being resourceful? What was the difference between trespassing and doing what had to be done to help your fellow man? All the normal rules seemed absurd and inapplicable.

By midmorning, the heat was almost unbearable. It's always that way after hurricanes pass. They suck the rain and clouds inland with them, leaving behind the clearest blue skies and most intense sun imaginable.

A local man stopped to ask if we needed anything. We thanked him and said we were fine. Amazing! His town was flattened by a hurricane, and he wanted to know if we were okay.

During a break in live shots, I finally got a chance to check my e-mail on the satellite truck's laptop. My inbox was jammed, but not just with e-mails from CNN. People were reaching out to me, desperate for help in finding missing family members or learning whether their homes had survived. Their anguish was palpable.

Subject: need help!

Kathleen,

Do you have communication with the police or sheriff's office? We are trying to find out if my home is still standing on 5th Avenue, just four blocks north of Hwy. 90 in Gulfport. It is located 2 miles east of the new Federal Courthouse. Would you be able to help me find out some information? I would appreciate any help that you can give me. My 75 year old mother, my daughter and I are staying in Thomasville, GA in a hotel. My cell phone is not working. I will check my e-mail.

Sheila Currie

Subject: Checking for Help

Kathleen,

I'm in Washington DC and trying to check on my sister and brother in law. I saw your report from Pass Christian this afternoon. That is the town they live in. We heard from them last night for about 45 seconds and know they are alive, but have not heard from them since. Their house is about 2 blocks off the beach off Hwy. 90 at Shadow Lawn (not that street signs even exist anymore). According to her brief report to us, they spent the worst part of the storm in their attic and came out to find a lot of destruction.

They stayed because my brother in law is a doctor and serves as the medical director for the local EMS. I don't know if you'll report from there again, but if you are back in that area and see folks could you ask about them?

Again, many thanks.

Kiki McLean

Subject: Need Information on James Hyre, Ocean Springs, MS

James (my Uncle), lives at 2 Gulf View Dr, in Ocean Springs. My mother spoke with him at 7 AM Monday morning, and we fear he didn't get out.

Too close to the ocean.

Ralph Hyre

Subject: Valorie (Young)—Bay High Classmate

Dear Kathie,

I am grasping at any lead or contact to try to find information about my father. I've had no success in phone contact with anyone.

I'm particularly concerned about Dad since he is a stroke victim and is wheelchair bound. As of 11:00 P.M. Sunday night before the storm hit, he and his wife had not left their house, even though several of us family members tried to convince them to leave. Most shelters are not set up conveniently to help handicapped people, so they thought they'd take their chances at home.

I'm writing on the chance that you'll be able to read this and if time and conditions allow, to ask you to add my dad's name to your list.

Thanks, Kathie!

Love,

Valorie

Subject: long shot—missing parents in bay st. louis

I unfortunately have not heard from my fam. They live in bay st. louis and . . . its bad there. They decided to ride it out, and they have a pretty old home, but i can't call or anything. I've seen some homes pretty trashed and i am kind of scared.

I have no clue if you can do this or anything, but i was wondering if you could see if its still standing. They live at 504 N. Second St., Bay St. Louis, MS. I would do anything to know they are ok.

Many (many) thanks,

Joshua

Subject: Treutels

Kathleen,

I saw your report this morning. I graduated from Stanislaus in '78 with Paul & Steve Treutel and dated Missy. . . . Did you find out anything about them? I heard that their parents planned to ride it out in their house on St. Charles.

Jim Murphy

Subject: looking for relative—Gulfport

My film professor from GW is looking for more info on his father and his property, including missing dogs, in Gulfport. His name is Gary Lorenz, they lived on Bayou Village Drive in Gulfport. My prof's name is Jay Lorenz.

Alexis

Subject: Hey! From Lydia Schultz

Just left a message on your phone. Was trying to get to MS when I got stopped cold in Atlanta. Am in Woodstock at Brooke's house hoping I can get some info about my house and Van. He stayed. It is soooooooooooo nerve wracking. Painful to not be able to get through and then you see these pictures that are sooooo God awful! Anyway, our house is on Breeden Place. I cannot imagine what it is going to be like in there.

Lydia

Most of the heart-wrenching e-mails were from strangers. Some, though, were from people I knew, like Sheila Currie, a local

Rotarian, and Valorie Young, one of my closest friends from high school.

The last one was from Lydia Schultz, my mom's best friend before she and my dad left Mississippi. Lydia, her husband, Van, and their daughters, Brooke and Marie, had lived around the corner from us in Bay St. Louis. Lydia was witty and sassy, a passionate woman who boldly embraced everything life threw her way. Van was the polar opposite—quiet and introverted. I babysat their girls regularly as a teenager. Brooke was a fun, spunky little kid who was always into mischief. Marie, a year and a half younger, was gentle and thoughtful and had a smile so sweet it could melt an iceberg. They were grown young women now, their parents divorced but still close friends. Van and Lydia had moved into a new home on a street built just a few years earlier. I couldn't believe Van had stayed. And I didn't know how I would find the street, much less the house, if Bay St. Louis looked anything like what we'd already seen.

I jumped on the satellite truck's phone to check my voice mail. Again, I was overwhelmed.

"Hey, Kathie. This is Lydia Schultz. I'm stuck in Atlanta and not trying to get down there just yet. But I've not been able to get in touch with Van in any kind of way. He stayed in the house on Breeden Place, and I was just wondering if there was some way you could possibly help me. My number is . . ." She barely finished her phone number before dissolving into tears.

The next caller was my brother-in-law, who had grown up in Long Beach. "Hey, Kathie. It's Mick. Just got off the phone with Mom. She talked to Kelly last night. They're doing okay. My cousin Monica that lived behind the Wal-Mart in Pass Christian, the house is gone. They have nothing but a slab. Kelly's house, they took a branch through the roof. Physically, everybody's okay. Just like everyone else, they're starving for information, specifically on access for roads. There's a lot of people that want to help—us included—trying to get supplies, relief supplies, in and out. So if in any of your clips you guys can find out what roads are open, what sections of I-10 are closed down, what bridges are shut down . . . I really appreciate everything you're doing down there."

Next was my older sister. "Hey, Kathie. This is Gerri. In case

Mom and Dad didn't call you, they've heard from Mark. Somehow, he was able to get out of the hospital and go to their location for their home. And believe it or not, in Ocean Springs at their location, their home is still standing. He said the pillars that hold up their front doorway area were pushed all the way from the front of the porch to the back of the porch. But he said that's totally easy for them to fix. He didn't say much about other damage. But he said they have a structure that they can live in. Now what they've been told by the National Guard is of course the homes aren't safe to go back to. No power. No water. And they're getting put in temporary, he said, Quonset-type housing on the Keesler Air Force Base for now. And at some point, they'll be able to go home. Do stay safe 'cause it's pretty unpredictable out there!"

Hallelujah! Mark and Maureen hadn't lost their home!

The next voice mail was from my brother himself. My heart leaped. It was so good to hear his voice.

"Kathie, this is Mark. I just wanted to let you know we got a chance to check our house today, and it has very minimal damage. Just a dozen or so shingles off. Mom was worried about our friends over in Bay St. Louis. Obviously, they took a pretty bad hit. I'm up on the roof of one of the buildings to get a good strong signal. We're all doing okay. Not sure when we might be released to go back to our house. I have my phone on. I don't know. I don't want to stay up on the roof too long. I'll probably go down and keep an eye on the kids. Talk to you soon!"

He sounded tired, but the news was all good. I so wanted to see him, hug him, tell him I was relieved he was alive and that I'd *kill* him if he ever did anything like this again!

My younger sister called next. "Kathie, this is Laurie. Missy Treutel is looking for Paul's family, for Steve's family, and for Pennie and David. And then your classmate Valorie Young called, and she's looking for her father, Tom Young. He is in a wheelchair. He's had a stroke. Anyway, she knows that they were staying 'cause he's difficult to care for other places. Hopefully, you'll get this message. I have called Missy to ask if she has any news of them, so you don't have to go if they've been located."

I hung up, drained just from listening to their gut-wrenching

~Remains of a Diamondhead neighborhood
Photo by Mark Proulx

messages. Suddenly, our live reports seemed so pointless. Lydia and the others needed help. People were missing, maybe dead. Homes were gone. No one could call into Mississippi's 228 area code. We were literally the only ones they could turn to.

"Kathleen, do you know where Diamondhead is?" Emmanuel asked, hanging up the truck's other phone.

"Sure. It's just north of Bay St. Louis. Why?" I asked.

Emmanuel, too, had gotten a frantic call from a friend, Kim Pierce, he'd known since he was a teenager. Her ninety-two-year-old grandmother was in a nursing home there, and Kim was anxious to find out if she was okay. That was all the encouragement I needed. Damn the rules! I was ready to leap across the line against journalistic involvement with both feet. But we'd do it on our own time, and we'd leave the camera behind.

"As soon as we're done, we're outta here," I promised him.

As other crews arrived at the satellite truck, we learned that CNN had secured a hotel in Ocean Springs for network personnel. A bed sure sounded a far sight better than another night in the SUV. But first, I needed information. Reporter Gary Tuchman had been to Bay St. Louis. I pumped him for details. How bad was it? Would the home I'd grown up in on South Beach Boulevard be standing?

Gary wouldn't look me in the eye. "It's bad," he mumbled, squinting down at his notepad, trying to look busy.

"Can I look at the tape?"

"Sorry, Kathleen. We've got to start editing soon." Gary turned away, peering at the monitor. He said nothing else. He didn't have to. I understood.

We wrapped and made our way to the hotel, only to find out it was full. CNN had forgotten to hold rooms for us. Luckily, the manager at the hotel next door somehow managed to find four rooms. We had no power or potable water, but at least we had beds.

After we checked in and threw our bags in the rooms, Emmanuel and I dashed west. It was dark when we finally reached the Diamondhead exit, the intersection ahead swarming with police. An eighteen-wheeler blocked the road north into the development.

I jumped out and found Hancock County sheriff Steve Garber. I explained we were with CNN and were looking for a woman at the senior citizens' center. And I asked about the dead. Did he have a count yet for the county?

"No. But Pearlington's bad. Pulled about a half-dozen bodies out of there," he said as he gestured to his officers to move the truck and let us pass. "Careful, now. Had some tornadoes back there. It's a mess."

There were no lights. Huge downed trees lay strewn across the road. We wove slowly around them. Street signs were gone, so we missed a turn and had to backtrack down the darkened roads.

Ahead, we spotted the taillights of a large vehicle, a bus parked outside the senior citizens' center. Aides were guiding hot, tired elderly men and women out of the building and into the air-conditioned bus. The seniors seemed to be in good condition despite the intense heat and humidity, and the building's structure appeared intact.

Emmanuel plunged into the group. "Has anyone seen Mrs. Lorena Hornsby?"

"Her nurse is inside," said one of the aides.

We entered the building. While hot, the interior was dry. Emergency lights cast a dim glow. A man with a flashlight guided us back. "I-10 saved us," he explained as we walked. "Water came under it and right up to the door here. Then it stopped."

A smiling young woman at the end of the hall was helping the last few residents gather their belongings. "Oh, Mrs. Hornsby?" she said. "She's a dear, and she's just fine. I put her on a bus to Wiggins not twenty minutes ago."

Mission accomplished!

Emmanuel and I drove back down the darkened interstate. When we hit the Highway 49 overpass, he e-mailed Kim the good news on his BlackBerry. We'd discovered a handful of spots where for one reason or another cell phones and BlackBerries sporadically got signals.

My BlackBerry vibrated to life as we drove down the other side. It was our Thursday assignment—Bay St. Louis.

~5~

Return to the Bay

"KATHLEEN!" JANET WAS POUNDING on my door. "Hurry! The Waffle House is open!"

I pulled aside the drapes. Sure enough. A generator was hooked up to the back of the restaurant next door, and a line was already forming into the parking lot. I dashed out with Janet and joined it. We'd been living on fruit, tuna, canned soup, granola bars, and Gatorade since Monday, so a hot meal was a godsend.

In line, we planned our day. CNN wanted something different, so we decided to put a microphone on me and do what it might be cruel to do to someone else—have the camera follow me as I saw what, if anything, was left of my hometown. I'd give viewers a guided tour of the devastation.

We sat down to find a scaled-back menu. But the food and the coffee were hot, and no one was complaining. A large, cheerful young woman with long, light brown hair pulled back in a ponytail took our order. She, too, was staying in a local hotel, she explained, since Katrina had destroyed her home. "But my husband's a roofer. And I work here," she added with a smile. "So we both have jobs. We'll be fine."

A few minutes later, when she was refilling our coffee and overheard our plans to head west, she confessed to one need. "The kids—my husband's with them now—they've got no toys. They are driving him to distraction! If y'all see any stores open . . ."

We promised to do what we could and downed our breakfast quickly, eager to get on the road. As we finished, an elderly couple who'd been in line behind us stopped by the table. They remembered me from my days reporting at Biloxi's WLOX-TV.

"Y'all have to get the word out that the infrastructure has to get up and running," insisted the husband, leaning in and gazing at me intently through his thick glasses. "The post offices have to open up. Senior citizens like us need our Social Security checks. The banks have to open up 'cause all the ATMs are down. People are running out of cash, and that's all anyone takes right now." He reached into his jeans and pulled out a fistful of crumpled dollar bills. "I'm seventy years old, and all I have in my pocket is fourteen dollars."

We were stunned. Before he could step back, I pulled my purse into my lap and dug for my wallet.

He put out his hand to stop me. "No, ma'am. That's not why I told you this. I don't need your money." He stood up straight and adjusted the American Legion hat on his head. "We'll be fine. You just have to let people know that things have to start working again."

We shook their hands and again promised to do what we could. We hadn't even left, and already I was moved beyond words. The courage and resilience of these people were astonishing.

In the parking lot, I made a quick satellite phone call to my parents—who'd retired to Colorado—for a list of friends and neighbors to search for. My mother read out Van Schultz's address, and I shook my head as I jotted it down. Addresses were ludicrously useless. "Mom, no street signs are left, much less mailboxes. And after what we've seen, I don't know if the house will even be standing. If you talk to Lydia, ask what color the roof is or what type of flooring they had—tile or hardwood or carpeting—because that could be all that's left."

I hung up, and we headed west. The empty steel billboard frames looming above the highway were bent like spaghetti and twisted beyond recognition. We passed one exit clogged with cars lined up at a gas station operating with a generator. People stood outside their vehicles, engines shut off to save gasoline, while armed police looked on to keep order.

As hard as I'd been trying to get home, a feeling of dread grew with every mile. We'd already seen the damage progressively worsen as we went west. I tried to persuade myself that some areas might still be just fine. But I knew that wasn't likely.

After forty minutes, we turned down the Route 603 exit for Bay St. Louis, and our mouths fell open. Unlike Gulfport and Biloxi, where buildings near the interstate were missing roofs or awnings, they were a shambles here. Unrecognizable. Mangled, muddy cars littered both shoulders, some flipped upside down and partially blocking the road. I imagined the line of vehicles racing north as Katrina's winds buffeted them, its storm surge overtaking the fleeing residents and . . . I didn't want to complete the thought.

A handful of people wandered among the cars, walking with no visible destination. Pieces of walls and roofs and sometimes entire houses flung off their foundations lay sideways and upside down along the road and in the woods.

We reached Highway 90 and turned left toward downtown Bay St. Louis. A hodgepodge of tents of various shapes and sizes had sprouted in the Kmart parking lot, which now resembled a refugee camp. A tattered sheet staked at one entrance proclaimed it "Camp Katrina." The only traffic on the road was military vehicles and a handful of pickup trucks, some with entire families riding in the beds. As we passed, a man in the back of one solemnly held up a soiled American flag. Most people were on foot, carrying their belongings in plastic laundry baskets or pushing them down the road in shopping carts. Every elevated sign on the businesses along the highway had been blown out. Boats were everywhere but where they belonged—in the woods, on top of cars, even in the bank and Burger King drive-throughs.

As we approached an intersection, a man with a shotgun motioned for us to stop and then grabbed Emmanuel's arm as we rolled to a halt. "I need that gas," he said, pointing to the red cans strapped to the tops of the SUVs. "I need it!" The man was sweating, wild-eyed, and desperate.

~A family drives past in Waveland solemnly holding an American flag.
Photo by Janet Rodriguez/CNN

"Listen, brother. I'm with CNN. I'm here to do this story. If it were up to me, I'd give you this whole goddamn car and the gas in it," replied Emmanuel. "But if I don't get this story out, you won't get the help you need. If we're done at the end of the day and have some left, I'll come back."

Somehow, his calm tone and demeanor resonated. The man stepped back and let us pass.

We turned left toward my high school, Bay High. Dozens of the lanky loblolly pines on campus had been snapped in two and lay scattered on the ground. A crowd of people milled about out front. When they spotted us, they began yelling. As we got closer, it grew clear this was no welcoming committee. "Give us your gas, goddamn it! Stop! We're gonna beat the hell out of you! You better give us that truck!"

"Keep going, Janet!" I yelled. "Don't stop! Drive around. Drive around!"

Janet and Emmanuel behind us floored it and sped past the angry mob, around the side of the gym, and out of sight. We pulled over, our hearts pounding. Two armed security guards approached the cars. The high school had been turned into a shelter, they explained. But it had no power, no gas, and little food and water. Understandably, some people were getting angry and wanted to leave.

Still, it was worth the chance to look for Van Schultz and some of my other missing friends and neighbors. The guards promised to stay with Janet, Emmanuel, and the vehicles while Gil and I saw what we could find.

Entering the gym, we discovered the laminate floor badly swollen from Katrina's floodwaters. Parallel sections had buckled, giving the odd appearance of wooden waves sweeping across the floor. The darkened hallway beyond was dank and dirty and reeked of urine and feces. Despite the lack of running water, residents had been using the bathrooms. Now that they'd become unbearable, people had resorted to relieving themselves in any private corner they could find.

I opened the door to the classroom where I'd taken typing. The roof had been ripped away, and electrical wiring and broken fluorescent light strips dangled from what was left of the ceiling. Papers and books were scattered across the floor, the desks and computers buried under pink insulation and ceiling tiles.

We made our way to the library, where I hesitated to open the door. But inside, the room appeared untouched. I leaned down and pulled a copy of one of my favorite novels, Boris Pasternak's *Doctor Zhivago,* off a bottom shelf. It was dry! I shook my head, not understanding how the books had escaped unscathed.

We stepped outside, where large sections of the school's roof were strewn about the courtyard. Under the breezeways surrounding the building and the gym, residents had set up makeshift rooms with coolers, melamine chairs from the classrooms, and what few belongings they had left. Shirts hung drying on clotheslines strung among the columns. Unfortunately, there was no list of who was at the shelter. And no one had seen any of the people we were looking for. I asked if someone was bringing them food and water.

"When they can get it," laughed a man, mopping the sweat off his face with a towel.

"They just brought water," said a woman in a blue sleeveless sundress, sitting on a stool next to her elderly mother. "Somebody had some gas. They were going to go all the way up to the Wal-Mart and get us something to eat."

"We're doing the best we can with what we got," said a smiling man, one of many wearing a Bay High Tigers T-shirt obviously taken from the cabinet of school spirit wear. "We're doing all right."

I didn't understand. It was Thursday morning. Katrina hit Monday. I had yet to see any signs of FEMA, the Red Cross, or the Salvation Army. How could all these people be left to survive with what they could cobble together on their own? In every coastal community, we'd found one main artery cleared by the Mississippi National Guard. We'd assumed that right behind us would come relief agencies setting up tents and trailers to hand out food, water, clothing, and more. Instead, nothing. Where were they?

One man in a sport shirt and shorts sat by himself, lost in his thoughts. When I approached, he told me he'd fled his home at the

~THE AUTHOR, GIL DE
LA ROSA, AND EMMANUEL
TAMBEKAKIS EDITING
BAY ST. LOUIS VIDEO IN
THE BACK OF THE SUV
Photo by Janet Rodriguez/CNN

height of the hurricane. "I was climbing from rooftop to rooftop. It was around thirty feet high. It was just horrifying. I mean, I've never gone through anything like this in my entire life." He spoke in a calm, low voice, betraying no emotion.

"So when I get to South Beach Boulevard, I'm not going to find my old house there?"

"I wouldn't think so," he responded.

We headed next to the Bay Bridge. I'd crossed it every day for years when I drove to work. It connected our little town to the rest of the Mississippi Gulf Coast. Enormous live oaks ripped up by Katrina's winds blocked the highway, so we parked and walked. It looked like a war zone. Military helicopters pounded overhead. The businesses that had lined the highway were gone. Vast swaths of sand had replaced the lovely historic homes that once graced the waterfront north and south of the bridge. At the water's edge, a couple squatted next to a swamped red van and rinsed off items they'd salvaged from the wreckage. Where the bridge was supposed to be, the asphalt of Highway 90 just dropped off, a few scattered chunks lying on either side of the roadway. Beyond that was nothing. Every single span was gone.

But people were congregating here. It was another cell-phone hot spot. I darted from person to person, running down the list of friends and neighbors I was looking for. "Have you seen Van Schultz? Any Treutels, Kergosiens, Gottsegens, Ogdens?"

"No, sorry," most replied. The sad looks on their faces told me I wasn't the first to ask about the missing and wouldn't be the last.

An excited scream erupted from a woman in a gray tank top who was on a cell phone. She began hugging her companion as he patted her shoulder reassuringly. "My son's alive!"

"I told you. I told you."

"He climbed on top of his roof!" she exclaimed, laughing and crying simultaneously. "I didn't know if he was alive. Last time we talked to him, he was taking on water."

Nearby on his cell phone, a tall, dark-haired man in muddy khaki shorts and a dirty white T-shirt leaned against the remaining highway guardrail and shook his head in frustration. "We ain't heard from nobody. I ain't talked to Erin. I don't know where she's

~Remains of the two-mile-long Bay Bridge connecting Bay St. Louis to Pass Christian
Photo by Mark Proulx

at, if she's okay or whatever. Y'all are the only friends I've been able to get in touch with."

Dejected, we were headed toward the car when two women in shorts turned and yelled my name. They were Diane and Debra Edwards, two of my Bay High classmates. Both blond-haired, blue-eyed beauties in high school, they were little changed except for a few more smile lines around the eyes. "Oh, my God!" We threw our arms around one another, the sisters talking at once. "I said, 'I think that's Kathie Koch.' Our homes are destroyed. But we're okay. We're alive. All our family's alive."

Diane lived in a two-story brick home around the corner from my old house. Debra's home was on Nicholson Avenue just north of the railroad tracks. Both had evacuated and had nothing left but the few clothes they'd taken with them. The roads were blocked, but they were hoping to return to their homes to see what they could retrieve. I offered them my extra clothes, lantern, and flashlight, but they declined. We exchanged phone numbers and addresses and promised to stay in touch.

"We have to check the Jesus statue," I told Janet before we continued our search.

Just two hundred yards from the bridge stood a statue of Jesus in front of a stone grotto. Erected in 1955 on the western grounds of St. Augustine Seminary, the first Catholic seminary in the United States to train African American priests, the display had survived Hurricane Camille in 1969. Since the bridge had proven no match for Katrina, I doubted the grotto or Jesus would be standing.

But as we rounded the toppled live oak tree, there he was. Arms outstretched, the white life-sized figure was intact. The highway sign for the bridge lay face down next to the steps leading to the stone grotto. Trees in the woods behind leaned sideways. A hundred feet away, a white minivan lay upside down next to the brick remains of someone's fireplace.

As we stood there, a car pulled up and a woman got out and opened the trunk. Inside were a few muddy possessions she'd clearly dug from the remains of her home. One was a camera. "I don't think the camera will work," she said, trying to find a clean spot on her shirt to wipe the dirt off the lens. She turned toward the statue and put the camera to her eye. "Somebody told me one time when his hands are open like that, it means, 'I love you this much.' "

In the passenger seat was her husband, his clothes stained and wrinkled. I walked around and said hello, but he offered no response. He stared through me with that dead, dazed look I'd seen in survivors' eyes days earlier. Storm zombies. The woman got in the car, and they drove off.

We turned south off the highway toward downtown and passed the grounds of St. Augustine's retreat center. I looked for the statue of the Virgin Mary that normally marked the entrance. Enormous uprooted trees lay right and left, blocking the way. In the middle of it all was the statue, almost completely obscured by limbs and branches but unbroken.

Weaving our way through an obstacle course of power lines,

mangled trees, swamped, crushed cars, and pieces of walls and roofs, we made it to Main Street. In the middle of the road, we found a tall black steeple ripped by Katrina's winds off the Main Street United Methodist Church, where it had sat for a hundred years. A plucky hand-painted sign dangled from the second-floor balcony of the apartments across the street—"We're Still on the Map."

We drove as far as we could, then parked and clambered over and around the debris. Most of the walls of the downtown business-es were gone. Where the walls held, the windows had been blown out. The roadbed was buried in sand, broken boards, and power poles, as well as glass and metal intertwined with pottery and other fragile items swept from the art studios lining the street. Where Main Street dead-ended at Beach Boulevard, the road fell away, disintegrating into a sea of broken asphalt chunks that stretched north and south as far as the eye could see. Bright yellow utility pipes wove through the shattered roadway, and odd concrete cylin-ders protruded three feet out of the sand at regular intervals where manholes had been.

~THE STATUE OF MARY GRACING THE ENTRANCE TO THE ST. AUGUSTINE
RETREAT CENTER IN BAY ST. LOUIS
Photo by Chuck Carr

I scrambled north over the crumbled road to try to find our old waterfront ice-cream parlor, which we'd shut down years earlier. It was now a popular seafood restaurant called Trapani's Eatery. All the businesses on the bay side of the boulevard were gone. Katrina had turned them into battering rams that relentlessly pummeled to pieces any nearby structures. All that was left of the white, one-story block building we once owned was a mass of broken bricks, boards, pipes, and wires.

A rifle-toting National Guardsman stood patrol on the waterfront, apparently to prevent looting, which would have made sense had there been anything left to steal. The only salvageable belongings I saw were far out of reach in the second-floor apartment over the Bay Euphonium antique store. The entire front of the building had been torn off. And while the ground floor had been swept clean by the storm surge, the furniture upstairs stood oddly untouched, like a life-sized dollhouse. Pictures hung on the wall, not even askew. A lamp sat neatly on a glass-topped wrought-iron foyer table behind a plump, rose-colored couch. I was beginning to realize that some

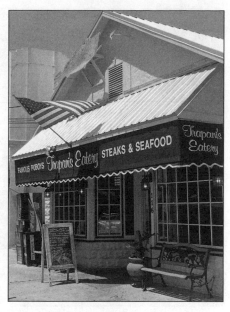

~Trapani's Eatery, the building
that used to be the Koch
family's Sunshine Ice Cream
Parlor, before Hurricane
Katrina
Photo by Mimi Heitzmann

things in this disasterscape would never make sense.

I looked north for the thousand-foot-long pier where children fished and couples took romantic moonlight walks out over the bay. During high school, after stuffing the senior homecoming float, classmate Patty Payne and I in a burst of misdirected school spirit had spray-painted "Go Bay High" on the pier's side. Now, only four small, tattered sections jutted out of the water. On the one closest inland, someone had strapped an American flag on a tall pole.

So much was gone. It was hard to even recognize this was Bay St. Louis. Every fiber of my being silently screamed that what I saw before me could not be real. But there was no waking up from this nightmare.

We got back in the SUVs and were about to drive off when an old gentleman, his long gray hair pulled back into a ponytail, approached Gil and Emmanuel, gesturing emphatically. Then the man came to my window. "This is the third day I've walked down this street. The third day," he added for emphasis. He pointed at the crumbled remains of downtown. "But this is the first time I've seen any of this."

The man looked around, confused by this new reality his mind was finally beginning to process. He was as shell-shocked as any

~The view north on what was Beach Boulevard. Trapani's Eatery once stood on the left. The destroyed Bay Bridge is visible in the distance.
Photo by Mark Proulx

~The view south on Beach Boulevard in downtown Bay St. Louis
Photo by Mark Proulx

~KATRINA LEFT ONLY A FEW BATTERED SECTIONS OF THE
JIMMY RUTHERFORD FISHING PIER IN BAY ST. LOUIS.
Photo by John Wilkerson

soldier who'd been blasted off his feet, only to waken and find everything foreign and unrecognizable. The dazed man turned and continued down the street.

Nearby was the church I'd attended and where two of my sisters had gotten married. Our Lady of the Gulf was right on the water, so I wasn't optimistic. The rectory, a small one-story brick building to the south, was nothing but a skeleton of two-by-fours holding up a roof. I hoped Father Tracey had evacuated.

Standing erect on a low pedestal next to the rectory was a two-foot-tall statue of the Virgin Mary holding a small baby Jesus in her arms. I studied it, astonished. Not a crack. Not a chip. I didn't understand how the small cement figure could escape harm when the entire building next to it had been battered apart by the hurricane. I wasn't looking for miracles, just a sign that God hadn't forgotten this small town of good people whose lives had been so suddenly and completely shattered.

I looked up at the Gothic-style structure built in 1908, one of the oldest Catholic churches in Mississippi. Though the entire roof had been peeled off by Katrina's winds, the structure itself looked intact, as did the stained-glass windows.

Inside was a different story. The pews had been swept to the front of the church, where they smashed through the gray marble communion rail. Large holes had been ripped in the floor. The beautiful four-foot-tall angel holy-water fonts and red carpeting from the central aisle lay in a pile covered with mud, branches, and other debris swept in on the storm surge.

"Kathie? Is that you?" called a voice from the vestibule. It was Kathy Cox, a middle-school classmate. She was with her brother, who'd driven in from Charleston, South Carolina, with clothing and supplies. As was the case with my other friends, her home had been destroyed. Exhausted, Kathy was consumed by the absence of relief aid since the hurricane four days earlier. "People are getting sick because they don't have food. I mean they're getting sick—vomiting and diarrhea," she explained. "And they don't have any way to cook food. And they're trying to, like, eat out of the cans."

"A lot of old people are on their front porches. They can't get water," added her brother. "The water drop-off is way up at Wal-Mart. It's so hot here."

"And nobody is shuttling it down?" I asked, stunned. The Wal-Mart was more than four miles away in Waveland, the town just west of Bay St. Louis.

"No one."

"I saw a man in a wheelchair in the road trying to get around the debris and up to the highway," Kathy said. "He knew if he stayed in his house another day he would die!"

I hugged her, as much to stop the rush of words as to comfort her.

I was reeling as I stepped out of the church. I was sick and tired of promising I would do what I could, then finding I could do so little. I felt like an ant trying to move a mountain. Furious and frustrated, I wanted to push aside the camera, rip off the microphone, commandeer the SUV, and drive up and down the streets honking the horn and giving out what food and water we had left. But then we would be the ones stranded and unable to do our jobs. Where was the help? Did the country even know or care people here were suffering?

It started to rain. "Come on. We've got to try to get to your house," said Janet, ushering me into the car.

We made our way back to the highway and the one road open to the beach. It was Nicholson Avenue, the first street we'd driven down the day my family moved to Bay St. Louis. As we approached the railroad crossing, we saw to the south a white house split in two leaning against the tracks, where it had been slammed by Katrina's ferocious winds and roaring tide.

When we came down the other side, the allée ahead was no longer a haven but a wasteland. In the towns to the east, at least the debris resembled something. But here, if I hadn't seen it with my own eyes, I would never have known this used to be a neighborhood. Every single house had been erased. In their place stretched an unrecognizable sea of boards, beams, bricks, and shattered glass, broken only by an occasional boat, refrigerator, or section of roof. It looked like the desolate World War II photos of Hiroshima and Nagasaki.

As we turned left onto the beach road, I started looking for

~TRAIN TRACKS IN WAVELAND, MISSISSIPPI
Photo by Mark Proulx

something, anything, I recognized. The giant live oaks were still standing, but their limbs as high as thirty feet up were now draped with a strange assortment of tattered fabric and the former contents of people's homes. They'd been stripped bare of leaves, just as the landscape had been stripped of most vegetation, leaving everything a muted brown-gray mud tone.

I stared at lot after empty lot, slab after empty slab. The Camille-ravaged ruins that had haunted me as a child were no longer the exception but the rule. I looked for the telephone poles that had ringed the perimeter of our hurricane-proof house. That's how I would find it. Instead, I spotted the white retaining walls of the driveway.

"Turn in here!" I shouted.

Janet and Emmanuel pulled the SUVs into the sloping driveway. I jumped out and walked past the cedar tree I'd hit with our Chevy Impala as a teenager when I was learning to drive. Its battered branches were stripped and broken. "And you thought I did a number on you," I said, patting its trunk.

~The remains of a Nicholson Avenue neighborhood just over a mile from the author's former home
Photo by Alec Miran/CNN

Just beyond was an empty foundation, raindrops splashing on the yellow linoleum kitchen floor. The phone poles that were supposed to hold the house together had been sheared off at the base. The walls and roof were gone. One iron railing from the central staircase lay where the living room had been. My parents had sold the home a few years earlier, so someone else's belongings were mangled in the wreckage. I wondered who they were and if they knew what had happened. In the backyard, the enormous sheltering limb of the old live oak had snapped off and smashed a red car that had been swept onto the patio. And where my brother's room had been was a tangled pile of bricks.

Nothing had escaped. All our neighbors' homes were gone. The Smiths', the Gottsegens', the Ogdens', the Coopmans'. In every direction

~THE AUTHOR STANDING ON THE CEMENT PAD THAT USED TO BE HER FAMILY'S
  HOME
  Photo by Janet Rodriguez/CNN

~Bricks and rubble strewn over what had been Mark's room in the former Koch home
Photo by Janet Rodriguez/CNN

as far as I could see, nothing—not even a wall—was standing. And I had no idea if any of our friends had made it out alive.

I had held them in all week, but now the tears coursed down my cheeks. We'd finished shooting, so I turned my back and sobbed. I cried for the dead and the missing and the town and the people and all they had lost—all *we* had lost. There is something about the place you call home that anchors you. Now, we were all adrift.

~6~

Final Search

THE BROKEN TRAFFIC LIGHT swung back and forth in the morning breeze off the water. Underneath, a mountain of debris shoved up to the base of the historic Biloxi Lighthouse nearly blocked the intersection. City work crews had frantically cleared parts of Highway 90 for President George W. Bush's motorcade. It was Friday morning, and after a storm of criticism he was finally coming in person to survey the battered Gulf Coast.

The lighthouse, one of the few waterfront structures to survive the hurricane, was the backdrop for our final day of live reports. "What would the people of Mississippi say to the president right now?" the anchor asked me.

I chuckled softly because I was too much of a lady to say live on national television what people were really thinking: I responded, "Where have you been? And where are FEMA and the relief agencies? There were CNN crews here—safely positioned—when Katrina hit. We made our way here from Mobile twenty-four hours later—in SUVs, not tanks. Our network didn't have any advance information that FEMA or NOAA or the federal government didn't have. And the Mississippi National Guard had cleared one major road in every city. Yet day after day, nothing! I don't know if anyone here died because of the delay. But people have certainly had to endure unnecessary suffering. And that's what they'd tell President Bush."

The anchor moved on to a New Orleans reporter. We were off the air.

"You have a call on the satellite phone!" yelled Janet.

My husband, Rick, and my daughters, Kaitlyn and Kara, were about to leave for school, and the girls wanted to let me know how their first week of classes had gone. I listened woodenly to their bubbly voices as they chattered on about their new teachers and friends and how volleyball practice was going. "Good. That's terrific. Super. Really? Wonderful. Okay. See you guys tomorrow."

I hung up the phone and stood there immobile. I was numb. I didn't care about anything they had said. It was all inane and frivolous and completely unimportant when compared to what I'd seen the last week. But these were my children! How could I feel this way? Tears welled in my eyes. God, I was a horrible mother. What was wrong with me?

"Kathleen, we've been cleared for the rest of the day!" said Janet triumphantly as she emerged from the truck. She was now as consumed as I was with helping families connect with loved ones. CNN was pulling us back to Washington and rotating in another correspondent, so we had twenty-four hours left to search. We headed west in our SUV while our crew stayed for live shots with the afternoon reporter.

We took the Long Beach exit and tried to backtrack to where we'd been on Tuesday to look for the Washington woman's sister and brother-in-law. But police cars from jurisdictions across the country were now positioned at every railroad crossing leading into the heavily damaged waterfront neighborhoods. They refused to let anyone through.

On our way back to the highway, we found my brother-in-law's sister's house with the tree through the roof. But the one-story brick home was fine otherwise and even had a generator, so we kept moving.

In Bay St. Louis, we made our way to an elementary school downtown that we learned had been turned into a shelter. We found a neat table with two lists and a bottle of hand sanitizer. "Hey, y'all!" said a young woman wearing a white baseball hat. "Are you locals or looking for someone? Just wash your hands and then you can check the lists. If you live here, be sure to sign the survivors' list."

It was a terrific idea. Those in charge were keeping not just a list of people in the shelter but a running tally of who was alive in town and where they were. That way, family and friends had one place they could come to see what had happened to loved ones, since virtually all other communication had broken down. Unfortunately, neither list had the people we were looking for.

Under the breezeway outside the school, adults and a few children sat at picnic tables chatting and playing cards. A school bus pulled in, and everyone jumped up and began unloading bags of ice into the school kitchen. The floor was wet and muddy. A metal table in the middle of the room held six boxes of canned goods and a case each of water, juice, and soft drinks.

"Hi, I'm Hope," said a pretty blond-haired, blue-eyed girl holding the door as the adults hauled the ice to waiting coolers.

"Whose shelter is this?" we asked, looking on their shirts for the insignia of a charity or relief organization.

"It's our shelter!" said a short-haired young man proudly.

Kevin Schroeder explained that the winds and storm surge had left virtually no home untouched. Many houses were missing roofs or walls. And even if the flooded structures were intact, people had no dry bedding, clothing, food, or water. So when no help came, some of the residents had decided to break into the local elementary school to look for something to eat and a clean, dry place to rest. "We set people up in the gym so they could sleep there," he said. "It's kinda hot, but it works for a shelter. It keeps a roof over your head." Everyone had started pooling their resources and assuming different duties—registrar, cook, driver. And they were managing just fine.

"Kathie! It's Johnny! How the hell are you?" A heavyset man with a broad grin and a tousled mop of light brown hair extended his beefy hand to me. It was Johnny Kersanac, another friend from high school. He told me how he'd been volunteering with the sheriff's department searching for bodies. Now, he was helping keep an eye on things at the shelter. "You like the survivors' list? That was my idea."

I asked about Van Schultz and the others, but Johnny hadn't seen them.

"Kathie, can you let my family know I'm alive?" he asked. "Shit. They've gotta be goin' crazy about now."

I pulled out my notepad and jotted down his information. The others running the shelter crowded around. "Say, we could really use a few things, if you find any stores open," someone said. I started a list—forty blankets, air mattresses, shoes, socks, underwear.

"And I need a new battery for my hearing aid," chimed in a balding man with gray hair. "This one's about to go." He pulled the pink device from his ear and showed me the tiny, round battery. I added it to the list, doubtful we could even find a store open, much less anything that specific.

"What about food?" I asked. What I'd seen in the kitchen wouldn't go far if they were serving forty people a day.

"No," someone said. "People are bringing what they can from their houses. We're good for now."

We headed south into downtown and spotted a police officer clearing debris from his mother's backyard. He hadn't seen Van Schultz or the others. Then we quizzed the owner of a local bed-and-breakfast. Jackpot! A friend had called her at eight o'clock Monday morning to say she'd just spoken to Van and he had six inches of water in his house. My heart sank. We'd heard so many stories about how one minute people had water covering the floor and within an hour were swimming out the windows. Unless Van had at that moment jumped in his car and raced north, he was probably dead.

"Damn," I muttered under my breath as the woman walked away.

"Let's keep going," said Janet gently. "We have others to look for."

We turned back toward North Second Street to try to find the missing parents a stranger had e-mailed about. We crossed Highway 90 only to find an impassable tangle of debris stretching up the road. Chairs, refrigerators, mattresses, and vases protruded from the mass of boards, shingles, tarpaper, and pipes.

~NORTH SECOND STREET IN BAY ST. LOUIS
Photo by Janet Rodriguez/CNN

We pulled into a collapsed gas station and climbed over the wreckage to see if we could spot addresses on the few homes on the road that appeared to be partially intact. Suddenly, a broken piece of the gas station awning on the ground next to us moved. Janet and I jumped back. Initially, we'd been worried we would encounter rats, snakes, and assorted wild animals in the rubble. But for days, the only creature we'd seen alive was a dazed pelican. A brown paw appeared now from under the fiberglass, and a white cocker spaniel half covered in mud dragged himself out into the afternoon sun. Panting, he looked up at us quizzically with his one good eye.

Janet ran to the truck to get water and a tuna pack while I poked around in the debris for a bowl. Nearby, we'd noticed two women pulling up pottery from the mud. A friend's gift shop had been there, they'd explained, and some of the stock had survived. "Floaters, we call 'em," said one of the women, holding up an unbroken vase. Her friend reached down and pulled up a large American flag as tall as she was, wrinkled and mud-spattered but untorn. We all reflected silently for a minute, then continued our search.

I found and wiped clean two white porcelain bowls with delicately painted pink flowers, and we filled them for the dog. He devoured one pack of tuna, then another, and slowly lapped up the water. We could see he was weak and that his left front leg was broken.

~Woman picking through the rubble of a friend's
Bay St. Louis gift shop
Photo by Janet Rodriguez/CNN

I wondered if he would bite if we tried to pick him up.

The growl of heavy machinery broke the silence, and the debris jamming Second Street began to surge forward. A front-end loader was clearing the road, pushing the rubble toward the empty gas station. I ran to the truck, grabbed my yellow rain slicker, and wrapped it carefully around the dog. He didn't even whimper as I picked him up and carried him to the truck.

The grinding mountain of debris came to a halt atop the broken awning where the dog had been hiding. The sunburned man driving the loader looked down at us, shut off the machine, and opened the window. "I'm from Biloxi. I lost everything I had in the storm. But the worst thing was I lost my dog." He looked wistfully at the mud-encrusted cocker spaniel cradled in my arms. "Y'all are real people." He swallowed hard, fired up the engine, and went back to work.

Janet and I looked at each other. What could we do with the dog? We should leave him with someone in Bay St. Louis if the owner were ever to have a prayer of finding him. So as we searched for people, we looked for a home for Lucky, as we called him. Any dog that had survived the winds and storm surge a block from where the two-mile-long Bay Bridge was smashed to bits certainly had earned that moniker.

But the answer everywhere to our inquiries was no. No to the missing, and certainly no to an injured dog. One soldier at a corner where military teams had gathered looked at me like I was crazy. "Ma'am, we can't do enough to help all the people. What are we supposed to do with a dog?"

We ran into Johnny Kersanac on another ice run in the school bus. "No luck yet?" he asked. Gas was a precious commodity, but he offered to take us to the street where Van Schultz lived. After a few blocks, he stopped. "Damn! I forgot. All those roads are blocked. You can't get back there yet." It was growing dark, so even if we got close it was too late to hike there and search through the rubble.

We returned to Ocean Springs and paid a visit to the CNN hotel next door. We'd discovered the night before it had a room stocked with supplies, so we chose some canned soup and sat down exhausted in the lobby to eat.

In walked Charlie Neiswenter, the truck operator, wearing surprisingly crisp, clean clothes. "I love the feel of a new shirt!" he exclaimed.

Janet and I sprang to our feet, the same question on our lips: "Where did you get a new shirt?"

"The Wal-Mart's open. Got power back this afternoon!"

We were up and out to the truck like a shot. We may have struck out at reconnecting families, but at least we'd be able to help the industrious folks in the shelter. But we pulled up to the superstore only to find the manager locking the doors. "Sorry, ladies," he said. "Try us back tomorrow. We'll be open at 9 A.M."

We were up and packed the next morning at seven. We had to hit the Wal-Mart, deliver what we bought to the shelter forty-six miles away, find someone to take Lucky the dog, and get to the Mobile airport by two that afternoon.

I desperately wanted to try one more time to reach Van and Lydia Schultz's house. I could still hear Lydia's tearful message, and I understood now what she was asking. She wanted us to get there and find him before the girls did, because Brooke and Marie wouldn't sit still for long with their father missing. But I also knew the odds were he hadn't survived, so there was probably nothing we could do for him. On the other hand, forty people camped out at the Second Street Elementary School shelter had many needs, and we finally had a way to help them.

"Janet, we have a choice," I said. "We either help the living or look for the dead."

She looked me square in the eyes and answered without hesitation, "You know what we have to do."

First stop, the CNN storeroom. We'd barely begun explaining our mission when Meg Cronham, the cheerful coordinator of supplies, stopped us. "Look, I've got stuff here that's just not moving, like the vanilla soy milk. You can take that." We pulled a luggage cart in as she began handing us cases of unwanted food.

Outside, CNN colleagues were helping us load the SUV when we brought up the next hurdle: Lucky. "You know, there's a billboard south of here past the interstate for an animal clinic. And I think it's just down the road," said one. But would it be open on a Saturday after a hurricane?

We drove just three-quarters of a mile south and found the Big Ridge Veterinary Hospital—with cars outside! We carried Lucky in and gave the staff information on where he was found. A young veterinarian in a T-shirt and shorts pulled the stethoscope from around her neck and gave the scruffy cocker spaniel a quick once-over. "We'll do our best," she said, making no promises. Lucky shuffled around the office floor, trying to understand his new surroundings. Janet and I knelt and petted him one last time before returning to the Wal-Mart just as the doors were opening.

"One cart per person!" shouted an employee to the waiting crowd as they pushed into the store. So many people had lost virtually all their belongings that the retailer had decided this was the only fair way to keep the lines moving.

Janet and I each grabbed a cart and devised a plan on the spot. She'd get in line with hers while I filled mine. I'd come back, leave my cart, and then fill hers.

~Lucky the resilient cocker spaniel in the SUV on the way to the vet
Photo by Janet Rodriguez/CNN

I dashed down the aisles like a crazed competitor on a shopping game show. The stock on the shelves was already thinning, so I took what I could find. Nine pairs of men's boxers, nine pairs of women's underwear, fifteen blankets, and the cart was full. I ran back, swapped it out, and grabbed the rest of the blankets on the shelf, as well as some board games and cards to fill the interminable hours at the shelter. We checked out at 9:44 A.M., loaded the car, and headed for Bay St. Louis.

At the shelter, the residents waved as we pulled up, then eagerly crowded around to unload the supplies.

"Stores are already open in Ocean Springs?" one man asked, incredulous.

"Underwear!" exclaimed another, holding up a plastic packet like a trophy.

After the bags and food were unloaded, Janet and I set our flashlights and rechargeable AM/FM radio lantern fans on one of the picnic tables.

"But aren't these yours?" asked Hope. The nine-year-old had been enjoying the morning's excitement.

"We don't need them anymore, and you do," I replied. I looked

~CNN PRODUCER JANET RODRIGUEZ AND THE AUTHOR WITH THE RESIDENTS OF
THE SECOND STREET ELEMENTARY SCHOOL SHELTER
Courtesy of Janet Rodriguez/CNN

down at her mud-covered sneakers. "These look like they might fit
you." I pulled out my rubber boots and handed them to her.

It was as if I'd presented her with magic slippers. "Wow! Thanks!"
she replied, clutching them to her chest.

"Kathleen, come on." Janet gestured to her watch. We had to get
on the road.

A quick snapshot, a round of hugs, and we headed for the truck.
We assured our new friends we'd keep the pressure on. "I promise I
won't let anyone forget what happened here," I vowed as we climbed
into the SUV and pulled away. I had no idea then how that promise
would haunt me or just how difficult it would be to keep.

On the road east, I began thinking about my brother and his
family. The whole week, I'd been unable to reach them. Local numbers were out of service. And no one knew when families would be
released from Keesler Air Force Base to return home. I hated leaving without seeing him or at least talking to him. I knew he had to

be wondering what happened to Bay St. Louis and all our friends there. And though I knew he was fine, I just wanted to wrap my arms around him and celebrate the fact that he and his family had made it through.

We pulled up to the CNN hotel to get our suitcases before racing to the airport. Meg helped haul our bags out.

"Guess who stopped by while you were gone?" she asked.

"Who?" I said.

"Your brother, Mark. He came in with his four kids. They looked kind of hungry, so I gave them some food from the supply room." She laughed. " 'Course, your nieces and nephews were only interested in the candy." Meg gestured to the cardboard box in the center of the lobby filled to the brim with candy of every shape and size. "The littlest one toddled right over there and grabbed two fistfuls. Your brother couldn't get him to put it down!"

I couldn't believe it. So close but yet . . .

"Meg, thank you. Thank you so much for taking care of them." I blinked back the tears in my eyes. "If he comes back, could you give him this?" I handed her a brick. When on Thursday I had left the rubble of the house we'd owned for thirty years, it didn't feel right to just turn my back and walk away. It was the only real home I'd ever known. In the other cities, we'd lived. But in Bay St. Louis, we finally belonged. So I picked up seven bricks, one for every member of the family.

Hours later, Janet and I were on a plane back to Washington. I kept having sharp pains deep in my chest. *Probably from lifting too many cases of food or my overstuffed suitcase full of bricks*, I thought. *Or maybe this is what a broken heart feels like.*

~7~

Bodies and Beds

A STRANGE FORM OF NORMAL was beginning to settle over the remains of Bay St. Louis. The buzz of chain saws slicing through downed trees and limbs dueled constantly with the thwack of hammers as residents nailed blue tarps into place over what was left of their roofs.

Congressman Gene Taylor was back in the ragtag Mercedes after spending days in a Humvee with the National Guard handing out MREs and water to storm victims in remote areas of the county. Food deliveries from FEMA had finally started, though to just one distribution point—the Wal-Mart parking lot in Waveland. Taylor had nearly come to blows with a federal official to get the food released without a constant military presence.

"Based on my experience in Florida, we can't pass out this food without the National Guard here because there'll be rioting," insisted Eric Gentry.

"Look, butthead," said Gene, finally losing his temper. "This is South Mississippi. We all know each other. There's not going to be any rioting. The only rioting that's gonna take place is if you don't feed 'em!"

As the congressman's car passed down Main Street, a man waved from the stoop of the funeral home. It was the owner, Edmund Fahey, who flashed Gene a weary smile.

It had been a different scene two days after the storm when the normally ebullient funeral home director tracked down the congressman at the Emergency Operations Center. "Gene, we gotta do something. There's no electricity, no water. I got a dozen bodies lined up in the shed out back." Fahey put his head in his hands, sighed, and looked up. "They're in bad condition and gettin' worse. You have got to get me a morgue!"

Gene checked with the Pentagon. But all the military's portable morgues that could be used in times of national emergency were deployed in Iraq and Afghanistan. Then he overheard a county supervisor reassuring the driver of an ice truck caught up in the post-hurricane chaos. "I don't have a checkbook with me," said Steve Seymour. "But you are going to get paid."

The congressman jumped into the conversation. "Sir, it's a national emergency," said Gene with as much authority as he could muster. "We're gonna have to take your truck."

The driver was more than a little skeptical. But just as Gene began to explain his rationale for seizing the vehicle, the head of the Mississippi Emergency Management Agency, or MEMA, walked in on the exchange. "We have legal authority to take your truck. You will be compensated for it," said Jim Maher. "We know that you'll never be able to carry ice in it again once we put bodies in it. But we have to have that truck, and we have to have it right now."

And so began the county's portable morgue, set up to handle the dozens of bodies being recovered. At first, they were found in the open—on streets, in ditches, by search teams in gutted houses. As time went on, remains were unearthed by heavy equipment moving the mountains of wreckage and by hunters slogging through remote wooded areas.

Nikki Cleveland's mother, JoAnna, was among them. It was not the news Nikki expected to get four days after the storm when she met her younger sister at a gas station north of Bay St. Louis.

"Nikki, they found her. They found Mom's body," said Jennifer, tears rushing down her cheeks. "I talked to the police chief, and he says a neighbor found her back on Third Street."

"No! No! No!" responded Nikki, shaking her head. True, neither JoAnna nor Nikki's dad, Ralph, had been seen since the storm. But they were strong and she'd convinced herself they could have swum through, just as she and Patrick did.

Days later, when Nikki went to the new portable morgue at the Alcan Cable site on Central Avenue to identify the remains, things were less definite.

"We can't let you see the body," said the coroner.

"But why?" demanded Nikki, looking at the refrigerated eighteen-wheelers where the bodies were being stored.

"Well, we don't have a positive ID yet," she responded.

"I don't understand. The police said it was her. Could my husband do the identification?" Nikki offered. "Patrick's a doctor. He could handle it. Let him look."

Nikki stared again at the temporary, anonymous resting place of her mother and other Katrina victims. *Here she is. She's just piled somewhere, and nobody cares who she is!* she thought. But the coroner wouldn't budge. She handed Nikki another missing person report to fill out. Frustrated and confused, Nikki took the paper and went home.

Home was now the guest room of a friend's wind-damaged house fifteen miles north in the county. The home she and Patrick shared on a canal off the Jordan River had collapsed on itself after being pushed off its pilings by the hurricane.

Up and down the Mississippi Gulf Coast, residents were relying on the kindness of friends, family, and strangers and on their own ingenuity. *Home* now had many definitions, some more acceptable than others. Home was a car. It was a tent. It was a shed, garage, or carport. It was the second story of a house where the ground floor had taken on less than eight feet of water. It was an armchair, couch, or mattress in any structure that was dry. And if it had a door that closed and access to a toilet, well, those were bonuses.

Every night, Mayor Eddie Favre rested his stout frame on the couch in the chief's office at the fire station. Nothing but a slab was left of the house he rented at the end of North Beach Boulevard. "We've got a great view of the stars," the mayor would say with a smile when anyone inquired about his home. "We can sit on the slab at nighttime and look up at the sky and nothing blocks the view."

Eddie joked that camping out at the fire station actually made it easier to begin the work of rebuilding the city. "We get right out of bed in the morning, and before we even get ready for the day we're dealing with city business." Of course, rising from bed at five-fifteen in the morning when the firefighters reported in was no easy task for a mayor known in the past to amble into city hall well after ten.

Getting the city's power and water up and running was job number one. People had been managing without either for more than a week. Residents with houses that were more or less intact and salvageable were anxious to start mucking out their properties.

Tommy Kidd was busy doing just that at his son's one-story house near Highway 90. It was in the ten-block area near the hospital that had priority on the electrical grid, so power was back there in less than a week. They'd already dragged the ruined furniture to the sidewalk, ripped out the muddy carpeting, and bleached the walls. As a disincentive to any looters cruising the neighborhood, a terse sign sat atop the rubble: "Dogs bite. We shoot to kill."

With all communications out, residents were finding their own ways to deal with would-be looters. Several nights after the storm, Pat Kergosien heard someone chopping away in a neighbor's empty house with what sounded like an ax. He grabbed a Q-Beam flashlight and his .357 Magnum and positioned himself on a chunk of broken concrete near the waterfront. It wasn't long before he noticed a small, red, laser-looking light moving around up by Main Street. Minutes later, three young Asian men dressed in dark clothes emerged from the night, passing just twenty feet from where Pat sat keeping watch. One held a black sack in his hand.

Well, look at this, thought Pat. *Okay. I'll just see what they do.* He flashed the light square on the teenagers' backs.

The three nearly jumped out of their clothes and took off running back into town. They disappeared before Pat could give chase. He went home, got ready for bed, and sat up for a bit in his underwear on the front porch, gun by his side. A bright moon high in the sky cast much-needed light over the silent, darkened city.

A few hours later, Pat spotted another red light across the street outside the Kerns house. Joe Kerns, who had a heart condition, had been evacuated. His wife, Janelle, was home alone. Pat made out two figures moving toward the back of the house. He stood and tried to ease out the screen door, pistol in hand, but the door slipped from his grip and slammed, the noise echoing through the deserted neighborhood.

The men bolted, one running down Carroll Street. Pat gave chase in his briefs, unsure what he would do if he caught the looter. The other raced up a driveway and tried to cut through a neighbor's backyard. Pat heard a racket as the young man attempted to climb over the fence and through a briar patch of sharp, broken wreckage. When the figure in the street hit the storm surge mud at the bottom of the hill, he continued slogging through, so Pat gave up his pursuit and went back home.

His brother, Jeff, who was staying with Pat, berated him for a second time that evening. "Playing Rambo again!"

"Man, people are looting everywhere!" said Pat, exasperated but relieved that he'd sent his wife and children out of town to stay with relatives in Conroe, Texas.

Tommy Kidd, too, had sent his wife, Linda, to safety, in Atlanta. So he was free to do what he did best—make things happen. Tommy was what some people called a "fixer." He'd grown up in Bay St. Louis, knew everyone, and understood what it took to motivate people. A smile and a wink from "Mr. Tommy," as most people called him, and pretty soon everything started falling into place.

"We can use cleanup stuff. Cleanup stuff is at a premium—brooms, mops, hoses, things like that," explained Tommy, his cell phone pressed to his ear as he drove through town. He was talking to an Atlanta supplier for food brokers, an old friend from Tommy's years in the restaurant business. "Don't worry about the power tools. We've got to get folks in their houses to clean them up. Otherwise, we're going to have a real problem."

Tommy slowed to a stop next to a giant blue tarp stretched over a slab on Coleman Avenue, which was once the main drag of Waveland, the town west of Bay St. Louis. Restaurants, quaint businesses, the post office, and city hall had been interspersed among charming historic homes and cheerful water-view condominiums. It was all gone now. A few hardy residents camped out on the empty concrete foundations.

"I tell you, what people need is cots to sleep on, mattresses,

~COLEMAN AVENUE, THE ONCE-THRIVING MAIN THOROUGHFARE IN
WAVELAND, MISSISSIPPI
Photo by Mark Proulx

those foam pads," said a sunburned man in a yellow T-shirt who
was sitting on a folding lawn chair. "And hand sanitizer."

"Got it," replied Tommy. "Do you need another tarp right now?
If you do, I've got some back at the house. I'll bring one to you."
After a round of handshakes, Tommy was back on the road. "Hang
tough. Keep your chin up!"

On Highway 90 near the hotel where Tommy had ridden out the
storm, relief workers were gathering in the Kmart and Wal-Mart
parking lots. "We need concentrations of people—fifty, seventy-
five, a hundred—so we can get set up," explained a Red Cross worker looking for another area to distribute aid and supplies. He pored
over a wrinkled map spread out on the hood of his truck.

"Pearlington—that's an area that really needs help," offered
Tommy, pointing to the last town in coastal Mississippi before the
Louisiana border. "I've wanted to get out there, but I haven't had
time yet."

"Thanks," responded the man, folding the map and tucking it

~THE FORMER SITE OF TOOMEY'S GAS STATION ON COLEMAN AVENUE
Photo by Mark Proulx

under his arm. "Local information is our best source."

Tommy also hadn't had time—or, more precisely, hadn't made time—to check his own home back on the bayou. Most of the roads there were still clogged with wreckage. He knew whatever he found wouldn't be pretty. "I've been avoiding the pain. I'm in denial," he admitted when anyone asked.

Two miles down the road, Dr. Keith Goodfellow was living in a tent outside his office near the hospital. A few weeks earlier, the gentle, generous obstetrician/gynecologist had operated a successful practice, delivering thousands of babies in town. The beautiful waterfront home in the Diamondhead development just northeast of Bay St. Louis where his family had lived for eleven years was their own personal paradise. It had a dock on St. Louis Bay and overlooked a protected marsh. An avid outdoorsman, Keith was living his dream, since bountiful hunting and fishing were accessible in minutes whenever he got a break from work.

Keith remembered that Sunday morning before the storm, how

he'd ushered their four children into the car while his wife, Darla, a local schoolteacher, walked through the house making sure the TV, computer, and all appliances were unplugged in case of electrical surge. Darla even pushed towels under the front door to stop any rain from blowing in on the gleaming hardwood floors. "I love you, house," she'd whispered.

Now, it was all gone. Keith had scrambled over an eight-foot-high pile of debris burying his street, only to find nothing but pilings left of his family's home. His office had lost some of its roof and been inundated with four and a half feet of water, ruining his medical machines, electronic equipment, and the majority of his patients' records. But the structure was salvageable, so he'd gotten right to work.

Hurricane Katrina was the great equalizer. Doctors, lawyers, and other formerly well-to-do residents struggled in the rubble like everyone else to recover what they could and start over.

Keith spent his first few days hauling out waterlogged furniture

~The remains of a home in south Diamondhead, Mississippi
Photo by Mark Proulx

and shoveling debris, taking meal breaks for Pop-Tarts in the morning and canned soup or tuna for lunch. At dinner, he stood in line at one of the portable kitchens that churches had begun to set up around Bay St. Louis to feed residents who had no way to cook for themselves. At night, he slept with a loaded shotgun by his side and the filler door to his truck's gas tank positioned next to the opening of the tent in case someone tried to siphon his fuel.

As he was in the middle of mucking out his office, an elderly patient showed up needing a gynecological device changed. Keith looked at his gutted office and at himself, filthy and dripping with sweat. Then he remembered that the army had set up a medical tent nearby. "Let's go see if we can do it over there," he suggested to the woman. The military accommodated the odd-looking pair. After the ten-minute procedure, Keith got back to his grimy work.

A few days later, three men showed up. "We're here to help you however you need it," said one.

"Thank you very much," said Keith, eying the three cautiously. "Well, I could use a hand hauling these charts out."

For two days, the trio and the OB/GYN worked side by side dragging out debris and clearing the heavy equipment and examining tables from the office. The men wouldn't say much except that they were from a religious organization. They hinted they had checkered pasts. It made him uneasy, but then Keith reasoned there was little of value they could take even if they wanted to.

"Let me give you something for your trouble," offered Keith, reaching for his wallet when the work was done.

"No, sir," one of the men replied. "We're doing it 'cause we feel like we owe God something. God helped us, and we're helping you back."

While Keith worked to salvage what was left of his business, his wife, Darla, and the children stayed with her sister in Birmingham. Their plan had always been to live temporarily in his office if their waterfront home was destroyed by a hurricane. But now that wasn't an option. The kids enrolled in school while Darla looked for an apartment. Though homesick, none of them was eager to see what Katrina had left in its wake.

I, on the other hand, desperately wanted to get back to the Mississippi Gulf Coast. Nothing in Maryland felt right anymore—having instant access to water, electricity and air conditioning, hot food and cold drinks. Everything was clean, easy, civilized, and intact, and I wanted none of it. I finally understood the soldiers who, when pulled from battle in what most would call a lucky break, longed to rejoin their buddies on the front. It now made perfect sense. I felt like I had deserted my friends, my neighbors, my hometown.

To make matters worse, no one understood the sense of urgency I felt about what was happening on the Mississippi Gulf Coast. No one who hadn't been there could comprehend how completely an entire section of the country had been flattened and how desperately people needed help. I talked about how virtually everyone I knew in Bay St. Louis had lost their homes—as had their parents, grandparents, brothers, sisters, aunts, uncles, cousins, and all their friends. The video that filled our network's air every day failed to convey the enormity. Words fell tragically short.

Even my colleagues who had no personal connection to Mississippi were having a hard time with the abrupt return to civilization.

Subject: Working in Gulfport

It is very *weird* to go from disaster to . . . this. Toilets with running water, no worries about food, cleanliness, etc. Sleeping in a bed.

I went to a kids' field hockey game yesterday. There's a small stream near the parking lot. Big signs which read: *"Danger! Area subject to occasional flooding."* I laughed out loud.

Alec

Executive producer Alec Miran had been supervising production of CNN anchor Anderson Cooper's live show, *AC360°*, from Mississippi. I responded.

> Subject: Working in Gulfport
>
> I totally understand. I'm only now—after a week back—starting to adjust. At night, though, I'm usually back in the debris field in my dreams. And it feels comfortable.
> It's good to talk to Jeanne, Jim, Janet, etc.—the other troops from the field. No one else speaks our language, right?
>
> Kathleen

Alec had covered armed conflicts in Panama and Haiti and spent time in postwar Sarajevo and Kosovo. He recognized the similarities.

> Subject: Working in Gulfport
>
> True. Just like leaving a war zone. I've spent a good deal of time looking at the pictures I took. It's like I have to *prove* to myself just how bad things were/are.

Indeed, as I had e-mailed Alec, the only time I felt comfortable was when I was asleep. I'd drift back to our first day in Mississippi and spend the night wading through the debris-covered streets. Mile after mile, I'd pick up twisted screen doors, push aside broken bicycles, drag nail-covered two-by-fours out of the way, and lift dangling power lines so Janet could steer the SUV through. We never encountered anyone. It was just the two of us struggling forward every night through an endless sea of wreckage toward some unknown destination.

In my waking hours, I poured myself into facilitating relief efforts, sharing information on what was needed by whom, and how to get it there. My husband and children wondered about this maniacal woman constantly on the phone, BlackBerry, and computer. "Mom, you're not the Red Cross," said my worried daughter, Kaitlyn.

At work, I pounced on any Katrina-related stories I could find. Some evacuees had fled north to Maryland and Washington, D.C. We took our cameras to Red Cross headquarters in Prince George's County, Maryland, where they were arriving at the rate of two hundred a day. The lobby was full, every seat taken. One exhausted little boy was lying on the floor. Psychotherapist Janet Kuhn told me how she would listen to people's stories, cry with them, and then try to get them focused on moving forward and establishing some stability in their lives. She understood she was little more than a band-aid on a deep wound. "I've done all that is possible at this point," she acknowledged. "But I realize a lot more needs to be done."

Many came to the Red Cross with family or friends. I could spot the hurricane evacuees in a heartbeat. They stood out as starkly as if they were purple. They had an emptiness in their eyes and a weariness, as though they were burdened by an invisible weight. Katrina had sucked out part of their souls and left a permanent void. It had aged them, down to the youngest child clutching a parent's hand. They had what I called the "Katrina face."

A planeload of New Orleanians ended up at the armory in D.C. One evacuee confided to me that they had been taken to the New Orleans airport believing they were being put on buses to a shelter in a neighboring city. Instead, they weren't even told of their destination until they were aboard the aircraft.

Among the group was a man named Rick who sold time-shares. "I just feel helpless. I just don't know where to go next," he admitted. "I'm sixty years old, and you would think a big boy like me would know. But you can't imagine what it's like."

I interviewed a tall, thin African American man named Charles Stewart, though everyone called him "Lucky." His son, daughter, and sister were missing, but he tried to stay upbeat. And at the armory, that meant avoiding the crying man. "He cries every night and every day, and I'm really scared to even talk to him and see what he's crying about. I thought they had moved him. And the next thing, I heard him crying again, and he walks off." Lucky shook his head. "Like I said, I'm really frightened to even talk to him, the horror that he has going in his mind."

I reported on the problem of doctors displaced by the hurricane, like seventy-five-year-old Antonio Stazio, director of the Tulane Multiple Sclerosis Clinic. He'd evacuated to his daughter's Maryland home but was desperate to get back to his young patients. "You know, they were all my kids in a way. And they loved me, and I loved them," he said. "And now I feel like I'm deserting them."

Even more poignant was the New Orleans psychiatrist who had lost her home and was now living in Washington, D.C. "I grew up there. Of course, I want to go back. They're going to need me. The city's been so traumatized," she explained to me over the phone. "But I'm a victim, too. I've lost everything. And I just can't . . . I may never be able to help them."

Hearing her choking back tears, I understood her predicament. She was so emotionally distraught herself that she might never be able to practice her profession in the city she loved, just when its citizens needed her most.

Perhaps the only consolation for the New Orleans evacuees was that they could track the status of their flooded city on the national news. Every new development, good or bad, drew massive media attention.

That was not the case for Mississippi. Only a fraction of Katrina stories focused on the near-complete destruction of the state's coastline. Most simply mentioned it in passing as part of catchall phrases like "New Orleans and the Gulf Coast." Still, that was less infuriating than when journalists talked or wrote only about how "Hurricane Katrina hit New Orleans." It was wrong and sent me through the roof. I even e-mailed a network anchor I knew when he committed the sin of omission.

Mississippians who knew I'd grown up there began emailing and calling me to find out what was going on.

Subject: Hancock County

Hi Kathleen—

My name is Tracey Favre Pullin. I am also from Bay St. Louis & I graduated from Bay High in 1985. I live in Sumter, SC
with my husband, Bryan.

Anyway, I am really curious, like many people that live there,
why is it not being talked about on the news? It is very discour-
aging for many people that do live there. Are we really being
forgotten? I know New Orleans is bad & it is bigger than our
little county, but there is a lot of bad stuff going on there too.
A lot of these people do not have any place to live either. My
parents, my brother & his family & my sister & her family included! My parents have people living under their carport as
they are in Alabama right now. Anyway, I could go on & on.
Can you help me to understand any of this?

Thank you,

Tracey

Subject: BSL Update

Kathleen,

What's the prevailing attitude with the TV coverage of this
nowadays? It almost seems like the TV media is purposefully
leaving out mentions of Hancock County—actually anything
between Biloxi and New Orleans. Not sexy enough? I'm trying to understand why there isn't more on TV about what's
happening there. Thanks for your thoughts.

Mark Proulx

I assured them that CNN had been there after the storm and
still occasionally had a reporter in Mississippi. But the size of New

Orleans and the ongoing struggles with the levees both there and in the outlying parishes made it a more compelling story for most of the news media. Plus, I knew from experience that so much had been destroyed that the Mississippi Gulf Coast offered virtually nowhere to stay. So it was a case of journalists plucking the low-hanging fruit. They found it much easier to drive a few minutes from their New Orleans hotels to cover a story and be back in time for dinner than to drive more than an hour east.

But just because I understood didn't make me like it or accept it. The situation grated even more when I would begin to describe to someone the horrors of what had happened during Katrina and they'd reply, "I didn't know you were from New Orleans."

Or I'd hear the stories of Mississippi evacuees like seven-year-old Peter Drackett, whose family had moved to Orlando, Florida. On his first day at Audubon Park Elementary, his teacher asked the red-headed, bespectacled student where he was from. When he said Mississippi, she replied, "Oh, then you were fine. New Orleans was the one that got hurt." Little Peter then proceeded to describe how his home and his uncle's home and his friends' and neighbors' homes in Bay St. Louis had all been destroyed. After his solemn recitation, the second-grade teacher declared in a huff, "Well, that's not what they showed on TV!"

I also received calls and e-mails for help. Everyone thought that as a reporter for a major cable news network, I had the power to fix things. Toughest, though, was when my classmates reached out. Beth Paul had been both a cheerleader and editor of our Bay High School newspaper, with short, sassy hair and a feisty personality to match.

Subject: Donate

Hi Kathleen,

   Heard from Diane Edwards that you were here after the storm, real big mess huh? I am on the Bay-Waveland School Board, and seeing *Good Morning America*'s outreach to the Pass Christian schools (mustered up by Robin Roberts), I

~PILINGS AND FLOOR JOISTS WERE ALL THAT REMAINED OF MY HIGH-SCHOOL
FRIEND BETH KEITH'S BAY ST. LOUIS HOME.
Photo by Larry Keith

started thinking that you might could muster up some CNN
support?

I've attached a copy of an "after" shot of our house. Don't
have a soft copy of a "before" but just imagine many houses,
all of which are now gone. In the photos, mine is (was) the
house with the green pilings.

Hope this gets to you.

Beth (Paul) Keith

The photos showed a desolate wasteland covered with gray
surge mud, dried and cracked into a million pieces. I searched for
anything identifiable. A bent bicycle tire. A metal folding chair. Beth
and her husband had painted their last name and address in bright
orange on their green pilings so FEMA personnel and insurance
adjusters could identify the property. The scene was heartbreaking.

I e-mailed network executives an article about anchor Robin
Roberts's efforts to help Pass Christian, where she grew up. *Good*

~BETH KEITH'S YARD
Photo by Larry Keith

Morning America was adopting the town and partnering with everyone from the Salvation Army to stars like Sheryl Crow and Geena Davis to raise money for cleanup, recovery, and reconstruction. I figured the nudge couldn't hurt. Maybe the drive not to be outdone by a competitor would spur action for Bay St. Louis.

As I was working late one evening putting together a story on Bay St. Louis with unused video we'd shot Thursday after the storm, my cell phone rang. It was my youngest sister, Krissy.

"Kathie, I've got bad news. Brooke made it to Bay St. Louis, and she found her dad's body today. Van is dead."

"Oh, my God," I responded. "Where?"

"In the wreckage of their house," she replied. "Underneath the rubble."

My heart was pounding. When we'd learned in Bay St. Louis that Van was still in the house as the water started to come in, I'd known he was probably dead. But this was horrible! I'd hoped a search team, a neighbor, or a stranger would find him. But not Brooke or Marie. This was precisely what Lydia had tried to prevent. This was why she'd called and e-mailed me in desperation. I had cared for the girls when they were children. They had trusted and relied on me as their regular babysitter. I protected them and kept them safe. Now, I'd let them down when they needed me most.

I ducked into the bathroom, hoping no one would see me crying. Images of Brooke digging through the crumbled remains of the house raced through my mind. It was more than a week after the storm, and the weather in Mississippi was brutally hot. I shuddered just imagining the smell. No daughter should have that as the final image of her father. "Damn! Damn! Damn!" I said, pounding the bathroom counter. "I should have gotten there. I should have found him!"

I looked up at my image in the mirror. It was me but different. Then I recognized that weary, distant look. I had the Katrina face.

~8~

Faith to Go On

Every day brought a steady flow of news, good and bad, from down south. My high-school friend David Treutel e-mailed from Mobile, where he, his wife, Angelyn, and their son were staying with David's sister, Missy.

> Subject: Heading your way
>
> Heard you were in town.... Tried to call but any phones with 228 exchange have not worked. Just missed you as you were making your way down to your old home and Nicholson Avenue. Been wandering through town the last few days talking with friends and insureds and taking insurance claims. Made a foray into Mobile to Missy's house to get a quick shower, supplies and phones. Pretty much lost all family homes and business, but everyone is safe. Sorry about your family home. The area will come back but it will take awhile.
>
> Take care.
>
> David

My classmate Valorie Young was still trying to evacuate her father, who we'd learned on our trip to Bay St. Louis had made it through the hurricane.

Subject: Locating Valorie's (Young) father

. . . Conditions there are still deplorable, but at least he, especially as a wheelchair bound invalid, and the others he was with made it. My siblings and I are trying to find out the best way to get him out of there at present.

On behalf of all the other people that you've searched for and for their families, I thank you. . . . I'm sure if you helped allay just one person's fear, it was well worth it.

God's best to you and your family!

Valorie (Young) Prater

My former neighbor Lydia Schultz was now living in Pennsylvania and grappling with the loss of her home, her former husband, and our town.

Subject: Hi! From Lydia

I know, beyond a doubt, that I am luckier than my neighbors who are left there to face the destruction daily. I mourn for the loss of Van *and* what I knew growing up in Bay St. Louis. I think, in my mind, the house is probably least of all to be mourned. What I mourn is what the girls and I knew as we all grew up there. You know how great it was! Well, take it back to *my* childhood. *Oh my God!!!* It was a treasure. The whole Bay/Waveland area. *Gone!!!* So, it is a very difficult time.

Take care.

Lydia

One of our few successes in Bay St. Louis turned out to be for naught. Lucky, the dog we rescued, had inhaled so much toxic water as he fought his way through Katrina's storm surge that his lungs were full of fluid. The Ocean Springs veterinarian had put a splint on his broken leg and administered antibiotics, but the cocker spaniel didn't respond and could no longer stand, so he was put to sleep.

"He was looking so good when we dropped him off," said Janet, who'd gotten the news from the vet. "It's just, I really felt like we'd helped. Dammit!"

"At least he had a peaceful death, Janet," I said. "It was better than being crushed beneath all that debris the front-end loader was moving. His owners, whoever they are, would be grateful."

It was frustrating to have done so little while we were in Mississippi. And now, to be watching from a distance while my friends and neighbors struggled in silence.

I went to church. But even there, I felt alone. The tumult of emotions churning inside me wouldn't be silenced. Even the refrain of the communion hymn—"I don't want to leave this place"—made me ache to be back in Mississippi.

"Kathleen, I saw your reporting on Katrina. Are you okay?"

It was Derek Baliles, a spokesman for the Montgomery County Police Department whom I'd met in 2002 while covering the Beltway sniper attacks. During the three-week rampage that left ten dead, he had even spoken briefly to one of the snipers when he placed a call to police.

"No, Derek, I'm not," I replied, surprising myself with my candor. We sat down, and the words just tumbled out. "It was awful. Everywhere I looked, people were suffering. They lost everything. And they weren't just strangers. They were friends, people I grew up with. There wasn't enough food or water, nowhere to sleep. I felt so overwhelmed. Everyone thought we were like the cavalry—that we could get the nation's attention, make things better. And we tried. But it wasn't enough."

Derek placed his hands on mine. "I understand," he said. "I really do. During the sniper shootings, everyone I knew was in danger. People were dying all around me. And it was my job to keep them safe." He shook his head. "It was frustrating. People counted on us.

And I remember feeling so angry and helpless, as if I had failed."

Derek did understand! He didn't think I was crazy. It was such a relief. "But I feel so guilty," I said. "I feel like I just didn't do enough, that I let them down."

"You did what you could. Just like I did what I could," he said. "Just like anyone would in that situation."

It was what I needed to hear. But the news I needed most came that afternoon from the managing editor of CNN's documentary unit, Kathy Slobogin. CNN president Jon Klein wanted me to do a series of ongoing pieces about rebuilding Bay St. Louis that would be compiled into a documentary. So on September 19, I headed back.

To my surprise, the city looked worse than it had the week of the storm. Then, it had been possible to drive by and not realize how many homes and businesses were under three or eight or fourteen feet of water. Now, the water damage to structures that from the outside had once appeared to be minimally impacted was painfully evident. Mountains of insulation, paneling, drywall, and water-sodden furniture threatened to obscure the buildings that once contained them. It was as if the few intact structures left were so sickened by the destruction around them that they'd vomited up their contents.

We turned off Highway 90 onto the service road and pulled up to the chamber of commerce building. A pop-up camper, a canopy tent, and a couple of card tables and chairs were serving as the new office of Treutel Insurance.

"Kathie, how are you?" David asked, mopping the sweat from his brow as he stood.

"David, Angelyn, it is so good to see you guys!" I hugged them and stepped back to survey their improvised workplace. "So this is it?"

"Yes, all the comforts of home," replied Angelyn with a wry smile before turning back to the man she'd been helping. They huddled together over a paper claim form, since the company had no electricity or computer connection at the site.

David's father, David Treutel, Sr., stepped out of the camper, came over, and shook my hand. "Kathie, good to see you! How are

~Mountains of rubble virtually obscured the surviving homes.
Photo by Mark Proulx

your mom and dad?" He was wearing a faded polo shirt and a pair of shorts that appeared one size too large. "Sorry for my appearance. It was the best I could do over at Goodwill."

Like David and Angelyn, he looked good but bone-tired. It was a quiet morning, so David offered to take us over to their house, where he had a meeting with a flood insurance adjuster.

The lovely white-brick one-story home surrounded by magnolias and loblolly pines was set back 150 feet from the street. Covering the yard was a huge pile of the house's entire contents, from soggy books, broken furniture, and moldy clothing to the drywall, carpeting, and insulation that had already been ripped out and thrown on top of the mound. It was hard to look at. What was left of the most precious possessions of David, Angelyn, and Alex lay bare to the world. I felt like I was invading their privacy.

"Did you guys haul all this out yourselves?" I asked.

"No, we had someone take care of it," said David. "But still, when Angelyn saw this yesterday, she lost it."

"Who wouldn't?" I replied, leaning down and picking up a muddy leather case from the wreckage.

"That was a school satchel for one of the kids," David explained. Taking it from me, he ran a hand across the bag sentimentally for a moment before tossing it back on the heap.

Inside, the adjuster was waiting. The floors were bare down to the cement and the walls stripped to the two-by-fours. The two men walked around discussing the height of the surge, how long it had been in the house, and how quickly the structure had been mucked out. "You're light-years ahead of most people at this point," commented the adjuster.

I kept staring at the insidious black mold that speckled the length of most of the two-by-fours.

"It's been sprayed," said David. "So the mold is basically dead, and we can drywall right over it."

I wondered how comfortable I'd be living in a house never knowing if that was actually the case, since there would be no way to check once the mold-flecked lumber was covered.

Out back, David pointed to evidence that a tornado had passed right over the property. The trunk of a tall pine fifty feet from the house had been twisted round and round like a corkscrew. I had never seen anything like it.

We headed to his parents' house near the beach, where David had grown up. As we drove, he described how clients' visits now resembled counseling sessions. People aching to share their stories of loss would spend twenty minutes pouring out their hearts. Finally, in the last few minutes, they would pass on the contact information David needed to get adjusters to their properties. We drove past David's ruined office downtown. "There's our contact information," he laughed, pointing. Spray-painted in black block letters on the front of the yellow Acadian cottage was "GO TO CHAMBER OF COMMERCE TEMP. CLAIM OFFICE," followed by the company's e-mail address.

"And it's amazing, 'cause over the weeks the contacts are changing," he continued. "The first couple of days, the first week, week and a half, most everybody was here. But as time's wearing on and there isn't a whole lot of assistance, shelter or otherwise, we're seeing people start to head out to Florida and to Jackson, Mississippi, and to Mobile and to Houston and to Baton Rouge."

We pulled up in front of what used to be David's parents' home on St. Charles, where in 1969 the entire family had retreated to the attic to escape Hurricane Camille's twenty-four-foot storm surge. Nothing was left now but the slab and portions of two walls.

"Thank God they didn't stay this time," I remarked as we poked around the debris. Nothing appeared salvageable save a few unbroken china plates and a bottle of wine.

"Dad and I were talking, and I was saying, 'I wish I had just the slab that you've got.' It would be a lot easier than dealing with the water damage, the gook, and still seeing a lot of your stuff. But it's pretty much not any good anymore." David looked around the empty foundation. "Here, you say, 'Just bulldoze it.'"

"That's hard to say," I offered, scanning his face for a trace of emotion.

"It is," agreed David. " 'Just bulldoze my house. The place I've been . . .' He more than I. He's been here since 1941 on this property. 'Just bulldoze it and move on.'"

It sounded so cold. But it was the reality thousands were dealing with now.

~A Bay St. Louis neighborhood after plows cleared the road
Photo by Brian Rokus/CNN

"Will he sell?"

"I've been telling him like my insureds, 'Don't do anything rash. Don't sell your land,' " he replied. "A lot of people are offering really low prices."

"I'll bet. But do you want this place taken over by out-of-town-ers and condos and beachfront hotels?"

"We want a community," insisted David. "We have room for de-velopment but also for families, and that's what we want to see. The families, the traditions, the history we've got."

As we climbed in the car, David said, "I have someone I want you to meet." He told me the story of Diane Frederick, who'd cleaned house for his family when he was young. "Thanks to her, my dad has a way to get around," he said. Two months before the storm, David Sr. had sold Diane a compact car to give to her daughter, Cookie. After the storm, when he and his wife lost everything and were stranded, Diane gave them back the car to use for as long as they needed it.

"Amazing," I remarked, touched by the image of the housekeeper now in a position to help her former employer. How tough it must be for such a kind, proud man, a pillar of the community, to accept charity and wear clothing fished out of a bag at Goodwill. David Sr. had always been such a calm, reassuring presence. Now, he was the one who needed reassuring.

As we drove, David talked about how the determination to re-build was bringing the town together. "People aren't waiting a lot of times for assistance. They're doing it themselves. They're helping each other," he said proudly. "The spirit of the community has really come alive. It's a shame that you have to have adversity to pull out some of the good things."

We stopped in front of a modest one-story brick rancher. In the carport were two chests of drawers, the bottom drawers pulled out and lined up in the sun to dry. Tree branches and black shingles from the roof dotted the front yard. A smiling African American woman emerged from the house. Her red T-shirt bore the words, "God Is So Good to Me!"

"Kathie, meet the hardest-working woman in Bay St. Louis," said David with a broad smile.

~MOUNDS OF DEBRIS AND TRASH IN FRONT OF BAY ST. LOUIS HOMES
Photo by Mark Proulx

"How do you do? Welcome to my home. Sorry it's such a mess," she said, ushering us in. As in David's house, the floors were bare of carpeting. "I cut it out with a kitchen knife," explained Diane. "It was stinking!"

A light brown stain ringed the walls three feet up. Diane described how every weekend she drove home from Panama City, Florida, where her husband, Allan, was in the hospital. She cleaned up what she could and then drove back. They had no flood insurance to pay for repairs, since their neighborhood had never flooded and insurance wasn't required.

"I sat in a long line at FEMA today for four hours. And I put my name down on the list for a trailer." She held both hands up, crossing her fingers. "I put on the form my husband is in the hospital, and if they discharge him he won't have anywhere to go. So I don't know if that'll influence things."

Diane walked us out the front door. "I'm blessed. My home can be fixed." She pointed to a brick rancher across the street that was missing the entire roof. A blue tarp extended from the side of the house to provide shade for a few coolers, shelves, tables, chairs, and a small red tent. "My neighbor Mr. Larry's been living outside with a heart condition. He's seventy years old! And they're still giving him the runaround about a FEMA trailer."

A small man in a white T-shirt, jeans, and a black baseball cap puttered about underneath the tarp.

Diane crossed the street to talk with him. "How are you doing today?"

"I'm doing fine," he answered softly. "I'm just waiting for my trailer."

"So when did you apply for your FEMA trailer, Mr. Larry?" Diane inquired.

"Day after the storm," he said.

"And no one has come out?"

"The guy came out, inspected the house, and said there would be a trailer in my driveway. They keep saying they're going to bring one out." Mr. Larry gestured to some exposed pipes on the side of the house. "They even came out and looked at the sewer line and everything. And they said I'm going to get one, I'm on the list. But I'm still sleeping in the tent."

Diane patted her neighbor on the back and headed down the street. "I promised Miss Alvina I'd help pick up the shingles in her yard," she explained. She followed my eyes as I looked at the debris still covering her own front lawn. "She's eighty. I can get to mine anytime."

"Kathleen, we have a problem. We need to find a family." Emily Probst was one of the two CNN documentary producers assigned to work with me. She'd been riding with the crew while I drove with David. We'd both noticed the same thing. The town was devoid of kids. Couples had rapidly and wisely decided Bay St. Louis was not a safe or healthy environment for children. The wind- and water-damaged library was closed. Three-quarters of the schools had been damaged or destroyed. The town was populated by grownups—dirty, tired grownups with no time or energy to care for kids.

We climbed in the van and began driving up and down the streets. Finally, on Washington Street, we noticed a teenage girl riding her bike next to a white clapboard house with a corrugated tin roof, much of it missing. As we got out, she ran inside and summoned her mother. The young African American woman introduced herself as Shannon Evans, a home health-care aide. She told us how she and her four daughters rode out the storm in their little rental house. The teenager and an older sister eased their way out the screen door behind their mother and began raking the leaves and downed branches that still covered the yard.

"Right now, we're trying to do a little work, in and out," the woman explained. "You know, it's so hot, and I don't want them to pass out or nothing. So we're just doing a little bit at a time."

A giggling two-year-old came scooting down the steps into the yard. The oldest daughter followed, keeping watch over her progress. Meanwhile, her sisters eyed us suspiciously.

"It's got to be tough managing here alone with four kids," I said.

"The hardest part is everything is gone." She gestured to the west. "You got to go way out of town to try and get meat and food and stuff in the house."

"And what about your daughter who's pregnant?" I asked, noting the fourteen-year-old's rounded belly.

"They brought us some prenatal vitamins—one of the National Guard," said Shannon. "One of them was saying a military clinic was open. So she's gone and checked the baby's heartbeat and stuff."

"What are your plans for school?"

"They say Gulfport is supposed to have school next week," she replied hopefully. "That's probably where they will be going because they can't sit out. They gonna have to go to school somewhere."

Janelle, fifteen, had planted herself next to her mother and seemed bursting at the seams to talk. "There's nothing to do here now. I ride my bike around. But I miss school and my friends." Tears began streaming down her face. "Everything's destroyed. There's no one here anymore. Everyone's dead or left. It's so lonely. Sometimes, I wish I was gone, too." She wiped her cheeks with the back of her hand and disappeared into the house.

What did she mean? I wondered. *Not dead. Surely, the situation isn't that desperate.*

I asked Shannon what their plans were. She said they hoped to get a FEMA trailer to live in while the landlord repaired the house. She definitely wanted to stay in Bay St. Louis. "Everybody really sticks together out here. They're really friendly," she said. "Everybody is working together with each other seeing what they need—water and ice. I guess it's the friends."

We continued our search for families, driving to one of the local elementary schools, North Bay, constructed in a *U* shape around an open inner courtyard. The brutal winds and storm surge had smashed in the exterior walls of every single classroom. The tidy rows of desks and stacks of fresh textbooks and school supplies were crushed together like a disaster layer cake, the smell of chalk dust replaced by the stench of moisture, rot, and muck. The library was saddest of all, its books dumped from the shelves and splayed across the floor in a ruined pile.

A car pulled up, and a sturdy woman in a red T-shirt and gray jumper approached us and introduced herself as the principal, Frances Weiler. "It's heartbreaking. It's really heartbreaking," she said as she surveyed what was left. "It looks like an overwhelming loss." The principal explained that some teachers had already contacted her, anxious to come by and salvage what they could. "Their first thought was, 'I must save all those supplies I've worked for.' But we have really just discouraged them from coming back."

"Have any of the kids returned here?"

"I hope not," she replied. "Because I'd like them to remember it

~Destroyed classroom at North Bay Elementary School
Photo by Chris Stasny

the way they left it—normal on Friday afternoon, looking forward to the weekend."

Normal. I had a feeling the word would not apply to much in Bay St. Louis for a very long time.

I noticed a football scrimmage under way in a field above the school. We wandered up and watched a ragtag bunch of young men without cleats, pads, or uniforms racing up and down the field. The scoreboard was gone, and the goalposts had been tilted sideways by their encounter with Katrina's winds. It was my alma mater Bay High's field, but these boys sure didn't look like high-school players. I made a mental note to follow up, since in the South the gravest sin next to skipping church is missing the local football game.

Nikki and Patrick Cleveland were meeting us at their house in Jordan River Isles. Navigating in town was difficult enough with all the street signs washed or blown away, but at least there were still some landmarks to go by. Getting to the neighborhoods on the bayous was like going on a scavenger hunt. Directions were given in miles, and intersections were identified in bizarre new ways. "Turn right at the white boat up in the trees" and "Make a left at the Santa Claus statue on the debris pile" were sentences residents uttered daily with straight faces.

The neighborhood on the bank of the Jordan River had been decimated, every home left in ruins. We pulled up next to what was left of a tan house with brown shutters that appeared to have folded in on itself. The roof had collapsed, some of the windows were blown out, and salvaging anything looked impossible.

"Our house was swept off of its pilings. And it moved north by about ten feet and west by about ten feet," explained Patrick, pointing as he walked around the structure. "We're pretty set for insurance. Our engineer says the wind took it before the water because the pilings are all lying in different directions. And the wind was coming in different directions. Water always pushes things in one direction."

It was a cloudy, overcast morning. Hurricane Rita was approaching in the gulf, and Nikki seemed uncomfortable. "Looking at the water today, I mean, it's just different. You just don't see it the same way you used to see it. I don't know." She glanced nervously at the river and struggled to explain. "I don't know if I'll ever see it the same way. It might not ever be so beautiful to me."

Patrick echoed his wife's sentiments. "I don't want to hear the wind howling or see the water come up. Never again."

Nikki's parents, Ralph and JoAnna, were still missing. But she would say little about how she was managing. "I don't know. We're just taking one day at a time, just trying to get through each day."

"And how hard is that—getting through each day?"

"Some days are a little harder than others. But we still have each other," she said, looking at Patrick with a smile. "We're still young, you know. We're gonna have a wonderful life after this."

They were unsure, though, if that life would be in Bay St. Louis. "We don't know. We're not sure what we're gonna do," Nikki confessed. "But we would love to rebuild here, and have children and raise them here. I had the best childhood growing up here."

"This is our home, and we don't want to live anywhere else," said Patrick.

"Family and friends right now—everybody's trying to help us out," Nikki added. "It's amazing how many people love us and care about us and want to help us."

But for the Clevelands and many others in Bay St. Louis, generosity was a two-way street. We followed Patrick to his veterinary clinic in the Kiln, where we found veterinarian Waddy LeBourgeois examining a cat. Tall and lanky with a shock of white hair, he was a close friend of Nikki's parents. Waddy had survived the storm on the roof of his Waveland office, along with nineteen animals he'd managed to haul out of their cages. "My practice is sitting there, and I can build it back. But there's nobody there now," he said.

So not only had Patrick invited Waddy to work out of his clinic, but he and Nikki set up an air mattress in one room so Waddy would have a place to sleep. The aging vet was wearing scrubs, the only clothes he had left. "I'm not going to buy pants 'cause I have no place to put them. I lost my house. I lost my hospital. I lost my two cars. I lost my best friend and his wife."

As we listened, we realized Waddy wasn't asking for pity. He was trying to share a message.

"You can buy new pants and new belts and a new hospital and

all that. But when you lose a friend, it's tough," he said. "Your best friend—find 'em. Go up and give 'em a hug. Give 'em a kiss. Tell 'em you love 'em. 'Cause you never know about life."

Waddy scooped up the cat that was purring around his ankles and headed back to the examining room. We left with lumps in our throats.

Our next stop was my friend Pat Kergosien's house, where we'd arranged to make a copy of the pre-Katrina footage his daughter Erin had shot the weekend before the storm. I'd already rushed a CNN crew over weeks earlier to dub the video Pat shot from the family's porch during the hurricane. But no one at the network was impressed.

"It looks like three feet of water in the street," complained the regional desk coordinator.

"That street is on a thirty-foot bluff," I pointed out.

"But no one knows that," he said, and the exclusive Katrina video died an early death.

It was strange in the middle of a disaster zone to walk into a completely undamaged house. No mud was on the floor. No windows had been blown out. Pat and Hope's bungalow sat just high enough to miss the surge. And the building to the east was wide and sturdy enough that it had held together and blocked the worst of the winds.

We hooked up the tape deck, and Pat hit Play. "This was downtown. There, you can see Trapani's and the Fire Dog Saloon. That's the old Merchant's Bank building." The camera whizzed past Our Lady of the Gulf Church and St. Stanislaus, the local private boys' school, and then past an endless parade of gracious historic homes that once lined the five-mile length of Beach Boulevard. Like a proud tour guide, Pat carefully described each house and the family that owned it. Though the video had been shot less than a month earlier, things had changed so radically that it felt like stepping back to a distant time and place.

When it was over, my producer, Emily, got up shaken and pulled me aside. "I think I'm going to be sick," she said, her face pale. "I had no idea. I didn't realize what was here. Oh, my God. It was beautiful."

~THE HOME AT 948 SOUTH BEACH BOULEVARD BEFORE AND AFTER
HURRICANE KATRINA
Photos by John Wilkerson

"I know. It was." It was sad but gratifying to see her epiphany. Bay St. Louis was such a hidden gem that, with so much of it gone now, those who'd never been here found it hard to comprehend the loss.

Perhaps no one felt it more keenly than the man trying to pull the city back together, Eddie Favre, mayor for the last sixteen years. We met him in the old downtown, where we found him chatting with a middle-aged couple who'd evacuated the area. "We're now residents of Charleston, South Carolina," said the bespectacled woman with thick gray curls.

"No, no, no," said Eddie, waving his finger in a mock scold. "You are *visitors* to Charleston, okay?"

As we strolled down Main Street, the mayor pointed to a cheerful placard—"Watch for Our Grand Re-opening!"—posted on the crumbled remains of what had been an art gallery. "That's the kind of sign we like to see." It seemed Eddie was genetically engineered to be mayor of this town of eternal optimists. Ninety-five percent of the homes and businesses had been damaged or destroyed by the hurricane. Fifty-six people in the county were dead or missing. The infrastructure was crushed. National Guard Humvees roamed the streets. Helicopters flew overhead. Practically the entire Mississippi Gulf Coast was on a dusk-to-dawn curfew. Yet he continued to look on the bright side. "We're taking it one step at a time. We're actually only crawling right now," he said with a chuckle. "We haven't started walking too well yet. But it's getting a little bit better."

Eddie insisted the disaster was giving the town the opportunity to redesign things to everyone's greatest benefit. Instead of another low-slung bridge with a draw span, a new Bay Bridge could soar high above boat traffic. A new beach road downtown would finally have a third lane for parking. "Don't go put something up just to solve an immediate problem," he said. "Let's look at it long-term. We don't need to rush into anything."

Still, when pressed, Eddie acknowledged his town had been through hell and had a long way to go. "I think for about the first two weeks, the adrenaline rush was such that people didn't . . . I still don't think people realize how bad it was. And now, every time we drive up and down the streets, you see something a little bit different or from a different angle. And it just hits you all over again, the vastness of the destruction."

We walked down the dirt slope that used to be Beach Boulevard. "Eddie, everyone's saying when it comes to the recovery so far, it's not so much been the federal government. It's the churches, the volunteer groups."

"It's the churches. It's the sister cities throughout the country, the police departments, the fire departments, the religious groups from all over the country. Individuals that would load up whatever they could in the back of a car, a pickup, or a small trailer. Anything from trunks of cars to convoys and semis were bringing in supplies to us. And that's what saved us. And they're still coming in."

~THE BAY EUPHONIUM ANTIQUE STORE AND THE APARTMENT ABOVE IT ON
  BEACH BOULEVARD DOWNTOWN
  Photo by Skip Nocciolo/CNN

"Are you confident that everyone will be back?" I asked.

"I think the people are going to be here. The biggest thing that I guess concerns me is that if our people aren't made whole again, whether it's by the insurance companies, or the state government and its agencies, or the federal government and its agencies, then a lot of people will not have the opportunity and won't be able to afford to rebuild and come back here. That's our biggest concern."

Eddie marveled at the attitude of Bay St. Louis citizens. "They've lost everything, but they still smile. They still believe it's going to be okay. And every day, as long as it's a little bit better today than it was yesterday, we're on the right track. We may not have a house, but we have a home. We may not have anything else, but we have each other." Eddie's voice cracked with emotion. "And one day, hopefully in the very near future, it's going to come back. We may not have the historical buildings that made Bay St. Louis part of what it was. But the biggest thing that made Bay St. Louis what it was, was the people. And the vast majority of them are staying."

One doesn't generally expect eloquence from a man in shorts in the middle of a disaster zone, but it was the most moving rallying cry I'd ever heard.

I found it hard to imagine the burden of being mayor of any of the towns on the Gulf Coast post-Katrina. But no one had gone into the job with a greater appreciation of what might lie ahead than Tommy Longo, mayor of Waveland. His father, John Longo, Jr., had guided Waveland through the aftermath of Hurricane Camille in 1969. "I'm glad I lived through that. You know that it can be done. But we're literally starting from scratch," said Tommy, gesturing to the endless debris field covering both sides of what had been the city's main street, Coleman Avenue.

We met the mayor at the site of what had been the historic three-story city hall, built in 1875. Only a knee-high mosaic mural of a beach scene that had decorated the supporting wall on the lower steps remained. "We lost every public building that we had," said Tommy. "The police department lost every single police vehicle that we had. Our fire department lost every single fire vehicle. Seventy-eight-thousand-pound fire trucks just turned into things the size of a cinder block."

~ALL THAT REMAINED OF FRIENDSHIP OAKS CONDOMINIUMS ON WAVELAND'S
COLEMAN AVENUE
Photo by Mark Proulx

Weighing heaviest on the mayor's mind were the residents who'd died, the people he'd tried but failed to persuade to leave. Twenty bodies had already been pulled from the rubble. "I just wish they'd listened," he said, shaking his head and looking down as we walked. "We told them it would be bad. I should have gone back one more time. Maybe I could have been more forceful."

I studied his face. Tommy blamed himself. He felt personally responsible. I wondered how he could deal with the pain of the losses. As it was, he was dealing with near-unbearable physical pain. Tommy had undergone knee replacement surgery two days before Katrina and hadn't seen a doctor since. "I got out of the hospital at 5 P.M., and we had our first EOC meeting at 6," he said, trying to smile as he limped with every step.

Tommy's phone rang. "Mm-hmm. Okay. What do we do about accounts receivable?" he asked. "We lost all our records. We lost all our invoices."

The crew and I stepped away to give the mayor privacy. Two men in hospital scrubs approached us. "We're doctors, volunteers from Florida," they said. "Anyone hurt? Got any cuts? Need a teta-nus shot?"

I had a sudden brainstorm and explained to them Tommy's situation. I also pulled aside FEMA's aide to the mayor, Troy Buck, a firefighter from Marion, Indiana. "He's not going to like this," said Troy.

"What will we use as an examining room?" asked one doctor. Not even a wall was left to crouch behind.

"That truck," said Troy, pointing to a late-1980s Chevy pickup a city worker was using to deliver water, ice, and MREs. "He can sit in the bed. You guys can stand here and block the view."

When Tommy hung up the phone, Troy put his arm around the mayor's shoulder. "Boss, these doctors are going to look at you—check the knee."

"Nah. I'm fine, Troy," said Tommy. "I don't have time."

Troy steered the mayor toward the now-open tailgate of the blue Chevy. "Listen, Tommy, if you go down, this ship goes down with you."

"Aw, all right."

Tommy hoisted himself onto the tailgate and removed his jeans while Emily, Troy, the camera crew, and I turned our backs and formed a human wall around the rear of the truck. After a few minutes, the exam was over. Tommy emerged with a fistful of painkillers and a prescription for more.

"We'll be back to check and see how you're managing the pain," said one of the doctors with a wave as he and his colleague continued down the street in search of more patients.

We followed the mayor to the end of the street, where an area cleared of rubble held a tan Quonset hut. "It's carpeted, and it doesn't leak," he said, giving us a tour of the structure that had been erected that day so residents would have a place to deal with city business until a more permanent town hall was built.

Tommy bristled at those who said he was crazy to try to rebuild a city that no longer existed. "A lot of things I've heard—'Mayor of no city,' or 'Mayor of a city that's not there.' My city is just as strong in that sense as it was before. Because I'm mayor of the people. And that's what the city of Waveland is, is its people." Tommy gestured

~Quonset huts housing Waveland's government offices
Photo by Mark Proulx

to the few residents who had stubbornly pitched camp along the destroyed street. "And by God, they're very resilient. They're brokenhearted. We've been knocked down. But we're standing up now, and we're putting one foot in front of the other. And it's going to take a long time. This is a long-haul kind of thing. But I promise you, if you come visit us in a year, you'll be amazed."

Storm clouds were gathering as the first bands of Hurricane Rita appeared on the horizon. We were driving past the historic L&N Train Depot when we noticed a green tent pitched alongside a damaged building. A blanket with an American flag design was tacked to the wall next to it. The weather would soon be difficult for tent dwellers like Richard Silva, but the carpenter and musician wasn't leaving. "There's no place left to go. I'm here." He looked solemnly at the wreckage around him. "Everybody just lost everything. I lost my home, my job. It's a whole different town here. It's like everything's turned upside down."

Many were focused on staying upbeat. Signs outside businesses bore slogans like "God Bless Bay St. Louis. We Will Be Back" and "Brave Mississippi. Be strong. Regroup. Rebuild. Return." But there were others like the black spray-painted tally marks on one brick house marking off fifteen days, followed by the words, "No FEMA?"

And the plaintive but futile requests like one sprayed onto the siding of a tan house next to the railroad tracks: "Need help finding mother's urn of ashes."

Father Michael Tracey, parish priest at Our Lady of the Gulf, felt the struggle between hope and despair. He himself had returned reluctantly to Bay St. Louis from his annual August vacation to his home in Ireland. Family members had told him, "Stay here. There's nothing to go back to."

Indeed, Father Tracey had lost all his belongings when Hurricane Katrina blew in the windows and ripped the brick walls right off the rectory. When we saw him, sunburned and wearing an olive-green T-shirt, khaki shorts and a canvas outback hat, he looked more like a hunter on safari than a priest. "Ah, Kathie! It's wonderful to see you!" he said in his gentle Irish brogue, folding his tall frame to give me a hug. "I'm sure things don't look quite as you remembered them."

Father Tracey had spent his first years in the priesthood at Our Lady of the Gulf and had been the adviser of our Catholic Youth Organization. In our own ways, we had both grown up in Bay St. Louis.

He ushered me to a small pop-up camper next to the remains of the rectory. On a picnic table beside it was a cardboard box filled with dirty, wrinkled photographs. Photos were perhaps the most poignant items in the tangled wreckage that now stretched along the Gulf Coast. Plump babies on blankets smiled up through a film of mud. Families posed together, their arms interlocked, blissfully unaware they'd been dismembered when the storm surge ripped away their legs. Not only did the happy events in the pictures contrast starkly with the devastation that now prevailed, but these were precious memories lost, graphic examples of how Katrina's ferocity had caught so many by surprise.

Still, people were determined to preserve them. We'd seen unclaimed photos tucked into the top of a chain-link fence. Another had been propped against the root system of a gigantic tree overturned by the winds. Father Tracey was collecting photos in his box, hoping to reunite them with their owners. "Because they're memories—family heirlooms, in a sense." He showed me a muddy family portrait he'd fished from the ruins. It was taken at a wedding he had attended in Ireland ten years earlier.

"Where did you find this?" I asked.

"Three or four hundred yards away in the rubble. And this one was in a frame—my brother's wedding in 1983." He gently wiped dirt off one corner. "It's something I treasure."

We walked over to the church, where the scene was little changed from three weeks earlier. The diocese was grossly under-insured, and estimates were that $2 million would be needed to repair the damage. "Everything is gone. Pews. The floor has been destroyed," Father Tracey said. It had been too much for some parishioners to bear. "There are people that came by the church here who just couldn't go in. There are people that cannot go and look at the water anymore."

Father Tracey had always been a gentle, sensitive man. It was clearly difficult for him to see his flock suffering.

Back at his tiny trailer, where the dark-haired Irishman could barely stand up straight, we sat at the fold-down kitchen table. I had to ask him the *why* question. I'd been trying to wrap my head around it since August 29. I knew that bad things sometimes happened to good people. I saw it all the time in my work. But why this unprecedented level of destruction? Why this place? And why, counting Hurricane Camille, twice in a lifetime? This was not Sodom or Gomorrah. Bay St. Louis was a small town full of good people who had done nothing to deserve this. I was furious! I just didn't understand it. Local children of my generation had been raised to believe that if we led good lives and cared for our fellow man that God would reward us, not smite us.

Father Tracey nodded. I wasn't the first to ask this question. "I think maybe it challenges us to have some kind of growing faith. To realize that there's something deeper here. That the things we surround ourselves with are passing. And that what really matters are people and relationships. And the bonding, the support, seizing the moments that we have and treasuring them."

"But it wasn't just things. People died! Van Schultz. The Dagnalls. Their families are suffering."

"Out of all this cleansing, there is new life, new growth. Just like in the cyclical part of nature. There's always a cycle going on," Father Tracey said. "And from this, from the ashes, will come your growth. And we've got to believe that."

I didn't know what I believed anymore. I just didn't understand how a loving, merciful God could let something so horrible happen to tens of thousands of people who had done nothing wrong.

A knock came on the camper door. It was Mike Gibbens, another friend from middle school. "We've got the tarps ready, Father Tracey!"

We walked out to find huge pieces of heavy white vinyl stretched across the parking lot. Mike, who now owned a construction company, had evacuated during the storm. "I told all my friends I'd get this church fixed when I got back," he said. But with Hurricane Rita bearing down on the Gulf Coast, Mike had no time to rebuild the roof, so he was improvising. He lifted a corner of the plastic to reveal the top of a whiskey bottle and the Jack Daniel's legend. "They're liquor billboards!"

"Just be sure you keep the bottle side down, Mike," cautioned Father Tracey with a wink.

We laughed out loud at the image of helicopters flying over the destruction and suddenly seeing gigantic liquor bottles stretched across the roof of the church. Now, that would be a hurricane moment worthy of Jay Leno!

A crane lifted the tarps over the open roof, where a team of Mike's workers began quickly nailing them into place. Just as they finished, the skies opened up with the first drenching rain since Katrina.

We got in our van and raced toward the interstate to catch our flight back to Washington, D.C. The surge from Rita had already pushed water out of the bayou and onto Route 603. In another hour or so, the city would be cut off. As we turned to exit east onto I-10, I noticed something the rain hadn't budged—the debris line from Hurricane Katrina on the south side of the interstate overpass. Seven miles inland, the brown slash of scum, sticks, and trash left behind when the storm surge receded was higher than an eighteen-wheeler.

~9~

Wake-up Call

PEOPLE IN BAY ST. LOUIS and up and down the Mississippi Gulf Coast were getting a lesson in patience. The words *quick* and *easy* were absent from the post-Katrina vocabulary. Every day, the choice was which line to stand in next. FEMA? Small Business Administration? Red Cross? And once residents reached the front of the line, the tension was ratcheted higher. Would their applications for living expenses, housing assistance, trailers, or other aid be approved, denied, or declared still pending? Would their records even be there? Or, as so often happened, had they gotten lost in the mountains of red tape, the residents condemned to start the mind-numbing process all over again?

Those with cars had the choice of a thirty-, forty-, or fifty-minute drive to a hardware or grocery store, then at least an hour-long wait in line at the register.

Those without cars lined up at the free food tents and distribution centers.

Calvary Chapel Relief was serving meals on St. Stanislaus's football field. In an odd pairing out on Highway 90, a band of social activists from Wisconsin called the Rainbow Family teamed with an evangelical Christian group from Texas to offer three meals a day and health care at the New Waveland Café and Clinic. Doctors with Virginia's Loudoun Medical Group set up shop at the train depot to provide free medical care to anyone who walked in.

Volunteers also established surprisingly efficient centers for distributing the truckloads of donated supplies that continued to pour in. CityTeam, a nonprofit Christian organization from California, ran one on the town baseball field, where residents could come and select whatever they needed. Foundation Hope turned an empty storefront in a shopping center on Blue Meadow Road into a drive-through operation. As cars pulled up, volunteers ranging from firefighters to United States Forest Service and National Guard personnel took the lists of needs and ran them inside. Those working the store dashed up and down the rows of wooden shelves filling bags that were then delivered to the waiting residents.

Other volunteers were gutting houses. One bright morning in early October, a group from Calvary Baptist Church showed up at Diane Frederick's brick rancher, where mold was fast creeping up the lower section of walls soaked by the storm surge. "This stuff right here is nasty!" said the foreman of the group, who directed the volunteers to cut well above it. They swarmed the structure, jigsaws whirring in virtually every room as they removed the damaged drywall and ripped out the ruined lower cabinets in the kitchen and bathroom.

Diane worked alongside them, shoveling up chunks of sheetrock as they fell. "They are just wonderful. They're all working for the Lord," she said, a blue dust mask dangling around her neck. "I am so blessed to have them!"

By the end of the day, Diane's house was ready for repairs, though she still had not figured out how to pay for them. Her husband, Allan, remained in the hospital in Florida, where she tried to spend most of her time. Diane was eagerly anticipating his return. Their FEMA trailer had arrived earlier that week. "Very homey and comfortable. Small and compact but nice," she said cheerfully. "This is going to be my home away from home until I can fix my house up and move back in."

Firefighter Monte Strong's family was also living in a trailer. It was set up at Waveland's Buccaneer Park, a state park destroyed by

Katrina but reopened as a trailer site for local first responders. The family shared close quarters, even though they'd sent Mallorie and Caleb north to Hattiesburg to live with relatives and attend school until classes resumed in Bay St. Louis. Unsure who was living in the campground, Danielle was reluctant to let four-year-old Dawson play outside alone. The tromping of his tennis shoes as he ran up and down the eleven-foot-long space could become maddening. "Could you just be still?" Danielle sometimes found herself snapping. "Watch TV!"

Casino Magic, where she'd worked, had been shredded by the storm, so Danielle was adjusting to being a stay-at-home mom, as well as trying to maintain some sort of routine for the family. Little Dawson, feeling the strain and the absence of his siblings, would awaken in the night calling for his parents. Often, he just got up, pushed open the bedroom door, and climbed into bed with Monte and Danielle.

After more than five weeks, Nikki and Patrick Cleveland had a FEMA trailer, too. It was set up on their friends' property in Pass Christian, where they'd been staying since the hurricane. "I'm a little nervous about the bathroom because my head is close to the ceiling," Patrick said, straining to fit his six-foot-two frame into the cramped shower.

"It's the only thing we have of our own right now, so we're proud of it," said Nikki. "Don't want it to be permanent, though."

But the list of those in Bay St. Louis without trailers was far longer.

Diane Frederick's elderly neighbor with the heart condition, Larry Pavolini, was still sleeping in his tent.

David and Angelyn Treutel were still driving back and forth every day from Mobile while they waited for their trailer.

Shannon Evans and her four daughters were staying temporarily in a hotel in Greenville, Mississippi, so repairs could begin on their rental house. They had thought they would be able to live on the grounds in a FEMA trailer when school started, but Shannon returned one October weekend to find the landlord had posted signs in the yard and on the house reading, "No Trailer By Owner." She was unsure what they'd do.

My classmate Beth Keith, whose home had been reduced to pilings, was still waiting. She, her husband, Larry, and three children were living with relatives in Hattiesburg. Every day, she drove ninety miles south to her job outside Bay St. Louis. The only explanation she got when she called FEMA contractors for help was that two Larry Keiths lived in Bay St. Louis. Perhaps their trailer had been delivered to the wrong person. Beth was so frustrated she dashed off a biting letter to a local newspaper complaining that "FEMA trailer contact information is a more well-kept secret than Dolly Parton's bra size."

Though nothing but columns was left of the home of Darla and Keith Goodfellow in Diamondhead, FEMA told them their loss did not qualify them for a trailer or living expenses. They were still trying to find an apartment in Birmingham. But bias against Katrina evacuees was rampant. "I don't know if y'all are the type of people we want here," they heard from the manager of one apartment complex.

"My husband's a physician. I'm a teacher," responded Darla, astounded.

But to the rental community, Keith was an unemployed homeless man with a wife and four kids. "You want me to pay for a year in cash?" Keith finally offered to break the logjam.

Bay St. Louis mayor Eddie Favre was also denied a FEMA trailer, though the home he'd rented had been erased by the hurricane. He was shopping online on the computer at the fire station, hoping to buy a trailer himself. Eddie's living conditions had improved. He'd graduated from the couch to an inflatable mattress on the floor of the fire chief's office. "It's still a whole lot better than what a lot of folks have right now," said Eddie. "A lot of folks don't even have this. We're still fortunate."

Frustration was also growing when it came to getting children back into classrooms. The district had learned that repairing or replacing the six public schools would cost $29 million. In the interim, officials needed seventy-six portable classrooms to reopen schools by the planned November 1 start date. It was mid-October, and only sixteen portables had been installed.

"We have a problem because FEMA isn't providing trailers

quickly enough," said Superintendent Kim Stasny when I called to check on the schools' progress. "They tell us we're in line, but . . ." She was exasperated almost to the point of tears.

Kim was worried that many of the twenty-four hundred students enrolled before Katrina might not return. If the start date was delayed several weeks, that could send a signal the district couldn't be relied on, and even more families might stay away. And that could lead to teacher layoffs. The domino effect of a late opening was potentially devastating.

In a CNN story meeting on the documentary, my colleagues expressed concern that, despite the compelling video of destruction we'd shot in Mississippi, there was a notable absence of conflict. "Isn't anybody angry?" asked managing editor Kathy Slobogin. "We need conflict."

"People are astonishingly upbeat," said Brian Rokus, the Washington, D.C., producer assigned to the documentary. "We're shooting a school board meeting this week, so maybe some sparks will fly there."

In fact, Atlanta-based producer Emily Probst had raised the same issue with me during our September shoot. "I don't understand how they remain so optimistic," she said. "Everyone says, 'We're fortunate. We'll be okay. We'll rebuild bigger and better.' And I look around and wonder, 'Are they seeing what I'm seeing?' "

I realized that attitude was tough to comprehend when one didn't understand the place or the people. Mississippi was not Louisiana. Residents were not going to scream from the rooftops for help. Mississippians were proud, hardworking people not accustomed to receiving charity. In fact, they were more comfortable giving. While the state ranked fiftieth in the nation in income, it was first in per capita charitable giving. Those who had the least gave the most.

After the hurricane, when no help came, Mississippians found it natural to pull themselves up by their bootstraps and start helping each other. Whining and complaining didn't do any good because everyone else had lost everything, too.

Also, when outsiders looked at the endless mountains of rubble, they had a hard time fathoming how to start over. But because of their experience with Hurricane Camille in 1969, Mississippians knew there was a light at the end of the tunnel. They saw the way through and knew it could be done. Not that anyone thought it would be easy, just possible.

But I *was* angry. How could so many people—including the mayor himself—still have nowhere to live? And why weren't the children in our county getting the trailers they needed to start classes when every other school system on the Mississippi Gulf Coast had already reopened? Letting both situations deteriorate to a crisis point would create the conflict and drama we needed for the documentary. Still, I had to do something.

My October 14 assignment presented the perfect opportunity. I was covering the White House and would attend the daily press briefing. It was my first day back on the beat since Katrina. To say I was highly motivated to get some answers would be an understatement.

But I couldn't launch right into Bay St. Louis, so I asked Press Secretary Scott McClellan if President Bush was satisfied with the ongoing relief efforts in the South. Among other things, Scott said the president had "great confidence" in the leadership of Homeland Security secretary Michael Chertoff and Coast Guard admiral Thad Allen, the point person in the response efforts. He added, "Though there's a lot work that continues . . . a tremendous amount of progress" was being made.

That was my opening.

"I'm just saying . . . Pick a town. For example, Bay St. Louis, Mississippi," I said. "They've been promised FEMA portables so that they can open their schools November 1, the last system on the Gulf Coast to open. They were promised those seventy-six portables on September 26. They have sixteen. They're not going to be able to start school if they don't show up. The mayor wanted a FEMA trailer. He can't get one. His house is a slab. He's sleeping in the fire department. It doesn't sound like things are working."

Scott's face turned red. He was clearly not pleased. "We're working to address those issues. You're bringing up one or two incidents here or there. You have to look at the overall efforts that are going on." He spoke briefly about how hard the government was working and ended with a terse admonishment: "Admiral Allen is the one that will be in the best position to address individual areas that you're talking about."

That was that. No promise to look into the situation. *At least I tried*, I thought. And at least the reporters in the briefing room and anyone watching now knew of a town called Bay St. Louis that still needed help. I headed home that Friday afternoon glad that I'd rattled the cage a bit, even if I'd accomplished nothing.

The next week, I called Superintendent Kim Stasny for a status check and braced myself for another depressing litany. Instead, Kim was positively elated. "We have trailers everywhere!" she said.

"What? When? What happened?"

"Friday, I started getting calls from the Education Department in Washington and from someone with, I think they said it was the Global Accounting Office—GAO," she said. "They wanted to see if we were happy with the rate the portables were coming in and how FEMA and the Corps of Engineers are working for us."

I was speechless. Not just the Department of Education but the Government Accountability Office, the investigative arm of Congress, had sprung into action!

"We had meetings with the Corps of Engineers Friday afternoon and Saturday morning. The trailers started coming in Saturday and Sunday evening," said Kim. "We've got two contractors working on the installations. The Corps is checking in with us two, sometimes three times a day. The word is out there that we need help!"

I couldn't believe it. I had never expected such a response. "So will you make the November 1 opening date?"

"It's going to be close," she said. "They've kicked it up to 24/7 on the installations. We may still have to delay by a few days."

I was thrilled! I decided not to mention the White House briefing. The important thing was what was happening—the children would soon be back at school—not why.

More upbeat news for the town's kids came from Ginny Vegas, whom I'd known in middle school. In 1969, her family had lost its home on North Beach Boulevard during Hurricane Camille. "We were living in total devastation. We had nothing. There was really no place for us as children to go. We were just playing on the debris piles and the fallen oaks." Determined to make sure the city's children this time had somewhere bright, beautiful, and happy to begin the healing process, she'd enlisted the help of the nonprofit organization KaBOOM! which built playgrounds in underprivileged neighborhoods. It agreed to construct one in downtown Bay St. Louis that would be designed by the city's children.

Subject: Bay St. Louis, Mississippi Playground

Hi Kathie!

Just wanted you to know that we will be having a Design Day on Wednesday, October 19. KaBOOM! has been so generous—they are paying for almost the entire project because they loved our story so much. . . . I think this is the first good news for BSL folks and it will lift their spirits so. . . . Hopefully, it will get everyone to push past the horror of the whole thing and focus on the future. . . . We'll see.

Best,

Ginny Vegas

But construction wasn't moving well on all fronts. Nor were efforts to push past the horror. David Treutel and his parents still hadn't made progress on rebuilding their homes.

Subject: How're Things

Hey Kathie,

. . . Have not had a chance to think about rebuilding yet, also almost impossible to get hold of good contractors. Will be heading to the house this weekend again to try and bulldoze some of the debris to the road. . . .

Pennie and Dave are looking for an apartment to move to and have no real plans to rebuild anytime soon.

See you when you next come down.

David

Lydia Schultz was struggling with reconstruction of a different sort.

Subject: How are you?

Kathie,

. . . Day by day, I am trying to rebuild. With Wilma in the Gulf it is hard to put this behind us. I find myself swinging *wildly* with the emotions. One minute up, the next out of left field comes a cry!!! I don't know how people left there are dealing with it. It must be very difficult. I'm not there and am having a hard time. Talked to a friend today who is in Monroeville, AL and she is having same thing. One day you wake up and ok! This is a good day. The next I am thinking of Van all day and *down*!!! I think that's the hardest part for me. He was a good man and father.

Oh, by the way, the Dagnalls are still *not* on the dead list. Van is. *That* caused some dreams.

Love to everyone,

Lydia

Many impacted by Katrina felt like they were riding a wave. The positive developments propelled them forward until the setbacks slammed them down face-first.

Like the day a press release arrived from emergency operations officials back home. The headline read, "Food Supplies Running Low in Hancock County, Mississippi." I was stunned. I knew people were still fighting to get shelter, but at least they weren't starving. I'd assumed food and water were a given. The advisory went on to explain that the volume of food donations was starting to drop off and that the supply for families and free kitchens in the area was beginning to run dangerously low.

How was this possible less than two months after the hurricane? Most people in Bay St. Louis and Waveland still had no way to prepare their own meals. Just a handful of restaurants were open—none, though, for breakfast. Residents had nowhere within fifteen miles to buy groceries.

I started forwarding the press release to everyone I knew. I posted it on CNN's in-house computer network and sent it to assignment editors at our now-permanent Gulf Coast bureau in New Orleans. I printed it out and started distributing it to anyone I thought could help.

I ran into Joe Lockhart, whom I'd covered back when he was White House press secretary for Bill Clinton, outside the CNN Washington bureau greenroom. "Joe, take a look at this. They're already running out of food on the Gulf Coast. It's unbelievable!" I handed him the release. "You've got to make sure President Clinton sees this." Bill Clinton and former president George H. W. Bush were leading a nationwide fund-raising effort for the Katrina-stricken areas.

"I'll be sure to read it," he said as he headed to the set.

But monitors throughout the bureau were filled with images of presidential adviser Karl Rove and Vice President Dick Cheney's chief of staff, Scooter Libby. The grand jury was in its final deliberations on whether or not either would end up indicted for his role in the leaking of the name of CIA operative Valerie Plame. All of Washington was salivating over the intrigue, political survival being a far more fascinating topic than actual survival.

That night, I handed out advisories at a Rotary Foundation reception for recipients of international Rotary scholarships. The Bay St. Louis Rotary club had sent me to study in Dijon, France, when I graduated from college. I knew the civic organization was deeply involved in the relief effort in Mississippi. A club in Hancock County, Indiana, had adopted our county and already made three trips down

~During a visit to Waveland, former president George H. W. Bush shook hands with the author's friend Mark Proulx as Mayor Tommy Longo looked on.
Courtesy of Mark Proulx

to bring supplies to first responders who'd lost their homes. Rotary clubs in Jonesboro, Arkansas, had sent truckload after truckload of food, water, clothing, gasoline, and medical and cleaning supplies for distribution throughout town. Rotary clubs in Great Britain had even sent tents for the people of Hancock County.

The generosity was inspiring, yet I was shocked at how quickly aid was drying up and how ready the rest of the country was to move on. People didn't seem to understand that every day was still a struggle for the Gulf Coast.

The next morning, my cell phone rang. It was the family from Waveland I'd met in Mobile who had asked me to check on their home. "I'm so glad you called!" I told the mother. "I'm sorry, but somehow I lost that piece of paper you wrote your address and phone number on. How are you? How's your house?"

"We're doin' all right," she replied. "We lost everything. The house had four feet of water in it. So we're workin' on fixin' it."

"Do you have a trailer?" I asked.

"No. But we signed up for one. Right now, me and my husband and daughter are stayin' in a tent in the yard."

"All three of you? That's not much privacy."

"Well, we feel safer that way. We heard gunshots across the street the other night. So it's better to stay together."

I cringed at the image of the teenage daughter and her parents crammed into a tiny tent that offered protection from the weather but little else. "Have you had any cold nights yet?" I asked, thankful that Mississippi's temperate fall climate made tent dwelling more bearable.

"Just a couple," she said. "We got in line the other day to get some winter jackets, but they ran out before we got any. So we're gettin' along."

Here, finally, was a problem I could solve. "Give me your sizes," I said.

"Nah, we can't let you do that," she said.

"Listen, I'll be there next week. I'm not taking no for an answer."

I got their information and headed to the office. I logged on to my computer and nearly started doing handsprings. The big news of the day filled my screen. It was in an e-mail from Beth Keith.

Subject: Elementary school in your hometown

Hey Kathie,

Just wanted to let you know that the power of the press worked. My letter was published in *Sun Herald* and *Clarion Ledger*. The same day we got a call from someone from FEMA asking if we were the ones that wrote the letter. We had a trailer the next day. The fact remains that the communities still need somewhere to go for answers. . . . Will keep you posted. Hope all is well.

Beth

~10~

Fall Rituals

SLEDGEHAMMERS CUT THROUGH THE AIR, smashing apart the damaged soft pink drywall still lining Dr. Irene Koskan's Bay St. Louis office. What didn't fall with the first blows was ripped off by hand or pried loose with a crowbar. Then the shovels moved in, scooping the wreckage into a wheelbarrow. Once full, it was rolled out to join the growing mound of debris in the parking lot north of the modest one-story building.

There was a precision to the process. Little chatter was exchanged among the young men wielding the tools. If they moved like a team, it was because they were—all members of the football squad at Bay High. The players still in the area spent their days mucking out buildings. It gave them something to do—a way to contribute to rebuilding the city. It was hard work, but they liked it.

In the evenings, the boys practiced football. On Friday nights, they played games, though school still hadn't reopened. But they were hardly fair fights. Teams north of the Gulf Coast had ballooned, their rosters replete with coastal players who had lost their homes. Meanwhile, Bay High was scraping by with half the normal team members, some even recruited from the junior high.

When we caught up with the players at work in early November, they were well aware of the odds they faced. "We play the teams up north, we're like, 'They didn't have to go through none of this. They have homes. They don't have to clean up. They're in school,' " said middle linebacker Trevor Adam as he swept up crumbled chunks of drywall and dust. Despite his ready smile, his frustration was clear. "This is us every day, morning time to evening time. Then we go straight to football practice. This is our life until we go back to school."

It showed. Most players had lost ten to fifteen pounds since the hurricane. At lunchtime, the boys piled into a Jeep and a truck and made a beeline for the corner of Sycamore and Old Spanish Trail, one of the regular stops of the Salvation Army canteen truck.

I rode with the players and asked if their experience was bringing them closer. Trevor, a senior, said that would be tough, since they were already a true band of brothers, having played football together since they were five or six years old. Still, they had taken a beating as freshmen, ending the season 0–10. "Each year, we've progressed. We just had no superstars on the team," he explained. "That was our thing coming into football this year. If we were going to win, we were going to win with all of us doing our jobs. And so far, we've done that." In fact, the team miraculously had a 4–2 record.

The white box truck with the familiar red emblems was there when we pulled up, a handful of residents waiting at the open window. The boys bounded out of their vehicles and joined the line. "How many today, son?" asked the volunteer inside as a slim young man, Tigers quarterback Tyler Brush, stepped forward.

"Two, please, ma'am," he said.

The players emerged with Styrofoam trays laden with barbecued chicken wings, potatoes, carrots, and peaches. The once-quiet group laughed and joked excitedly about the next night's game against the Pearl River Central Blue Devils. It would be the final home game for seniors like Teddy Morris. "Us playing on Fridays, just to give the people in this town a relief, just for a couple of hours—that's amazing for us, just to get something off everybody's mind," he said.

The boys quickly devoured the Salvation Army fare and headed back to work. I left in search of a restaurant with producer Brian Rokus and our crew. My personal rule when on the Gulf Coast was to not accept free food. That was for the residents. Visitors with the means to pay needed to support the few restaurants that had managed to reopen.

At the last intersection heading toward the water, where a few businesses were still standing, we saw a sign for Southern Delights. It had a spare menu but every day featured a local staple like red beans and rice or jambalaya. We ate and were getting up to pay when an attractive middle-aged woman with shoulder-length blond hair approached me.

"You're Kathleen Koch, aren't you?" she asked.

"Yes," I said.

"I'm Mimi Heitzmann. I don't know if you remember me. I just wanted to thank you for everything you've done, all your reporting on Bay St. Louis. It's meant so much to us here."

"Mimi, I was just doing my job," I said. I was uncomfortable with her praise, since I felt I'd accomplished so little.

"Well, since you left, I've become a writer and photographer. I wanted to give you something to say express my gratitude." She held out two paperback books she'd written. Local waterfront scenes graced the covers. The pages were warped and discolored. "They're the only copies I have left. I'm sorry. They got wet in the storm surge."

I took them from her and looked at the titles—*Fantastic Stranger* and *No More Tears in Heaven.* "Thank you, Mimi. They're perfect," I said. "I wouldn't want them any other way."

Her gifts reminded me that we had some of our own to deliver. We made our way down the back streets of Waveland and stopped next to a modest one-story home raised three feet off the ground. A quick glance inside made it clear the house had been inundated by the storm surge. On the left side of the yard under the shelter of a small stand of trees was a red tent with chairs and camping equipment outside.

"Hello! Anyone here?" I shouted.

No answer. We checked with neighbors and found we had the right house, so we left the three new winter jackets inside the tent and zipped it up so no passersby would see them. It was bad enough that the family I'd met in Mobile had to endure life crammed in a tent. At least now when they left it, they'd be warm.

Tommy Kidd's house was our next stop. He'd finally made it there, only to find that his fears—or at least half of them—had been realized. Katrina's winds had blown out windows, peeled the vinyl siding from the south side, and ripped off the roof over the eaves, exposing the rafters. The storm surge had roared through the main floor of the elevated home, smashing and scattering the beautiful white cabinetry and beige upholstered furniture. The centerpiece of the main floor—a ten-foot-long antique table—was missing, apparently swept out when the water receded.

~Plaintive plea at a former Bay St. Louis homesite
Photo by John Wilkerson

"See, there's your water line," said Tommy, pointing to a dirty brown mark ringing the room ten inches below the ceiling.

"How high is that from the ground?" I asked.

"Oh, about twenty-seven feet," he said.

But the upstairs, incredibly, was untouched. Beds sat perfectly made next to neatly arranged slip-covered chairs sprinkled with decorative pillows. The Mardi Gras posters and memorabilia from Tommy and Linda's years in the Krewe of Nereids still hung intact on the walls. Even the white carpet had been pristine until Tommy and others walked upstairs in boots caked with the bayou sludge coating the lower floor.

Tommy dealt with it all with his usual unflagging optimism. "Everyone has losses in life. Some may have more than others. If you let it get you down, you're miserable. What can you do?" he asked, picking his way carefully through the overturned furniture and down the front stairs. "My theory of living is that into each life some rain must fall. Sometimes, it's a flood. But pick it up and go again. I just don't believe in crying. It's not anything that makes it any better. It'll all come together once again."

We stopped by the restaurant Tommy had helped manage with his daughter, Kelyn. The Daddy O's sign was the only thing intact. The roof was gone, and most of the structure over the dining area of the cheerful peach-colored building trimmed in turquoise had collapsed. The rust-colored banquette seats and white attached tabletops sat exposed to the elements.

"Our fritters are to die for. Apple fritters are the best," said Tommy proudly, unconsciously speaking in the present tense. He caught himself and began to reminisce. "It was a friendly place. It just had a lot of good memories for people, and people enjoyed themselves. It was family-oriented all the way through."

Tommy said he and Kelyn were anxious to start rebuilding. "Every day, I run into people that wanna know when we're gonna be open again." But first, a fundamental question had to be answered: What caused the damage, wind or water? They had no flood insurance, since the area wasn't in a flood plain. Still, Tommy was confident they'd be taken care of, since officers—including the chief—at the Waveland Police Department across the street had seen the roof fly off well before the storm surge came in. "I feel they're credible witnesses," he said with a wink.

It was four o'clock and time to get to Bay High's football practice. Coach Brenan Compretta had persuaded thirty-four players to return to keep the team going. Quarterback Tyler Brush was in Fort Walton Beach, Florida, when he got the call. His dad didn't want him to come back, but Tyler knew it would be tough to rebuild the team without a quarterback. "I needed to come back for everyone else who came back."

Safety Robert Labat returned from Florida with Tyler. They were stunned when they went to the field house to check their gear and found the door wide open. "We was just walking around looking, like, 'Where's everything at?' It was just mud, and our old pads were on the floor." The handsome young African American shook his head, remembering the chaos. "All the jerseys—they were gone. We saw people on the streets walking around. They had our jerseys on. They had our cleats on and everything."

The coaches knew they were starting over from scratch with boys who had to rebuild their homes from nothing as well. For a

~THE HURRICANE-BATTERED WAVELAND RESTAURANT TOMMY KIDD HELPED
RUN FOR HIS DAUGHTER, KELYN
Photo by Mark Proulx

while, they toned down their usual coaching style. "All of them are usually hard. Cussing and screaming all in our face and stuff. When we first came back, they were like women. They were all nice and everything. But now after a few weeks, it's back to normal," said Robert with a smile.

Senior Buddy Schultz had joined the team from rival St. Stanislaus, which hadn't managed to scrape a team together. He, his dad, his grandmother, and his two sisters had tried to ride out the hurricane in their business overlooking the water. The Big E was an old movie theater that they'd turned into a grocery store. The stocky, square-jawed young man calmly described how the windows blew in and the building collapsed, forcing them to cling to a telephone pole, scramble onto the roof, and then cross floating debris into a boat. His grandmother drowned.

I listened, amazed that he could even function. Football, it turned out, was his therapy.

"Being back on the field helps?" I asked.

"A lot. Like, I guess you can take anger out. You just lost a whole bunch, and it makes you mad," he said. "So you can take it out on the field instead of walking around all day and being mad."

After practice, I rode with Tyler Brush to see what was left of his home on the beach. He told me how he had moved to Bay St. Louis just as I had and fallen in love with the people and the place. There was determination in the way he talked about his decision to return alone, his military-style buzz cut enhancing the image he projected of a rookie soldier committed to a risky mission. "I didn't realize what I was getting myself into when I came back," said the young man who'd spent his first few nights sleeping under a teammate's aunt's carport. "I made my decision, though, so I knew I was going to have to tough it out."

We pulled up in front of a lot where an array of white pillars and beams supported a rectangle of floor joists. Everything else was gone except a tattered sheet tangled around one pillar. The sheet moved gently with the breeze off the water.

"This was actually a two-story house. My room was right upstairs," Tyler said. "I had a balcony that overlooked the water."

As we walked the empty lot, Tyler reflected on how he and his teammates had to grow up virtually overnight. "We lost our homes. Most people lost their cars. We don't have anything. Football's the only thing a lot of people on our team do have—two or three hours to get away from all of this and to go out and just have fun and be teenagers again."

I found it heartbreaking as a parent to hear him ache for what most adults hadn't even taken time to ponder. They were busy trying to replace physical objects—lost homes, cars, and possessions. There was nothing anyone could do to recapture a lost childhood.

The next day, we stopped to visit Mayor Eddie Favre at his new trailer—not FEMA-issued, though. The portly mayor had given up on the bureaucracy, bought one himself, and parked it on the grounds of the now-destroyed Casino Magic.

The battered casino barge that sat rusting in the bay was a constant reminder of how the town's tax base had been decimated. Before Katrina, the casino had pumped $300,000 a month in taxes into city coffers. Sales taxes had added another $125,000 a month. Property taxes were about the same. Now, all those sources of in-

~Eviscerated homesite just off the water in Bay St. Louis
Photo by Mark Proulx

come had virtually dried up. "That's where the concern is. Where is the money going to come from?" worried the mayor. "They tell us no municipality has ever gone under because of a natural disaster. Well, we're about to find out."

Still, Eddie refused to lay off any city personnel. "Twelve out of twenty-three firemen lost everything. Thirty-two or thirty-three of our police folks out of forty-five, including secretaries and dispatchers, lost everything. Of the ten public-works guys that are still here, nine out of ten lost everything. Our administrative folks lost everything," he said, shaking his head. "So, you know, they've been here ignoring their personal losses to take care of the needs of the public. And they don't need to be kicked out because of that, and won't be."

Eddie confirmed that county officials had extended the eight o'clock curfew for the Bay High Tigers football game that night. It was the one occasion every week when people got together and laughed and smiled again. Players like Trevor Adam knew how important the games were, not just as a refuge from reality but as a demonstration of the town's refusal to quit. "This is for Bay St. Louis," he said as he arrived at the field to suit up. "This is for every single person who went through this. We represent the community of Bay St. Louis and Waveland every time we step on that field, you know."

The scene had improved since our September visit. The goalposts had been straightened, though the scoreboard was still missing. National Guardsmen were on the sidelines tuning up their instruments. The conductor explained that they were the 129th Army Band from Nashville, Tennessee, filling in, since all the school's instruments had been ruined by the storm surge.

In the locker room, the players put on donated blue-and-gold uniforms. The tension was building. Not only was this the last regular-season home game, but if the team won, Bay High would host the playoffs on its own field for the first time in history.

"You come out and play hard, every single play!" urged Coach Brenan Compretta.

The players recited the Lord's Prayer on bent knee, then charged toward the end zone chanting, "What time is it? Game time!" They smashed through a poster held aloft by the cheerleaders.

On the other side of the field, the Pearl River Central team filled the benches. They were more than seventy strong, compared to the thirty-four players on Bay High's side. When the teams lined up for the kickoff, the Blue Devils seemed bigger, too.

Still, the Tigers took an early lead, scoring a touchdown after a Blue Devils fumble on the three yard line. The Blue Devils managed two field goals, but Bay High answered with two of its own in the second quarter. Pearl River tied the score with a touchdown just seconds before halftime.

In the stands, fans who'd lost nearly everything had somehow managed to find plenty of blue-and-gold shirts. Connie Cuevas's daughter Savannah even had her ponytails tied in matching blue-and-gold ribbons. "We *need* this! We need *normalcy* back in our life," said Connie.

But when the teams retook the field, it was clear the Tigers were fading. The fatigued first string had been playing both offense and defense. The Blue Devils leaped ahead with two touchdowns in the third quarter. Then the Bay High field lights started shorting out, just like the home team's energy. The power boxes on the light poles had been underwater too long during the hurricane and hadn't been right since.

In the fourth quarter, Pearl River scored again but missed the extra point. The Tigers managed a final push, scoring a touchdown with less than four minutes to play. But it wasn't enough. When the final whistle blew, the score was Pearl River Central 33, Bay High 20.

The exhausted Tigers struggled from the field. Some dropped where they were, overcome by emotion. A blond cheerleader knelt and hugged one player. A mother in a yellow sweater tried to comfort her sobbing son. But the image that struck me most was the hulking player who sat with his head buried in his hands while his grandfather in a corduroy jacket and camouflage hunting hat stood stoically next to him, patting his shoulder and staring into the distance.

Tyler, ever the leader of his plucky platoon, stood resolute in the midst of it all. "We played hard and came up short. It hurts."

"You've been hurt worse," I pointed out.

"Yeah, yeah, I have," he agreed. "It's definitely . . . It's nothing compared to what I've been through the past two months. I mean, at least we're out here playing football."

Coach Compretta gathered the team members and reminded them they'd be playing more football, since they had still qualified for the playoffs. It just wouldn't happen on their home field this year. "Going up to Mendenhall, okay? Hey, look, anything can happen once we get to this point," he said. "We're good enough to play with anybody in the state, okay?"

As the boys headed to the showers, Compretta acknowledged he would probably never see another season like this. "I can't imagine a season topping this one as far as surprises and as far as just having a group of guys like this. They're like men now. It's been something to see that happen. We have to go on the road, but that's okay. At least we get to keep on playing until somebody knocks us out."

Down the hill to the east of the field, another set of lights glowed in the night. The Corps of Engineers was racing to install portable classrooms at North Bay Elementary School. It had already missed the November 1 goal, so a new opening date of November 7 was the target.

Teachers were already back on the job, trying to organize their classrooms and all the new books and supplies. Virtually everything in every school had to be replaced. The teachers, most of whom still had no permanent homes, couldn't even buy basic classroom material. Donations had been pouring in. One contact was providing used desks. Another, library books. Others gave office supplies. School districts around the country were adopting individual teachers.

That very morning, trucks packed with donations had lined up outside district headquarters over near Second Street Elementary School. Teachers had pulled up in cars and climbed into the trucks to count out what they needed for their students. They emerged giddy and smiling, carrying load after load of the unexpected bounty.

Superintendent Kim Stasny said teachers had also come back early for emotional support, following the advice of Florida educators who had recent experience with hurricane recovery. "They need to sit, talk, vent, get it out of their system," she explained. "So when the kids get back, they can get back to the business of education."

The business of education had become a guessing game, given the district's uncertainty over just how many students would return. Though the teachers were on a contract through the end of the year, the superintendent was worried about a teacher-student imbalance. "What happens if you have 50 percent of your students and a bunch of teachers you don't need?" she said.

As the buses rolled out Monday morning, Corps of Engineers crews hurriedly conducted final checks on the rows of portable trailers. Sixty-eight had been installed—eight short of the total promised. But with initial attendance expected to be low, the school district hoped the trailers would be enough.

New rules prevailed for the bus drivers. They were to run down any roads that were open. Many wouldn't be. They were to pick up children even if they were not at the regular bus stop or didn't normally ride the bus. No preregistration for school or bus transportation was required. As the superintendent put it, "We'll take whoever we can get."

The mayor and the superintendent were at North Bay Elementary School for the official ribbon-cutting marking the resumption of the school year. But all eyes were on the buses as they pulled up to school for the first time in two and a half months. The doors folded open, and children came bounding down the steps. Some had backpacks, but others carried very little.

"How are you doing? Welcome back to North Bay! We're so excited to see you!" said Principal Frances Weiler as the children exited the buses. Few were on board, though. One bus carried only three students.

If the teachers were worried, they didn't show it. They stood on the gravel entrance to their trailer school holding signs for their grades. When the children caught sight of their teachers, they dashed to their sides. "I think I remember your name," said a six-year-old boy wearing a white dress shirt and blue pants.

"Do you?" responded a woman in a bright blue shirt with cheerful sailboat appliqués.

"Miss Ferguson," he answered hesitantly, putting a finger to his lips.

"You got it!" she said, wrapping him in a hug.

One little girl dressed defiantly in all white ran from her car and leaped into her teacher's arms, throwing her legs around the woman's hips.

"How are you?" the teacher asked.

"Good!"

"Oh, I missed you," said the teacher, planting a kiss on the child's forehead as she lifted her to the ground.

I had never seen children so elated to return to school. I could almost feel the healing taking place, the hugs and emotional reunions as important for the teachers as for the students. Weiler said the school would offer counseling sessions to the children and encourage them to express their feelings about the hurricane. "Every teacher will ask them to write. That's where they're going to express those things. They can share if they want." She surveyed the children milling around in front of the trailers. "But I truly feel that's not what they want to talk about with us. They want to talk about coming back to school."

The teachers shepherded their students down the wooden ramps and into the portable classrooms. Corps of Engineer workers and National Guard troops who'd helped install the trailers clapped as the children walked by.

The final count citywide that day was 932 of the 2,387 students who had started back in August—just 39 percent, well short of the 60 percent the district had hoped for. Still, this was a time for celebration. The principal refused to let a low turnout spoil things. "It's the happiest day because our children are back in school. It's been perfect, a perfect day," she said.

Parents, too, reveled in the moment. "This is just an emotional roller coaster. I am so thrilled that my kids . . . This is the first day of normalcy," said Ellen Hoffman, struggling to hold back tears. "There wasn't a whole lot of children back. But I think that once the word gets out that we're coming back strong and our kids are happy and they're healthy and they're safe, this community's just going to start bustling again."

Her son, Joe Joe, saw it all with the simple clarity of an eight-year-old. "I'm just happy to have somewhere to go again," he said.

I watched a third-grade girl walking hand in hand with her teacher toward their portable classroom and overheard the child comment, "The school doesn't have walls or anything." I wondered if she meant the two rows of eight trailers that were now North Bay Elementary. Or was she referring to the old school—the crumbled walls, smashed classrooms, and ruined contents visible just beyond the neat, new installation? It was a graphic reminder of what had been lost and how different life had been just two and a half months ago.

~11~

Thanksgiving

It was mid-November, but the Norman Rockwell image of families crowded around a Thanksgiving dinner table burgeoning with food repulsed instead of beckoned. I couldn't stomach the ritual. The thought of millions of Americans gorging themselves while people on the Mississippi Gulf Coast were hungry and living in tents seemed obscene.

I was getting used to feeling isolated. I'd changed. I had lost interest in gardening. The classical piano pieces I once loved playing now seemed infuriatingly placid. I needed angry, passionate music that screamed at the top of its lungs. In the car driving to and from CNN, I couldn't bear to be alone with my thoughts. So I was constantly on my hands-free cell phone, working stories and talking with friends.

I was driving home one evening when Brooke, Lydia Schultz's older daughter, called. As much as I wanted to talk to her, I was also afraid. How could I apologize for letting someone down the way I had her family? What words would I use to say it should have been me who found her father's body, not Brooke herself? She should never have had to endure that horrible experience.

Brooke was calm and reflective as she described how she'd tried to persuade Van to evacuate. He had refused, insisting that he'd just get stuck in traffic, and that he had nowhere to go anyway. She rebuffed my efforts to apologize. "Kathie, I think it was meant to be this way. I was the last person to talk to my dad. So I was the one who was supposed to find him."

Brooke insisted she was doing fine. We talked about getting together in Atlanta on one of my trips south. The conversation was brief. And while I appreciated her interpretation of events, it didn't lessen my guilt.

Her younger sister, Marie, who lived in Shreveport, Louisiana, was reaching out to me as well. The loss of her father had left a deep void in her life. They had been very much alike. She told me she could talk to Van about anything. Not only was he always there for her, he understood her.

Marie confided in one e-mail that, while people could understand mourning a lost father, grieving for a lost town left even her husband clueless as to what she was going through.

Subject: From Marie

Joe is supportive, but he doesn't truly understand, I don't think. Who can except for the people who still have such love for the community because they grew up there or have fallen in love with it at some point? I always wanted to move back there 'cause I did/do love it so much. It's so beautiful . . . and the people *are* nice. . . . There *is* that southern hospitality. . . . I haven't found it here or anywhere else I've ever been. . . . A large piece of my heart will *always* live in Bay St. Louis and with the people there. I have some framed post-cards in my bedroom of the Bay . . . water-colored pictures of the Train Depot and OLG church. And then there's one of an oak tree by the water with a sailboat off in the distance that says, "Heaven seems a little closer when you stay in the Bay."

Love and hugs,

Marie

I could feel her pining for understanding. My own husband and children had been patiently tolerating my obsession with helping my hometown. But I wanted more than that. I wanted them to "get it"—to feel the loss I was experiencing. I was also unsure what difference, if any, our CNN reports were making. I needed to get my hands dirty and physically set something right again.

So on November 20, my family was on a flight to Gulfport, toting suitcases packed with jeans and scruffy work clothes and boxes full of workbooks, flashcards, educational games, backpacks, and other supplies donated by Maryland schools and Girl Scout troops. The plan? Deliver the donations to North Bay Elementary School and then spend the week volunteering, doing everything from mucking out houses to serving meals at a citywide Thanksgiving dinner organized by several Arkansas Rotary clubs. The nearest intact hotel with a vacancy was forty-five miles away, so we were prepared to sleep in tents.

But Bay St. Louis being the place it was, no one would hear of that. Father Tracey found friends to stay with and loaned us his FEMA trailer for the week. And when my mother, three sisters, and their families decided to join us, room was found for them, too.

After we left the airport in our rental car, my husband and daughters were stunned by the miles of brown, dead timber and the now-rusting hulks of bare, twisted billboard frames still lining I-10. The damage that was such a familiar sight to me was new and shocking to them.

As we drove down Route 603 to Bay St. Louis, they marveled at the bizarre hodgepodge of wreckage, like the little red cottage tipped completely on its side that still lay wedged against a phone pole, a superfluous white sticker declaring it "unsafe." Once in town, they couldn't believe the level of destruction and the amount of debris piled everywhere.

I, on the other hand, kept assuring them how much better things looked. Slowly but surely, the yards and yards of towering wreckage that had turned the city streets into canyons were being removed. And the few buds that weeks after the storm had miraculously popped out on what appeared to be dead bushes and trees were now fully formed leaves.

~A cottage Katrina swept off its foundation and onto the north side of Route 603
Photo by Gerri Koch

We pulled up first at the town's ball field to help my sister and brother-in-law unload a trailer full of supplies they'd brought all the way from Mount Pleasant, South Carolina. "We didn't think we'd make it here," said Gerri as Linn slid open the back of the silver U-Haul. "We got a flat tire right in the driveway before we even left, and another while we were on the road. This stuff weighs a ton!"

The trailer was packed to the roof with shovels, cleaning supplies, tents, blankets, lamps, toys, clothing, towels, medicine, and crockpots and other kitchen appliances. "Incredible!" I said as we began hauling the booty out. "I can't believe you collected all this."

"My Jazzy girls were wonderful. Linn was wonderful," explained Gerri, a devotee of Jazzercise whose classmates had made generous donations. "Everyone was great."

Volunteers gathered around, their exclamations ample evidence that the load was much-needed. An African American woman in a burgundy sweatshirt, jeans, and yellow work gloves jumped onto a forklift and quickly laid pallets in place to accept the donations. "C. C.," she said with a wave, introducing herself as she worked. "Great job, all this stuff."

"Kathie, Gerri, how are you?" called a familiar voice. It was Tommy Kidd. He was helping with the citywide Thanksgiving dinner later in the week and had stopped by to pick up the cooking supplies Gerri and Linn had brought from a South Carolina restaurant, Coconut Joe's. The owner had contributed industrial-sized pans, chafing dishes, and coffeepots perfect for a mass cooking event. "Y'all have quite a nice load here."

"They're amazing, aren't they?" I said as Gerri and I helped carry the items to his truck.

"See y'all Thursday," said Tommy, jumping in to continue his rounds. He seemed to be in constant motion. And it wasn't an accident. "My therapy is helping other people," he'd confided to me shortly after the hurricane. "I might be criticized for not taking care of my own business, but this makes me feel a lot better than I'd be feeling otherwise."

I checked in with a pretty young blond woman from Jackson, Wyoming, Margaret Balliet, the coordinator of the volunteer group

~C. C. WHITE MANEUVERING A FORKLIFT WHILE MARGARET BALLIET (FAR RIGHT) AND ANOTHER RELIEF WORKER UNLOAD SUPPLIES FROM GERRI KOCH AND LINN GREENWOOD'S TRAILER.
Photo by Gerri Koch

Disaster Corps. Margaret was planning our house-gutting schedule for the week. We would start the following afternoon in Cedar Point, a neighborhood annihilated by the hurricane. My team would be my daughters, Kara and Kaitlyn, my sixteen-year-old niece, Kelly, and a group of teenagers from her Colorado church. They were staying in trailers donated to Our Lady of the Gulf so volunteers there to help repair the church and its adjoining schools—Bay Catholic Elementary and Our Lady Academy—would have roofs over their heads.

We were privileged to have a FEMA trailer to ourselves. Still, we were glad we'd packed light when we saw the tiny "camper," as locals called them. Storage space was nonexistent. A few days' worth of groceries and the cupboards were full. We stored silverware in the little oven. It was virtually impossible to exit the shower without stepping in the toilet. My husband's feet dangled off the end of the only real bed in the trailer. It had about a foot of space around it on each side. "No wonder Father Tracey was happy to go stay with friends," Rick joked, angling his six-foot-one frame across the bed. The girls had to wedge themselves into tiny bunk beds across from the sink. They hated the lack of privacy, a thin curtain the only thing separating them from the rest of the trailer.

I wondered how families along the Gulf Coast could live in these little boxes and not end up killing each other or at least going slightly crazy. Still, they were better than tents, particularly now that the weather was getting cold. Ever since an arctic snap sent late-October temperatures plunging into the thirties, the Hancock County Civil Defense Office had been passing out fliers to tent dwellers with tips on staying warm, avoiding frostbite, and preventing fires. Since so many dry, dead trees had been left in Katrina's wake, officials were worried that sparks could drift into surrounding woods and ignite uncontrollable fires. The United States Forest Service estimated four million acres of woods in Mississippi had been damaged by the hurricane.

Restoring some much-needed green to the barren landscape was job one in the morning. My younger sister Laurie had worked the phones and gotten nurseries in Georgia and Oregon to donate 350 cannas and 96 small shrubs, while family and friends brought junipers, hydrangeas, and boxes of bulbs, perennials, and annuals.

Before anything could be planted, volunteers had to shovel out the thick layer of sand and sludge deposited over the church grounds by the storm surge. They then dumped and spread wheelbarrow after wheelbarrow of soil to give the new plants some chance of survival. It was tedious work. But once the first few flowers were in place, the bright spark of color seemed to energize everyone. Inch by inch, they were reclaiming what the hurricane had stripped away.

As gratifying as that feeling was, my daughters and the other teenagers were eager to start helping residents. We reported to our first house-gutting assignment, at 1000 Dunbar Avenue, a block from David and Angelyn Treutel's home. The narrow one-story brick house had a small front porch, but its most striking feature was its solitude. Every structure to the north and the east between it and the bay had been flattened.

Our Disaster Corps coordinator introduced us to the owner, interfaith minister Gayle Jordan. Improbably in the middle of all the mess, the petite woman in her mid-sixties was wearing white sweatpants and a white turtleneck that matched her short white hair, along with a blue fleece pullover. "My house has a special distinction," she explained before we got started, as if to impress upon everyone that it must be treated with care. "It's the first house standing."

The Disaster Corps team passed out masks and gloves and explained that we'd empty the house first, then rip out the paneling, drywall, and insulation. The Reverend Jordan had been in the hospital recovering from back surgery and was unable to muck out the house herself.

Before we got started, the reverend had instructions of her own: "You'll find a lot of my ministerial robes. Please lay them out here. I'm going to have them dry-cleaned. Then for the weddings I perform, I often do the flowers myself. So please put all the vases and other glassware here." She pointed to open areas on the ground next to the house where volunteers had already begun to deposit her belongings. "My pots, pans, and other dishware can go over there." She was clearly organized and had a precise plan for how she wanted to proceed.

We split into pairs and each took a room of the house. The smell was horrible, and as we began hauling things out we understood why. The structure had been underwater, so every pot, pan, bowl, glass, and cup in the kitchen and every trash can, storage bin, bucket, and container in the house was full of a putrid, stagnant brown brew. The trick in carrying the containers out was to carefully dump the acrid liquid on the ground. One misstep, one wobble and we were doused with a concoction guaranteed to make us *persona non grata* for days.

The kids carefully followed the reverend's instructions. But they couldn't help noticing the ministerial gowns were stained, mildewed, and rotting. The pots, pans, and trays were rusted. And when they dumped the liquid from the glasses and dinnerware, dark brown stains remained etched into the surfaces. Everything had what locals called the "Katrina patina."

After an hour or so, the teenagers approached me out of earshot of the Reverend Jordan. "This stuff is all ruined. We should just throw it away. We're wasting our time!"

I looked at the clearly unsalvageable belongings and back at their frustrated faces. "Kids, these are her things. They're all she has left. She's the one who has to make that decision."

I went back to work in the rear bathroom, where the storm surge had pushed the toiletries, towels, household cleaners, and other items into a muddy pile. Since nothing was usable, I shoveled it all into a wheelbarrow and started rolling it out front to dump.

"Wait! We can't throw this away!" exclaimed the Reverend Jordan, stopping me and plucking a muddy, heart-shaped pincushion off the refuse. "This is an antique hatpin." She pulled out the pin and held it up so I could appreciate its worth.

It was a poignant illustration of her determination to save all her possessions, no matter how small. Friends in Bay St. Louis had told me that was how many people felt initially—that with a little soap, some elbow grease, and will power, they could clean up everything. But then they started scrubbing and scraping and realized the Katrina patina couldn't be budged. Finally, looking at the enormous and futile task ahead, they relented and threw it all away. The Reverend Jordan had not yet experienced that epiphany.

In a few hours, we emptied the home. The Disaster Corps site manager began passing out crowbars and sledgehammers to smash and pry off what was left of the walls and ceilings. The kids went at it with joyous abandon. All their lives, they'd been cautioned by adults to be careful, to slow down, to not scuff the walls or scratch the furniture. Now, they were being told, "Take this place down to the two-by-fours!" They found it so liberating that they worked until dark without breaks or complaints.

In our enthusiasm, we novices neglected one thing—to keep a path through the house clear of nails. By the end of the day, we'd flattened the tires on all six wheelbarrows. This was a crisis in a disaster zone where no hardware or tire store was open for forty miles.

Our punishment? The next morning when we reported to muck out a house on Main Street, we were allotted one wheelbarrow. What that wheelbarrow couldn't handle, we had to carry out. We improvised where we could, shoveling debris on sheets of plywood and dragging them to the curb.

~Taking a break from mucking out Gayle Jordan's Bay St. Louis home. From left to right are Tim Quinlin, Hannah Radner, Gayle Jordan, the author, Kaitlyn McNaney, Kara McNaney, and Kelly McLean
Photo by Margaret Balliet

"Y'all make sure you pile that in front of the phone poles or they won't take it," cautioned a city inspector surveying the property.

It was a new and ridiculous FEMA rule. All debris had to be deposited at the roadside or on sidewalks in front of the utility poles lining the streets. Anything inside those invisible lines would not be picked up for disposal. But Main Street in Bay St. Louis was a narrow, two-lane road with no shoulders. Not only was I loath to have the kids walking in the road, we were not about to block Main Street. So we dumped the drywall, bead board, insulation, and other refuse as close to the road as possible and hoped that would do.

This house was easier than the first. Most of the belongings had been removed, so water wasn't an issue. That is, until one of the boys' sledgehammer blows went astray and hit a pipe in the kitchen. We assumed all the utilities had been shut off, but water came gushing out. "Turn it off!" he screamed, trying to stem the flow with his work glove.

We raced through and around the house, trying every valve we could find, but nothing worked. Suddenly, I remembered the two men who'd driven up to the church in a blue pickup that very morning and offered their services. "We're plumbers from Vicksburg. We thought y'all might need a hand down here." Father Tracey had put them to work on some of the school buildings.

The site was just five minutes away, so I jumped in the car and dashed back to the church. "Hello! Vicksburg plumbers? Anyone seen the plumbers?" I called as I ran through the wrecked school buildings.

"Ma'am, is everything okay?"

"Come on! We need you over on Main Street."

I explained our predicament as we jogged to the vehicles. They followed me to the house, where volunteers had formed a bucket brigade, wedging construction buckets beneath the shattered pipe and swapping them out once they were full. The men opened their toolbox, pried the lid off a utility compartment next to the road, and used a long T-shaped metal tool with a notch on the bottom to turn the shutoff valve. Crisis averted!

Exhausted from two days of hard labor, we were about to head back to the trailers when I remembered that Father Tracey had mentioned Pat Kergosien's mother needed help moving her debris pile. It was still light out, so we drove over to Carroll Avenue and parked at the address we'd been given. She was a victim of the new FEMA rule. Despite her wide-open yard and the mound's location far from any structure, the debris removal contractor had sliced the roadside pile neatly in half, leaving the portion that was behind the utility poles.

"Okay, guys. You know what we have to do," I told them.

Since we had no shovels or tools, we began picking up and carrying the debris over the imaginary line and depositing it on the edge of the road.

"Hey! What are y'all doin'?" shouted a man's voice.

I looked up and saw Pat Kergosien striding down the sidewalk from his house at the top of the street. "Hey, Pat! We heard your mom needed a hand here. And as you can see, we have plenty of hands, so . . ."

"Kathie, it's you! I got a call that someone was down here on Mom's property. Y'all don't have to do this," Pat protested, looking at my dirty band of teenage workers. "We'll get a Bobcat and take care of it."

"Look, Pat. We have the time, and the kids have the energy."

In about an hour, we made the debris pile conform to FEMA standards.

Pat motioned toward his mother's one-story Acadian brick house, mostly obscured by a huge pecan tree Katrina had toppled over the entrance. "You know, if y'all are looking for something to do, I could use some help pulling up the rest of the floor in there."

"Kids?"

The team was game. The girls and I carried out the strips of white oak flooring that were piled inside while Pat and the boys used crowbars to pry up the heavy plywood subfloor.

Sweating and tired, our job done, we were about to leave when Pat asked for one more favor. "Can y'all give me a hand with this?" It was a refrigerator wrapped several times with duct tape.

The teenagers helped Pat haul it to the curb, but then curiosity got the best of them. "Open it!"

"No!"

"Come on! How bad can it be?"

Before I knew it, they cut the tape and exposed the rotting three-month-old contents for all to smell. The stench was so foul that Kelly quickly slammed the door shut. "That is so disgusting!"

The combined odor of rotten eggs, spoiled milk, and all manner of degrading meat, fish, and other food hung in the air. "Sorry, Pat," I said, covering my nose. "Come on, kids. Enough fun for one day."

"Appreciate your help, everybody." Pat shook hands with the group, then headed up the street. "Better get some more duct tape."

The next morning was Thanksgiving. Everyone was ready for a day of rest. We got up and donned the gold volunteer T-shirts designed by an Arkansas artist for those helping in the citywide banquet that day. The front had familiar local images—crabs, shrimp, a gracious southern home, and a pier reaching out over the bay. The back bore the symbol of Rotary International and a telling quote from Mayor Eddie Favre: "This is a day of Thanksgiving. We are counting our blessings."

Blessed was how most people I knew in Bay St. Louis described themselves, though the word normally wouldn't apply to a city that had lost 70 percent of its homes and businesses, where a third of the population was still missing. It certainly applied this day. Nearly a hundred people from three Jonesboro, Arkansas, Rotary clubs had given up the holiday with their families to come to Bay St. Louis not just to prepare a Thanksgiving meal but to serve it restaurant-style to every citizen of the city. That simple gift of dignity meant so much. "No waiting in food lines like everyone's been doing since August 29," said Eddie Favre, beaming. "A true sit-down meal."

We showed up bright and early to find the Rotarians and volunteers from the Calvary Chapel Relief team preparing food under what looked like a massive red-and-white-striped circus tent. Bob Warner, a Jonesboro surgeon who'd grown up in Bay St. Louis, had rallied this group and also organized the convoys of tractor-trailers full of fuel and supplies that had rolled in from Arkansas right after the hurricane. "It's home," he explained. "You know how special a place it was and how you want it to be that way again." As we walked past the steaming vats of vegetables, he said the volunteers had also arranged a booth for people to take their first family photos since the hurricane. "You're dealing with a whole city of people who've lost all their tangible memories—pictures, keepsakes. I think these pictures become more special in that context."

Outside, a dozen silver turkey fryers were lined up in the morning sun. Already, men in stained aprons were lifting the birds fried to a crispy golden brown out of the bubbling oil and wrapping them for transport to the dinner location outside the historic L&N Train Depot.

"Turkey for breakfast?" asked one chef, who introduced himself as a volunteer from Albany, Georgia.

"Sure," I replied, taking the piece he offered. The outside was slightly crunchy and the meat inside succulent and juicy. "Delicious! So is this the way you cook them in Georgia?"

"That's it. Good eatin'!"

We went to work carrying trays of green beans, sweet potatoes, cranberry sauce, and other food to the waiting trucks. The teenagers loaded bags of ice for the beverages. We followed the delivery trucks to the banquet site, a wide-open area underneath the generous branches of a grove of live oaks in front of the depot.

When residents began to arrive, volunteers ushered them to their seats and took their orders. As they waited, the Killer Shark band from Waveland took the stage. "We live two blocks off the beach. We lost our houses and everything, just like everyone else," said the lead singer. "But we have our friends and our families alive and well, and for that we're very thankful. We're going to try to make you feel better with a little music right now."

As the families at the tables leaned back and enjoyed the music, I could almost see the stress melt from their faces. The children, who'd made sure to stop for free face painting on the way in, reveled in their parents' relaxed state and undivided attention. They sat in their laps or leaned their heads on their parents' shoulders, everyone savoring this rare respite from the endless cleanup.

Eddie Favre circulated through the crowd wearing his apron bearing the Bay St. Louis slogan: "A Place Apart." "Today's great," he said. "Absolutely. Quite a showing. It's amazing."

Still, Eddie confessed he didn't feel quite right being exiled from the kitchen. "I got up early this mornin', put my only apron on, and was prepared to start cookin'. And they haven't let me do anything all day long! It's like, we're having a cookin' celebration in Bay St. Louis and I'm not allowed to participate other than enjoy? I can't deal with it."

"Mayors deserve a break, too, don't they?" I asked.

"When everybody else is taken care of, then we can take a break. Not until."

Eddie remarked how some volunteers who'd been in town before, like the mayors of the Mississippi towns of Pontotoc and Crystal Springs, thought things looked much better. "I guess we see it every minute of every day, and it's just not getting there fast enough."

"Is there still reason to be thankful?"

"Very much," he replied after a moment. "We're still here. And we have the opportunity to come back. And we will come back. And it's the great people that make Bay St. Louis a place apart, and always have and always will, and that's why it will be again."

We rounded up our family and got ready to drive to my brother's home in Ocean Springs for our Thanksgiving celebration. On the way, we did what I'd told myself we didn't have time to do, but what in reality I'd been avoiding—the disaster tour. We stopped where the old ice-cream parlor had been and where our house had stood on South Beach Boulevard. My daughters had never been to Bay St. Louis. And my mother, who'd been working with my sister on the church landscaping, hadn't been to either spot to see what was left.

The girls and my nieces and nephew who'd just arrived with my sister Krissy from Virginia walked across the slab and through the pile of broken bricks, poking at the belongings still tangled in the rubble. I described what had been there, but it meant little to them. They had no connection to the place.

"Look! This is the only thing that made it through the hurricane." I pointed to a small rectangular barbecue pit near the base of the giant live oak in the backyard. "Uncle Mark and Grandpa made this from the bricks of the house that was destroyed in Hurricane Camille."

The children listened politely but didn't appreciate the irony.

My heart ached for my mother, who walked the property quietly, immersed in her thoughts. I knew she was holding in her emotions because she was surrounded by her grandchildren. I noticed a ceramic wall plaque on the ground next to a neighbor's slab. A cheerful lavender, it bore the word *Dreams* painted in script. It was broken.

The celebration that evening in Ocean Springs was low-key, many of us reflecting on the losses our town had experienced and the long road ahead. My brother and his family were happy to be back in their home after evacuating to Colorado for more than a month while the region's schools and infrastructure got back up and running. Unfortunately, Keesler Air Force Base, where my sister-in-law worked, had sustained nearly $1 billion in damage. There was talk the family might be transferred to Arizona until repairs were complete.

The next day, we said our goodbyes to Father Tracey. My husband, Rick, a skilled carpenter, had spent most of his time working on the church's community center and schools, but I had found few opportunities to talk with the priest. "I'm sorry I didn't help more here on the church grounds," I told him as we left.

"Ah, Kathie. No need to worry. It's time we go out into the community and start helping the people," he said.

"It felt good. I just wish we could have done more."

"You know, every accomplishment, no matter how small, moves things forward."

We returned the keys to his FEMA trailer, which Father Tracey accepted with a begrudging laugh, and headed to the airport. On the way, my cell phone rang. CNN wanted to send a camera crew over from New Orleans to shoot my family doing recovery work. I had told only the documentary unit we were going, since it was personal volunteer time and not something we were doing to get attention. Still, I agreed to go on the air the next day back in Washington to talk about the serious need for volunteers in Mississippi.

A few weeks later, I got an e-mail from a prominent Georgia attorney that made me glad I had.

Subject: Bay St. Louis Story

    I just wanted to let you know that the report on your family's efforts over Thanksgiving in Bay St. Louis inspired me to join forces with Disaster Corps and spend my vacation week in Bay St. Louis with relief and clean up. As you obviously know, it is a powerful motivator when one sees what is really going on—or more aptly, not going on in the area. The concept of passing it on is clearly at work—your story led me to Mississippi and in turn I hope I can use my legal skills and my own media ties to help further. Thank you for keeping the problem in the public focus and for the more personal work you are doing on the issue.

Sincerely,

B. J. Bernstein

~12~

Holidays

IN NEAT PRINT, Bay Catholic Elementary School teacher Connie Heitzmann wrote the traditional holiday assignment on a donated whiteboard: "What do you want for Christmas?"

The third-graders worked excitedly for several minutes, then dropped the index cards on Connie's desk as the bell rang to end the school day. She picked up the stack and thumbed through it, expecting the cards would contain the usual catalog of toys, games, and other childish wishes.

A knot formed in her throat. The number-one request? Sheetrock. One child wrote, "I want things to be back to normal." A couple of students penned the simple request, "I want to be happy."

The fact that children who had lost so much—some everything they owned—were ready to forgo their own material desires was telling. Though their pupils romped on the playground with their usual abandon, teachers knew Hurricane Katrina had deeply affected them. This was poignant proof.

Connie and her husband's home had been swamped by the storm surge. When I saw her shortly afterward, she told me how her husband had discovered just three salvageable items while raking through the debris. One was a laminated prayer card from Mother Teresa, who'd been an inspiration since Connie visited one of the nun's schools years earlier. The second was Connie's class ring from St. Joseph's Academy. The third was a tiny blue ceramic truck that had been on top of a cake served at our family's ice-cream parlor for her son's fifth birthday party. "Sunshine Ice Cream Parlor" was painted on the side. "I want you to have this," she said. "I know it was a family business, and you shared some wonderful times there."

Despite everyone's efforts to stay upbeat, Christmas seemed to magnify what was missing. The town had no decorations, just a spindly Charlie Brown–style Christmas tree propped up at the end of Main Street where the roadway crumbled to dirt at the water's edge. Citizens put up few decorations, though some did string lights and erect trees and manger scenes outside their FEMA trailers. One sardonic trailer dweller decorated a wreath with bleach, rubber gloves, a dust mask, MREs, a water bottle, and a FEMA banner.

My high-school classmate Beth Keith, preparing to celebrate Christmas in a trailer with her husband and three children, explained it this way: "We were going on adrenaline for a while. But during the holidays, that's when it hits home, when you realize your family traditions are gone."

Her words rang in my ears as I spread our red-and-green quilted tree skirt under the lush spruce in our den and began carefully hanging ornaments we'd collected over a lifetime. My friends and neighbors in Bay St. Louis had lost all such heirlooms. I felt guilty enjoying mine.

I was having difficulty enjoying anything about the holidays. Christmas carols like "Away in a Manger" and "I'll Be Home for Christmas" reminded me how few people in Bay St. Louis had a permanent place to lay their heads. Giving my family a wish list was unthinkable. Shopping seemed positively hedonistic. My daughters got used to covering their ears when store commercials would ask, "What do you get for the man or woman who has everything?" I would jump up and scream at the television, "You get them nothing, dammit! You write out a check and send the money to the Mississippi Gulf Coast!"

We'd seen for ourselves how bad things were. But some, like my mother's best friend, Lydia Schultz, still couldn't bring themselves to go.

Subject: just a note

   . . . There are so many people trying to help. But I just hear
things are kind of stagnant down there! Of course, you get
12 perspectives from 12 different perceptions so one never
knows unless you go down for yourself. And I just don't seem
to be in a space that will allow me to do that. . . . When I reach
for things that I had in my house and that are now gone, I find
myself crying uncontrollably! . . .
   Anyway, take care and I love you.

   Lydia

   Times were particularly difficult for Nikki and Patrick Cleveland. Nikki's parents' bodies had finally been identified. The couple
held a service at the local funeral home to lay Ralph and JoAnna to
rest. Father Tracey officiated, and a large crowd turned out to support Nikki and her two sisters.
   Nikki was still angry that the identification process had taken
months, leaving them all in limbo. "A funeral home actually called
us and said, 'We have your parents here.' We were shocked because
we had not heard from the coroner. We thought for sure they must
not have the right bodies. So we really hesitated to try to make any
arrangements because we weren't sure."
   Patrick acknowledged the mixed emotions. "We're sad and relieved at the same time. Very sad because now it's real. But relieved
because at least we can move on."
   As if their losses and the starkness of the holidays weren't
enough, many families in Bay St. Louis were coming face to face
with a troubling reality—they may never be able to afford to rebuild
their homes.
   Though just a third of the town was in a flood zone, where residents were required to buy federal flood insurance, 95 percent of
Bay St. Louis had been inundated by Hurricane Katrina's massive
storm surge. Many residents didn't have insurance to cover the
damage because they had been told they lived on high ground and
didn't need it. Unfortunately, the FEMA flood maps everyone had

based their decisions on were twenty years out of date.

Sustained 125-miles-per-hour winds had strafed the town for six hours before the peak storm surge rolled in, so most homeowners started out confident the wind and hurricane coverage from private insurers that they'd paid premiums on for years would at least cover that damage. They were stunned to find claim after claim up and down the Gulf Coast was being denied.

Because of Katrina's unprecedented storm surge, some insurance companies were taking the position that the hurricane was an all-water event, so the federal government's flood policies should pay for the damage. And even in cases of wind damage, some had little-known clauses in their policies stating that if another force like a flood or a rising tide also damaged the structures, then the insurance companies owed nothing. Such "anti-concurrent cause" clauses meant that even if homes were entirely ripped apart by wind, homeowners couldn't collect a dime for wind damage if a flood or a storm surge followed and pushed down just one board or brick. I was amazed that such clauses were legal and suspected most homeowners whose policies included them didn't know it.

Mayor Eddie Favre was denied payment for damage under his renter's insurance.

Lydia Schultz's wind damage claim was denied.

The wind claims of Nikki and Patrick Cleveland, Gene and Margaret Taylor, Darla and Keith Goodfellow, and Beth and Larry Keith were also denied. The four couples had all purchased both wind and flood insurance and thought their homes were protected no matter what happened.

Others like Tommy and Linda Kidd and Angelyn and David Treutel had been offered some compensation but were going to dispute their companies' findings to try to get more of the damage covered.

"When you see part of your roof blown off and you see all the siding above the water line gone, it's got to be evident that wasn't water. That was wind, small tornadoes," argued Tommy Kidd. Because his insurance company hadn't yet agreed to pay for the roof damage, Tommy couldn't make repairs. So the ceiling was starting to fall in on the previously undamaged second floor. "It makes you feel that all the years of insurance you pay, that it's a waste of money and time."

Though twenty-seven witnesses across the street at the Waveland Police Department had watched the wind tear the roof off Tommy's daughter's restaurant, Daddy O's, the insurance company had assigned two engineers to determine if water instead had wrecked the building. "Here we are three months down the road, and our business, we can't destroy it. We can't finish bulldozin' it to rebuild because the money's not there," said Tommy. "And it's very, very disheartening."

Back in Jordan River Isles, Nikki and Patrick Cleveland's home also sat untouched. "We can't do anything. We can't take our house apart and see if there's anything left in there that we might could salvage. We can't change anything," said Patrick. "So, around us, people can start rebuilding homes and we can't. And who knows how long it's gonna be?"

In fact, by December, the neighbors on either side of the Cleveland home had cleared their lots. Both had been paid by their insurance companies for wind damage. Patrick gestured to the east. "Apparently, somewhere down there, because that's the direction the wind came, the wind parted and missed our house, got both of theirs, but didn't get ours. Just water got our house," he said sarcastically.

On North Beach Boulevard, Congressman Gene Taylor was also having a hard time understanding his insurance company's rationale for denying that Katrina's winds did any damage to his waterfront home. On one of my trips to Bay St. Louis, Gene pointed out a piece of metal wrapped taco-style around a tree branch thirty feet in the air. The bark at that height was intact, and green leaves had sprouted on many of the branches. But a few feet below, the branches were bare and the trunk scarred, most of the bark stripped away by the floating debris that had battered the trees for hours. "That was a part of my tin roof," said Gene. "Tin does not float. That piece of tin flew up there."

"That piece of tin is over the water line," I said. Granted, I was no expert at interpreting hurricane damage, but I wasn't blind.

Gene described how two female adjusters had walked the property with him. When he asked about payment on his homeowner's wind policy, they said, "Oh, we don't know that you had any wind damage." When he pointed out the tin pieces up in the trees, "they just kind of shrugged and said what they'd been coached to say: 'It was all water.' So we'll go to court and hopefully the right thing will happen," Gene said.

The house where Van Schultz died was the only one on Breeden Place that had partially collapsed. All the other houses had damage from a different direction. A private claims adjuster told Lydia the house was hit by a tornado. The insurance company's inspector agreed, but the claim was still denied, so Lydia was suing, too. "I am not expecting anything. Nothing," she said dejectedly. "I have written off that house investment. In my mind, it is gone."

As I talked to each of them, I became angrier and angrier. True, if only water damaged a home or business covered by flood insurance, then the federal flood program was responsible for paying for those repairs. But if clear evidence of wind damage was visible even to the most untrained layman, how could private insurance companies simply deny it existed? Particularly when the entire structure was gone, how could they claim that sustained 125-miles-per-hour winds had played no role in the destruction? I'd stood in 70-miles-per-hour winds in Virginia Beach in 2003 and watched the roof peel off the hotel next door. People who had lost everything in Katrina did not deserve to be victimized a second time by their insurance companies.

Not all of them were bad players. David Treutel, who two months earlier had graduated from working in a tent to a twenty-by-sixty-foot office trailer, could attest to that. As an independent broker, he dealt with roughly twenty different insurance companies. "I have about four or five companies that I think would get an A or a B. Probably four or five companies have failing grades. And we've got the rest of them that are probably somewhere in between."

David confessed, "I've had to call the insurance commissioner to complain about my own company because they weren't doing what they were supposed to. Some of them got mad with me. That's why I'm glad to be an independent agent. I'm not an employee of any one of these companies. I have a fiduciary responsibility to the companies, but I also have a responsibility to my insureds."

Like the client David ran into one morning at the Emergency Operations Center. "Finally got to see my insurance adjuster today," the woman said.

"Well, that's a good thing," he replied.

"No. I equate that to going to the dentist and getting my wisdom teeth removed."

Many of his clients were upset. One man even came in carrying a handgun. But David used his easygoing nature and his own family's loss to defuse the crises as they arose. "Once you realize that you're kind of all in the same situation, it takes away a little bit of the stress that we see right now."

Stress was evident at city hall, too. By the holidays, just a third of the debris burying the town had been removed. "It's just a slow process," said Mayor Eddie Favre. "There's so much debris on private property. It's gonna take awhile to get that."

As many as a thousand residents were still waiting for FEMA trailers. Eddie knew that if the people didn't come back, the town wouldn't either. "As soon as we can get shelter for them here, then they will come back home. We're hopin' possibly for the holidays, if not soon after the holidays, we can bring our people back home."

Fortunately, volunteers continued pouring into the area to help do the work residents otherwise couldn't afford. My own place of worship, Cedar Ridge Community Church, was about to send a delegation to help at a Baton Rouge, Louisiana, relief center when I intervened to chide the men's group organizer. "Big, strapping guys like you are going to hand out supplies? You've got to go to Bay St. Louis, Mississippi, and gut and rebuild houses. You won't believe the damage there." So the group rerouted to Bay St. Louis, though finding a place to stay was still a major challenge.

Tommy Kidd was preparing meals at a volunteer village set up in Waveland by a Utah charity, the Morrell Foundation. For a minimal fee, the village provided food, tents with cots, a laundry, bathrooms, showers, Internet access, and meeting space.

Tommy, himself a one-man relief team, was stunned by the dedication of complete strangers who before Hurricane Katrina had never even heard of the towns of Waveland and Bay St. Louis. "There's just been an outpouring like I could never believe. I'm flabbergasted. Just so many good, good people. These churches that are sending down these folks. They just, you know, get in that mud, cleaning out, throwin' a foot of dirt with shovels. I mean, you know how bad my house was. And they come in and they thank us for lettin' them come to town. It's amazing. It's restored my faith in human nature." Tommy shook his head and laughed. "I really believe out of all bad comes some good. And this is proof positive."

The holiday spirit motivated even more good deeds. The construction team working seven days a week since September to rebuild the CSX railroad bridge passed Our Lady of the Gulf Church at dawn and dusk every day as it commuted to and from its base camp. Two weeks before Christmas, the team appeared with a towering fir tree complete with lights and decorations for the front lawn.

A week later, a truck from the nonprofit organization KaBOOM! rolled in packed with the brightly colored beams, bars, chains, and plastic roofs and platforms needed to construct the town's new playground. More than six hundred residents and volunteers shook off the chilly temperatures and rallied to complete in one day the first new permanent structure in town since Katrina struck.

My middle-school friend Ginny Vegas, who spearheaded the project, sent me an e-mail that, like so much this Christmas, was sprinkled with hope and pain.

Subject: Bay St. Louis Playground Build

Dear Kathleen,

We missed you so much. You would have loved it. The mayor cooked jambalaya, we had over 650 volunteers on a cold, wet day and they built the playground, five planter benches, five picnic tables and garbage cans in record time. There was laughing, singing, just old fashioned joy. . . . We were awash in happiness! So many people said that it was the first uplifting day since the storm. . . .

Our little community is very much still on its back. Seems the government is AWOL. I think they would still be pulling bodies out the swamp if it weren't for the Christian groups.

Thank you again for your help keeping the Coast on the radar screen. I know there are so many other stories around the world. Bay St. Louis needs you. . . .

We best focus on our blessings.

Ginny

And so they did all over Bay St. Louis that Christmas morning, in whatever structures remained for them to worship in and with whatever family and friends had stayed to start over. At Our Lady of the Gulf, parishioners stood in a nave bare of pews and virtually everything else. But the roof had been replaced and the walls were sound, so they gathered for the first mass in the church since the hurricane. Father Tracey told them they were, as the holiday carol said, home for Christmas.

As he spoke about the birth of the Christ child, a young couple in the congregation shared knowing smiles. Nikki and Patrick Cleveland in seven months would celebrate the birth of their first child.

~13~

Disaster Tours

As the confetti flew and champagne corks popped at the stroke of midnight on December 31, I'd never been more relieved to see a year end. I just wanted 2005 to be over. No matter what happened in 2006, it had to be an improvement.

The Schultzes felt the same way.

Subject: for you my friend

God, Kathie! It has been an atrocious year! And I am the eternal optimist but I was thinking that I am sooooooo glad to see 2005 leave. . . . I still feel this is all so unbelievable and I wish it could go away. But . . . we will all be ok at some point.

Love you,

Lydia

Subject: How well said is *this*???

Kathie,

   I meant to write to you a long time ago, but I'm either running, running on my days off or in a weird funk here and
there . . . sorta in a daze. I'm not as depressed as I was . . . but
sometimes I get online and have to look up things about the
Bay . . . and inevitably get in a funk. I want to know what is
going on. . . . I can't not know . . . about my home. Joe and I are
going to the Bay on Saturday. Mom wants us to go down and
try to go on a treasure hunt as dad's old neighbor Gayle, who
is re-building, will have a Bobcat there Sunday. Gayle found
my mom's stained-glass + brass $700 antique lamp the other
day . . . unbroken. It was on a table in the living room. I don't
know how it didn't break. I don't want to go . . . yet I need
to. Ugh!
   I agree about merely celebrating that 2005 is over. Joe and
I went to bed at 7:45 P.M. on New Year's Eve. I didn't care
to celebrate. I also agree that moving forward *is* our only
choice. . . . Thank you for your love and support. . . . I send
you and your family the same.
   Take care.

Love,

Marie

   Both also asked me why they had seen so few reports about the
Mississippi Gulf Coast lately. Resentment was building that the majority of the coverage still focused on New Orleans.
   So I was thrilled when the White House announced President
Bush would make a January trip south to Katrina-ravaged areas
including Bay St. Louis. I had told many of my White House colleagues about the unimaginable destruction in Mississippi and even
shown them pictures, but I knew that a person had to see it to fully
appreciate the magnitude of the disaster.
   It was a brisk day but the skies were bright and clear when our

press plane landed at Stennis International Airport. We boarded buses to St. Stanislaus, the private boys' school where the president would speak to a crowd of four hundred. I asked our Secret Service handler which route we'd be taking.

"Highway 90, ma'am."

"But it's a straight shot to continue directly south from the airport to the water down Nicholson Avenue," I pointed out. "Then you go left down Beach Boulevard. That takes you right to Stanislaus."

"I'm afraid that's not possible. The beach road is not capable of handling buses."

"That road is perfectly fine," I said. "I drove it the week Katrina hit and dozens of times since. It is drivable all the way to the school."

"Please take your seat, ma'am."

I was floored. The worst damage was in the areas closest to the water. The Secret Service route steered completely clear of "slab land." Reporters would see only houses and businesses that had flooded, many with the blue FEMA tarps still in place on their roofs, and the shrinking piles of debris that still covered roadsides and filled parking lots. I didn't know if it was deliberate, but it certainly seemed someone was trying to put the best face on the unprecedented destruction the town had suffered.

At St. Stanislaus, several dozen residents waited outside the auditorium for a glimpse of the president. Unlike the angry crowd that had gathered in Jackson Square to protest Bush's visit to New Orleans, most of these people were just glad Mississippi was being noticed. Only two carried signs. One read, "We Need Help. Lost Everything," the other, "Rebuild Waveland, not Iraq."

As reporters were ushered into the gym to set up in our temporary workspace, I smelled a familiar rich, spicy aroma wafting from the back of the room. It had to be gumbo. I walked back and was surprised to see a virtual banquet spread out on folding tables. The traveling press, particularly when accompanying the president on trips to small towns and disaster-stricken areas, was accustomed to a steady diet of sandwiches, chicken, and barbecue.

The chef, wearing the traditional white double-breasted jacket and tall white toque, noticed my look of astonishment. "We've got some Mississippi Creole love going on. So we've got all the good stuff," said Steve D'Angelo, lifting the lids on the silver chafing trays. "We've got fried green tomatoes, gumbo ya-ya. We've got shrimp jambalaya, pecan-crusted pork loin."

"Stop! I'm in food heaven!" I laughed.

Steve explained that he was chef and owner of Bay City Grill, which had just reopened down the street on New Year's Eve. The roof had to be replaced and the interior completely renovated since it was flooded by Katrina's storm surge. The restaurant staff had dropped from thirty to three.

While repairs were under way, the normally busy chef had time to be with his family. His second child, Mia Belle, was born just two weeks before the hurricane. Steve savored their rare 24/7 relationship, from mundane feedings to baby milestones like her first toothless smile and her initial successful attempt to roll over. "Having her fall asleep on my chest every afternoon was just incredible. If the restaurant had been open, I would've missed all that," he said. "I know it sounds crazy, but in some ways this has been a gift. I wouldn't want to be anywhere else. I mean, this is the place I need to be."

Yes, I was home.

Mayor Eddie Favre strode in wearing a blue windbreaker and shorts.

"Still in shorts, Eddie?" I asked, amazed. "You've got to be getting cold now."

"Yes, baby." Eddie laughed. "The president's going to get another look at my chubby knees!"

Back in the fall, Eddie had wanted a way to express his frustration with the lack of help the town was getting. But being the affable mayor of a committed town of non-whiners, he couldn't exactly carry a protest sign. So he decided that since Katrina had left him with nothing but a shirt and a pair of shorts, he'd stay that way until Bay St. Louis was put back together. "Wearing long pants sends a signal that everything is okay. And everything is not okay," Eddie explained. "And until such time as everything is okay here, I'll wear my shorts."

Not everyone was pleased. State and local officials even offered to send pants for this, Eddie's second meeting with the president. But the mayor said no, though he was glad Bush was finally visiting the town. "His presence alone says that four and a half months out, we're not forgotten." Still, Eddie was worried. "What has not been talked about up to this point is what funds are available to make up for the lost revenue the cities and counties will have over the next three, five, seven years. We can rebuild all we want to, and if we don't have the money to maintain it once it's rebuilt, it didn't do a whole lot of good to rebuild it."

"You can't run the town?"

"That's it."

Eddie headed in for the speech not long before President Bush's motorcade arrived. I was glad to learn that Bush, at least, had taken Beach Boulevard and seen how Katrina had reduced entire gracious waterfront neighborhoods to kindling.

In his talk, the president touted the $85 billion the federal government had made available for hurricane recovery, though just $25 billion had been spent. Bush commented on how he now saw "a little bounce in people's step." Leaning over the podium, he noticed Eddie front and center in his shorts. "I arrive here at this important school and he's got short pants on," said the president with his trademark chuckle. "Eddie, I like a man who sticks to his guns."

After his brief remarks, Bush met with local leaders and business people before flying to Florida for a Republican National Committee fund-raiser. Since it was a closed event, the press corps stayed behind in Bay St. Louis to file reports. That meant we'd have time to kill at the end of the day. I had an idea and cornered the mayor.

"Eddie, it's such a shame the press buses never made it down the beach or to Cedar Point. The other reporters never got to see what really happened here." I paused and sighed. "It's too bad I don't have a car or anything because all this downtime would be the perfect opportunity to drive folks around to the worst areas."

Eddie stroked his chin. "You know, I think we have a city van outside that no one's usin'. Maybe Dave could take y'all for a drive."

Pay dirt! That was precisely what I'd hoped for. I dashed through the filing center, letting everyone know of the opportunity for a tour of the disaster zone. Several reporters, including the Associated

Press and *Washington Post* correspondents, took me up on my offer. A few White House staffers joined us as we piled into the white ten-passenger van.

Our driver, Dave Stepro, a tall man with clear blue eyes, neatly trimmed, graying hair, and a mustache, introduced himself as the town's deputy police chief. He headed toward the water and then steered south down Beach Boulevard. He talked about the storm and the longtime family homes that had lined the beachfront and given the town a sense of pride, heritage, and identity. All were empty foundations now. Only a handful had FEMA trailers, most with American flags flying proudly out front. I had wondered if the flags would be a short-term phenomenon. They'd sprouted spontaneously after the hurricane on everything from battered pilings to Katrina-smashed cars. But they were still here, red, white, and blue symbols of the community's determination to survive.

"Are people still living in tents?" asked one reporter incredulously as we passed a green-and-blue tent pitched next to a toppled tree on a lot still covered with a mountain of rubble.

"Not many," Dave replied. "Some folks do that to keep the looters

~Grateful Message at what used to be a home in Pass Christian
Photo by Mark Proulx

off. It makes it look like someone's living there."

He turned right onto Whispering Pines and described the families who'd lived at each slab. Dave gestured with his right hand to an empty lot where only a huge magnolia was left standing. "That was my house. Cleanest slab in the county." At the end of the street farthest from the water, some homes looked repairable. But Dave pointed out how they'd been lifted and moved several feet off the foundations and so were structurally unsound. They would have to be demolished. He guided the van back to the beach and north toward St. Stanislaus.

"Turn left at this driveway up here," I said. "This was where I used to live." The van fell silent as we pulled up the hill and onto the circular shell driveway. Everyone got out. I walked the slab, pointing out where the kitchen had been, the living room and dining room, my brother's room. I described my room upstairs, with its views over the water and the pecan grove behind the house. I talked of going crabbing in the bay, of our bonfires on the beach, of my sisters' wedding receptions on the backyard patio under the giant live oak. I desperately wanted them to understand how special this place was. But it was like conjuring up a ghost. I was trying to breathe life into something long gone.

One of the White House staffers wandered into our neighbor's yard and noticed on the front stoop of the slab a small collection of items—a glass bowl, a metal goblet, and a few pieces of silverware. I'd seen such displays since the week of the hurricane—generally small, unbroken relics of little value, like plates, trophies, and children's toys—set up in spots visible to passersby. They were like sad little memorials to the lives Katrina had shattered.

Dave explained that's what people did when they found items in the rubble that weren't theirs. And since the hurricane had swept belongings inland for miles, it was a frequent occurrence. Residents would set the possessions out where the owners might see and reclaim them. Dave said it was Bay St. Louis's own form of disaster etiquette. Though the items might appear worthless, anything that survived the storm unbroken now had special significance.

After we drove back to the school, my colleagues thanked me for arranging the tour.

"My pleasure," I said. "All I ask is that you remember what you saw and let others know about what happened here in Mississippi."

An hour or so later, we boarded the buses and this time took the beach route back to the airport. But now it was dark. The absence of streetlights made it impossible to see the extent of the damage or the massive debris fields, so only those who'd ventured away from the school had any idea how much of the town had been erased.

As we left, another group was making its way south to get its first glimpse of the damage. The Goodfellows had decided to bring their children back to visit friends and see what, if anything, they could recover from their lot in Diamondhead.

Darla and the children were determined never to move back. "I can't do it again. I just can't," the longtime schoolteacher would declare.

Keith, though, was a different story. "I am so homesick for this area that you just couldn't believe it," he told a psychiatrist friend he ran into when the family stopped for lunch at Sonic, the first restaurant in Waveland to reopen and a major gathering place.

"I'll hypnotize your wife and tell her to stay here," joked his friend.

"I would love that," said Keith with a weary smile. "There has to be a lot of depressed people in here."

"It hasn't hit yet. A lot of people still have hope. But over the next twelve months, it's going to kick in."

David Treutel heard the same thing in a meeting with community leaders from Pensacola, Florida, which had been hit by Hurricane Ivan in 2004. They were a year ahead in the recovery process and came to town to give local government and business leaders an idea of what to expect. "You can tolerate almost anything for a short duration. But as the months wear on, things get more frustrating when the short-term adrenaline runs out and you see the scope of what remains to be done," warned an Escambia County official. "You're no longer in the spotlight. You're fighting the bureaucracy. You must prepare yourself mentally."

Ridiculous! thought David. *How can people feel worse a year after the storm than they do now?* Things were slowly getting better. He and Angelyn had finally been able to move their independent insurance business out of the trailer and into a brick-and-mortar building with heating, air conditioning, indoor plumbing, and phone lines, luxuries they'd managed without since August. It had taken the building's owner two months to get two weeks of repairs made, since skilled, reliable construction workers were scarce. They would either fail to show up or would begin the work but then get pulled away to bigger, better-paying jobs.

David and Angelyn had decided not to even compete to find a contractor to work on their home. They still had no word on the FEMA trailer they'd applied for in late September. They were keeping their eye on one of the few rental properties in town, a six-hundred-square-foot house that was being repaired, so they could stop the exhausting 112-mile commute each way from Mobile.

Alabama was still home for the Goodfellows when I caught up with them in late January. It was tough to see a six-person family jammed into a cramped one-bedroom apartment. Their trip home the weekend before had yielded a handful of precious belongings—an unbroken snowman Christmas plate, a Jackson Browne record from Darla's collection, and a snow globe, bracelet, and picture frame that belonged to the children. A CNN camera crew had gone along to capture their return for our documentary. But I could hardly bear to watch the video of their drive down the street and Darla's face when she saw that their home was gone. The look of shock and pain was too familiar.

Devout Catholics, they couldn't understand why they and the Gulf Coast they loved had been dealt such a severe blow. Darla told me their children had asked why it happened and why God was punishing them. "I mean, you keep wondering, 'What did we do wrong?' You know? I worked very hard to be a good mother. I worked very hard to do the right thing," she said. "We go to church on Sunday. I worked in a Catholic school. My children went to Catholic school. I've tried to teach them right from wrong and to always do the right thing. And it's important to do the right thing and treat people fair. Where did I fail? Is it something I did?"

Keith was grappling with guilt over leaving his practice. He'd concluded he simply didn't have enough patients left to support it. "Some of them are calling and saying, 'Please come back, please come back. What are we going to do? We don't have a doctor. We don't have any doctors down here.' That makes me feel sorry for them. That makes me feel like I should be there."

But for the four Goodfellow children, their first trip home had cemented their determination not to return to the Gulf Coast.

"It made me feel good that we aren't going back down there because all the stuff we were used to was, like, destroyed and everything," said twelve-year-old Thor.

"It's not the same. Things are always going to be different," insisted seventeen-year-old Samantha, the eldest. "You're always going to have to think about how it was."

Seven-year-old Desiree looked at me with her big brown eyes and said simply that going back was scary " 'cause you didn't know if people were there or not."

In fact, that was a traumatizing factor for children along the Gulf Coast, whether they evacuated or stayed. Most didn't know what had become of their friends. "I didn't really know if they were alive and stuff 'cause I didn't have time to see if they were evacuating," said Thor. "It was hard."

"It was scary 'cause, like, you knew where people lived and stuff," added fourteen-year-old Hillary. "And if they stayed where they were, that they'd be dead."

When the children visited Bay St. Louis, they managed to reconnect with some of their friends. Though Hillary refused to look for anything in the rubble of their home, Samantha was grateful for the few small objects she was able to find. "I took those because those are . . . It's like the only proof that the last eleven years of my life were real, and it wasn't just some dream."

Indeed, dreams were where many continued to wrestle with what they'd experienced. Darla dreamed almost nightly about walking through her house and touching everything that was gone. But it always ended badly. "I'm sitting on the chair with one of my kids. And it's just, the water rushes in and we're ripped apart."

Keith, too, dreamed about being back in their home and sleeping in his bed, instead of on an air mattress on the floor, as he did now. For him, it was an idyllic paradise lost. "I'll dream about going out at night and looking up at the stars in my backyard. I dream about getting up in the morning, seeing the sun rising over the Bay of St. Louis. I dream about sitting out on my dock, fishing with my kids out there." I found it heartbreaking to see him choke back tears.

My cameraman on the Goodfellow shoot was Mark Biello, a CNN videographer who had spent seven hours in a boat after Katrina capturing the first horrific images of New Orleans' Ninth Ward. That night, Mark and the men piloting the boat had saved what people they could. But there were many they couldn't. Mark had covered wars and suffering in the most remote corners of the globe. Still, he told me it was his Katrina experience that haunted him at night when he tried to sleep. "I dream that I'm in a bus full of school kids and it plunges into a river. As the bus goes underwater, I kick out the back door and start bringing the kids to the surface. Finally, it's sinking, and as the last kid floats up I go down with the bus." Perhaps strangest of all was Mark's reaction in his dream as he sank to his death. "I wasn't panicking or fighting at all. I was happy that I got everyone out."

"Maybe in some weird way you were at peace because you had done in the dream what you weren't able to do in Katrina," I offered.

"Exactly."

We talked about how on this story both of us found it impossible not to get involved. And we were both paying a price. But our work loads were such that we just kept plowing forward, figuring someday we'd get around to dealing with the emotional residue. It was as if by remaining in constant motion we could stay a step ahead of the demons pursuing us. Plus, a sort of bulletproof bravado prevailed in the news business. Correspondents, producers, and videographers routinely careened from one tragic story to the next, always maintaining they were unaffected.

Back home a few nights later, I began to realize how deeply I'd been impacted. I was in the basement watching *War of the Worlds* with my daughters. Aliens had invaded, and Tom Cruise and his children had one of the few working vehicles. Most cars were useless, strewn hither and yon. It was night. As the teenage son drove down a country road, figures began to appear out of the darkness. People were on foot, carrying their belongings, looking for help.

Some pushed their possessions in grocery carts. A flood of emotions rushed over the faces of father and son. They were shocked and wanted to help. But as the crowd grew thicker, they realized if they stopped they would risk losing their food and transportation to safety.

I was overwhelmed by the familiarity of the scene and nauseated by the guilt I felt inside. It was like watching a movie of myself the week of the storm. Was that me, protecting what I had, concerned only about my own survival? How could I be a good person if I averted my eyes and kept going? Yes, I had deadlines and a job to do. But how could I live with myself afterward? I jumped up from the couch and sat at the foot of the stairs and cried. What had I become? I didn't know anymore. I didn't want to know.

My eleven-year-old daughter, Kara, came and put her hand on my shoulder. "Mommy, are you okay?"

"No, sweetie, I'm not."

Two weeks later on my birthday, I was on another flight south. We were shooting the opening and closing segments for the documentary, which was to air at the end of February. Every flight to the Gulf Coast I'd made since Katrina had the feeling of a military mission. No tourists were on board, only residents or people committed in some way to being part of the recovery.

On this flight, my seatmate was the pianist for the Preservation Hall Jazz Band. Rickie Monie told me how he and three other band members had lost their homes and all their possessions in the hurricane. But while most escaped with their instruments, pianos are not exactly portable. The flood had claimed both his grand piano and an irreplaceable antique organ, a vintage Hammond B3.

Anyone who has played an instrument for years knows how it becomes a friend—in some cases, almost an extension of you. It is there when you celebrate the good times, and it is where you turn when your soul is aching and empty. You become so attuned to its touch and sound that you recognize when the tiniest thing is amiss. I had played the piano since I was seven. I told Rickie I knew he must miss his precious instruments. I couldn't imagine what it must have been like to see them warped and ruined.

This was my first flight into New Orleans, and I felt deeply conflicted. Since Katrina, I had maintained a single-minded focus on Mississippi and put any thoughts of New Orleans in a box. Yes, I loved the city—the food, the music, the architecture, the history. I'd even lived briefly in the French Quarter. But I was so frustrated by the attention the city garnered from the national media that any sympathy for New Orleans almost felt like a betrayal of Mississippi.

As I drove from the airport into New Orleans East, my anger began to melt into sorrow. On both sides of the highway were dead trees, dead bushes, dead grass, dead neighborhoods. Katrina's water line slashed like a scar across every building. Everything looked desolate and abandoned.

I was relieved when I reached Mississippi and the rubble I recognized. I met my crew and producer to shoot the documentary's opening scene down where Main Street crumbled into the water. It had by now become an iconic image included in every report on Bay St. Louis. The challenge was to find an equally compelling location for the closing segment.

The crew followed me to Cedar Point, where the damage progressed from wrecked homes flipped topsy-turvy to debris fields to empty slabs near the bay. Everywhere, belongings still hung in the trees. Box springs. A computer. Clothing, sheets, and towels drifted gently back and forth in the breeze. In the middle of the wreckage, the crew spotted an empty playground. Not a single small footprint marked the mud-crusted ground. No children's voices rang through the devastated neighborhood. The crew stopped to shoot it while I continued scouting a location.

I saw the Bay St. Louis Little Theatre sign and turned left onto Boardman Avenue. I'd driven past many times but couldn't bring myself to go down the road. For me, every memory of the theater— singing, dancing, friends, family, the hours of rehearsing and performing—was pure joy. And since I hadn't seen it destroyed, I imagined it could still be standing. It was possible. The wind and water might have swept past it at a forgiving angle. A fallen live oak might have redirected the storm surge around it. I would drive right up to the red barnlike building, open the door, and walk down the aisle past the rows of seats to the upright piano. I would sit and play a stanza from *Fiddler on the Roof* or *1776*. I would look at the stage

~A SMASHED TRUCK IN THE REMAINS OF A HOME IN BAY ST. LOUIS
Photo by Mark Proulx

and remember dancing the "Matchmaker" song in long, flowing skirts with my sister Laurie. I would hum strains from my plaintive solo, "Far from the Home I Love."

I pulled to a stop. All that remained were the concrete blocks that had supported the floor. The rear of the structure around the stage had folded in on itself and collapsed. The homes behind the theater had all been lifted and tossed off their foundations, their contents spilled across their backyards. It looked as though nothing had been touched since August 29. It was awful. And it was the place we had to do the closing segment.

The crew members pulled up. As they unloaded their gear, they asked if it had been an open-air theater. I assured them it once had four walls, a roof, a floor, and seats. And a piano. I began poking under the eaves of the collapsed building to see if it was underneath. Finally, I spotted it in a nearby clearing, toppled on its back. The lower panel was missing, leaving the strings open to the elements. They were brown with rust. What keys remained were swollen and immovable. I touched them, but the piano was mute.

"Hey, look at this. This would be a great souvenir!" said my cameraman, Jonathan Schaer, pointing to a small swinging door from the theater that lay on the ground. Screwed to it were the traditional comedy and tragedy masks and a slightly cracked ceramic banner reading, "Est. 1946." "We could unscrew this and take it back," he said.

My first reaction was to consider schooling him in post-hurricane etiquette. I abhorred the idea of taking "souvenirs" from the rubble. Everything around us may have looked like junk, but it belonged to someone and was not free for the taking.

But then I thought perhaps I should take it, have the cracks repaired, and return it to the theater. I brushed aside some mud and leaves covering the left side of the banner, and my heart sank. A two-inch section was missing. I started looking around on the ground. If I could find it and it wasn't too badly broken, maybe I could reinsert it. I lifted boards and began moving downed branches as my crew returned to setting up the shot. It was several minutes before the futility of the search dawned on me. What was I doing? Entire buildings were in ruins around me, and I thought I could find a two-inch piece of ceramic? Without a word, I turned, walked quickly back, and climbed into the car. I put my head down and let the tears flow. What was wrong with me? Why was this damn banner so important? Why did I need so badly to make one thing whole again? It would do no good in the grand scheme of things.

Leave it behind. Just leave it, I told myself. Everyone here had learned how to let go. I had to learn, too.

~14~

Mardi Gras

HER HEART POUNDING, Cyndi Meyer climbed the steps into the Mardi Gras float and took her position next to a rack of purple, green, and gold beads. It wasn't the prettiest float the statuesque blond had ever ridden. But it looked far better than it had the day after the hurricane. Cyndi, den lieutenant of Bay St. Louis and Waveland's all-female Krewe of Nereids, had raced to the eighty-by-hundred-foot building housing the twenty-five floats, only to find three of the walls gone and the tin roof collapsed. Ten feet of water had surged through the building. What hadn't been crushed by the roof was covered with a thick layer of mud and debris. It looked like a total loss.

Most of the 120 members of the Krewe had lost everything, too, but they weren't about to give up Mardi Gras. After a contractor removed the roof and large debris, the women got to work. For three months, Cyndi and her friends painstakingly scraped off the old paint, replaced ripped sheeting, and repainted the floats in bright, vibrant hues. It was their therapy, a chance to get away from gutting their destroyed houses and work on making something better. They managed to repair a dozen for the Nereids Parade, held every year a week and a half before Mardi Gras.

As the floats began to roll down the ten-mile parade route, Cyndi stood proudly in her glitter-gelled sweatshirt. No ornate costumes this year. She braced herself for the onslaught of parade goers, who normally rushed the float clamoring for beads, doubloons, and stuffed toys. Instead, Cyndi was puzzled to see people standing from their lawn chairs and cheering as the floats passed. "Thank you!" shouted a woman, approaching and reaching up to touch the Krewe members' hands. "Thank y'all for having Mardi Gras."

More people surged forward. "Y'all are the best! Thank you so much." Tears poured down people's faces. Cyndi and her friends threw their beads and trinkets and cried, too.

Four days later, I was on a plane south to report on how Mississippi was managing Mardi Gras and its ongoing recovery. I was still stunned by the reaction to our documentary, which had just been released to coincide with the six-month anniversary of the hurricane. My husband, Rick, had wanted to throw a viewing party the night it aired. I wanted to hide under a bed. I feared the documentary simply couldn't do justice to the people and what they had been through.

Afterward, family, friends, and colleagues called to assure me it had. But I never expected a response from viewers. The CNN public information staffer forwarding the e-mails said that only once before, for the 2004 documentary *Warsaw Rising*, had she seen this kind of outpouring. I read every single e-mail. But one paragraph stuck with me, since it lay to rest my fears that we hadn't conveyed to America what the Mississippi Gulf Coast suffered: "In one hour, Kathleen and her team managed to sum up our lives for the last six months. I can't think of one aspect that she did not hit on. She managed to capture every emotion, frustration, challenge, and triumph we have experienced. When telling everyone to tune in, I just simply said, 'Turn it on CNN at 7:00 and in one hour you will experience what I have been telling you about for the last six months.' Kathleen managed to express everything we were all feeling to the rest of the world. She absolutely 'gets it.' "

Also coming in were requests to speak at fund-raisers for Bay St. Louis being held from New York to Kansas City. At city hall in

Bay St. Louis, calls offering help poured in. A teenager all the way from Canada reached out, explaining she had started a collection for the city and wanted to know where to send the money. Bay Catholic Elementary School invited me to be the grand marshal of the city's Mardi Gras Children's Parade. My alma mater, the University of Southern Mississippi, wanted me to be the first inductee into its journalism alumni hall of fame. As a reporter who preferred to keep the focus on the people I was interviewing and not me, I found it all rather overwhelming.

Once in Bay St. Louis, the crew and I got right to work on our Mardi Gras rubble story. One of the eeriest and most distinctive features of the post-Katrina ruins was that they were laced with purple, green, and gold beads, as though Mother Nature had staged a macabre party. My skeptical cameraman, Skip Nocciolo, worried we were on a wild goose chase until I explained that people on the Mississippi Gulf Coast had a habit of saving their beads year after year. The hurricane had scattered the mementos across the landscape.

We went to a massive debris field around the corner from my old house and didn't even have to search. Beads dangled from trees and lay strewn on slabs and wrapped around bricks in the wreckage. One set had jester faces, their upside-down smiles mocking the rubble around them. I found a bejeweled box with even more beads inside. It sat open on the remains of a roof, as if carefully placed there. Nearby lay a Christmas wall plaque with a grinning Santa face and "Ho, Ho, Ho" painted down the middle. The symbols of joy and celebration mired in the twisted remains of people's homes seemed almost hideous.

While the crew shot, I wandered the debris field, carefully avoiding the nails, broken glass, and splintered metal. I still couldn't get used to walking on people's roofs. My neighbors' roofs. Maybe our old roof. I had no way to tell now, just as with all the possessions. It was impossible to know who they belonged to or how far they had been swept in the storm surge. Garden tools. A foam kneeling pad. A yellow toy bulldozer half-buried in mud. A broken baby crib.

We loaded up and drove half a block to the home of my high-school classmate Diane Edwards Bourgeois. Though I had run into

~Diane Edwards Bourgeois, the author's high-school classmate
Photo by Kathleen Koch

her at the foot of the destroyed Bay Bridge the week of the storm, she'd never shown me what was left of her house. As we got out, it was evident the storm surge had swept through the first floor of the two-story home, blowing out many of the walls and windows and cracking the brick chimney top to bottom.

Diane welcomed us inside and apologized for the mess. Furniture was flipped over. Piles of ruined belongings intertwined with leaves, branches, and pine needles covered the floor. Much of it wasn't even hers. "In fact, that's not my chair, the tan one over there," she said, pointing to a La-Z-Boy in the middle of her family room. "There's no telling where our things are."

Beneath the muck that coated everything, Diane said, were her once-beautiful brick floors. "I would wax, and no one could come in the house for two days with shoes on, until it was completely dry. I was a fanatic about my floors. You could see yourself in them."

As at Tommy Kidd's house, Diane's second floor suffered little damage, so she and her family had been able to salvage the furniture and possessions upstairs. Unfortunately, they'd stacked their family photos, videos, and yearbooks in the stairwell in case wind ripped off the roof, so they'd lost them all except for a box that floated out and was discovered by a neighbor. One of our high-school yearbooks lay open, waterlogged and ruined, on the steps. Visible through the dried mud was the smiling face of one of my favorite teachers, James Blanchette, who taught biology. "You don't think there's any way to clean that up?" I asked, trying to brush the book off. It didn't seem right to just leave it there.

"No, no." Diane shrugged. "I lost so much that I haven't had time since Katrina to realize what all I've actually lost. You know, it will be a moment when I reach for something or want something and I say, 'Oh, I don't have that anymore.' Not even my address book. But you know, our family is way more fortunate than most. We're blessed. We are," she said. "There were people who had nothing to come back to. We just thank God we have our lives, truthfully."

Diane said the home would have to be bulldozed and that she and her husband, Gene, planned to build on land they owned north of I-10 in Kiln, Mississippi. "I couldn't handle this happening again. Bay St. Louis will rebuild. We know this will once again be a beautiful place. But I don't see that far. All I see is the devastation and the pain and the suffering of looking at it and remembering and coming back to it. Oh, Kathie, it's just been a nightmare."

"Diane, I'm sorry. It's just so frustrating. You, all these people I went to school with, losing everything."

"I know, but I'm numb now. I don't have tears anymore. You get to a point when you're all teared out. You become numb because you can't deal with the feeling over and over. Even though you feel it, you suppress it. It's a fact of life. It's a mechanism that keeps me going."

Such raw emotion was rare in Bay St. Louis, where it seemed a citywide pact to remain upbeat was in force. Angelyn Treutel even had a plaque she kept on her desk at the office: "No Sniveling." But as they maintained a stiff upper lip in front of one another, people also needed a safe outlet. Increasingly, they vented to me.

We left Diane and drove east to Gulfport. On this trip, we were covering other towns, a change I welcomed, since I knew compelling stories could be found up and down the Mississippi Gulf Coast. On the way, I reflected on the trauma Diane and so many of my friends had suffered. I hoped perhaps time would blunt its intensity.

We went first to the gas station on Thirtieth Avenue down by the water, where we'd done live reports in the days after the hurricane. It looked like time had stood still, except that now the food on the shelves I'd wanted to give to residents was covered with black mold and swarms of hungry flies. A man inside surveying the damage introduced himself as Norman Barrentine, manager of a chain of Fast Trac convenience stores in Mississippi. When I expressed astonishment at the building's condition, he explained the company was having trouble finding workers to make the repairs. "You know, all of your construction people are just swamped—plumbing people, air-conditioning people, electricians. Everybody has just got more work than they can do."

In the meantime, the ten former employees were out of work, though the plan was to reopen by the end of the year. "It takes time. It doesn't happen overnight. Storm'll take you out overnight, but it'll take you a little while to come back," explained the manager with a patient smile. "We'll rebuild it. It'll be a better store, nicer store, more modern store."

The next morning, our focus was volunteers. As in Bay St. Louis, most home repairs were being made by people who had poured in from around the country to help. We met up with the Grassroots Volunteer Network at the Biloxi home of seventy-three-year-old Baptist minister Arcell Magee. Nine feet of water had surged through the modest house during the hurricane, ruining everything. Magee had no insurance. "I didn't know where to go. I didn't know where to get help. In rides this little lady to check on me. And she asks me what I was doing, did I want help, and I told her yes."

Samantha Brann, a brunette whirlwind, was unloading supplies for the volunteers getting ready to hang sheetrock in the reverend's home. The twenty-eight-year-old former high-school teacher had been at the University of Southern California getting a political science degree when Hurricane Katrina hit. The New Hampshire native quit school and came to Mississippi to help in the recovery. After a few months, when other volunteers were heading home, Samantha couldn't bear to leave. So with one chain saw, a handful of tools, and twenty-five dollars, she and a determined group of diehards formed the Grassroots Volunteer Network. They worked out of a tent city at an old VFW facility in Biloxi and relied on donations and her parents' generosity to operate. "I call home and say, 'We have no groceries this week,'" said Samantha with a laugh. "And they send us money to buy groceries." Her parents were understandably concerned at first about the responsibility she'd taken on. "They wanted to know, 'How are you going to do that?' And I had no idea. They just kind of went along with that. They are just incredibly supportive."

Grassroots' volunteers for Mardi Gras week were an Arizona couple, three students from North Carolina, three retired couples who'd driven all the way from Canada, and a group of friends from California, Massachusetts, and New Hampshire. I wondered if the allure of New Orleans' bawdy celebrations made it difficult to keep the work on track, but Samantha insisted the volunteers were committed. "If they're here for a week, they want to help for a week. They do not want to take a day off, period."

Volunteer Ray Hebert said they were not tempted to join the Louisiana revelry. "I'll tell you, frankly, we were turned off at that. All the drinking and what's going on in the street, when these people should be out here helping."

~GRASSROOTS VOLUNTEER NETWORK FOUNDER SAMANTHA BRANN OUTSIDE THE BILOXI HOME OF THE REVEREND ARCELL MAGEE
Photo by Skip Nocciolo/CNN

The Canadian women took us a few streets north to see the project they were working on. They cautioned that we may want to wear masks. The humble rancher hadn't been touched since the hurricane, and fuzzy gray mold hung down eight inches from the ceiling tiles.

"There's no rodents in here. Lots of cockroaches, but no rodents," said Wilma Hebert as we stepped gingerly through the disheveled family room.

"That's a good thing," I said.

An eighty-three-year-old woman had drowned in the home, and relatives who'd evacuated to Alabama couldn't bear to come and remove her belongings. "We found wrapped Christmas gifts that I guess her grandbabies will never get," explained Anita Gagne. "We pulled out, I don't know, fifty, sixty pieces of ceramics with her name on the bottom." Though the house stunk and had unsafe amounts of mold creeping everywhere, the women saw their dirty job as an honor. "I think we really felt like we wanted to treat her with respect."

"Yes. And then you take her things and you drag it to the street. And it's for everybody to see, to be thrown away," added her friend, clearly disappointed.

"It broke my heart. We were both crying," Gagne said.

More tears fell later in the day when the group finished at the reverend's house. "If it wasn't for Grassroots, I don't know what I would have done," he said, hugging and shaking hands as the volunteers loaded their tools. "When they start something, they bring a group and get it done. I mean, they don't play around."

Next, we drove east toward "the Point," a working-class neighborhood on the eastern tip of Biloxi surrounded by casinos. Though the massive barges that held the gaming floors had all been destroyed, the casinos' land operations and hotel rooms were salvageable. Their reconstruction was providing much-needed jobs. A few establishments had already reopened. But the homes in between remained largely in a state of complete disrepair.

We turned onto Esters Boulevard, a narrow street hugging the railroad tracks, and stopped in front of the only house where we saw signs of life. A few children played in the street next to a small portable basketball goal. Upon seeing us, they ran to a trailer positioned between two houses and got their mother, Sheila McIntyre, a large, energetic woman with an even larger voice. She showed us the repairs volunteers were busy at that very moment making on her home. Sheila had flood insurance and so could afford the necessary building supplies.

But her next-door neighbor, Lucy Williams, was another story. The petite elementary-school janitor had no insurance on her small two-bedroom home. Her husband, a seasonal seafood worker, had been ill. And though they owned their home and had paid off their furniture and car, they couldn't afford both his medication and insurance payments. "Miss Lucy," as everyone called her, didn't qualify for government aid.

Because Biloxi is a peninsula, water from Katrina rushed into the Point from virtually every direction. It flowed over the rooftops and threatened to sweep Miss Lucy away until her six-foot-three husband plucked her out of the surge and saved her life. That was just one of the reasons she met with friends on her front porch every morning to thank God for all his blessings.

Inside what was left of the fragile structure, she didn't appear to have much to be thankful for. The wind and water had stripped the interior bare, blasting out the windows, ripping up part of the floor, and leaving behind just a shell. Of all her furniture, Miss Lucy found only one dining-room chair. She told me she planned to keep it to remind her of what she once had. As for the house, the city told Miss Lucy it was no longer safe and should be torn down. "But I can't tear it down because this is all I have. If it be torn down, you know, who gonna help me to rebuild it?" She looked wistfully around the shattered structure. "I'm not gonna tear it down. I'm just going to leave it like this until someone come in and help me."

As we stood on the front porch, several casino limousines crossed the railroad tracks and headed north. They stood out in sharp contrast to the destruction around them.

"We see it a lot," said Miss Lucy.

"VIPs?"

"They'll be going to the boats," she said with a sigh. "It's very hurtful and painful because, you know, they're more concerned about the gambling and stuff. And it's just like they forgot all about us."

"The government doesn't care?"

"The government don't care. The mayor don't care. The president don't care. Don't nobody care."

Still, as we loaded our gear, Miss Lucy was buoyed by the fact that we cared. "Praise Jesus! He sent you to me, and now everything's gonna be fine. I been prayin'. I been prayin' that somebody will come in and want to help me."

My sound technician, Ron Helm, was uncomfortable with her effusive response to our interview. "Someone has to tell her this was just a news story. It probably won't change anything for her. I mean, some viewers might send her a gift certificate or something. But—"

"Ron, I understand," I interrupted, pulling him aside. "But all she has left now is her faith. We can't take that from her."

As we pulled away, I noticed an e-mail on my BlackBerry. House Speaker Dennis Hastert wanted a copy of our Bay St. Louis documentary to play aboard the plane later that week as he and a thirty-

~THE AUTHOR WITH LUCY WILLIAMS AND OTHERS IN WILLIAMS'S HURRICANE-
DAMAGED BILOXI HOME. FROM LEFT TO RIGHT ARE JOSHUA MCINTYRE,
THE AUTHOR, BOBBY WILLIAMS, LUCY WILLIAMS, AND SHEILA MCINTYRE.
Courtesy of Lucy Williams

five-member congressional delegation flew south for their first look at the devastated Gulf Coast. "Way to go!" quipped one colleague on the e-mail chain. "You're an in-flight movie!"

People *were* listening. I was glad we hadn't burst Miss Lucy's bubble. Who knew what might happen?

At the same time, the thought of a planeload of lawmakers and staffers focused on our documentary was a bit unnerving. In the first segment on the storm, my editor and producer had used virtually every second of video in which I'd become emotional during our post-Katrina trek through Bay St. Louis. When we had discovered my childhood home in ruins and I thought we were done taping, I turned my back to the camera and stood sobbing in the rain, releasing the pain and despair I'd been holding in for days. But the cameraman kept rolling, and the documentary included that vulnerable moment. At first, I felt violated. Then I worried whether or not anyone would still take me seriously when I reported from the Pentagon briefing room or the front lawn of the White House.

A wise colleague, correspondent Zain Verjee, put things in perspective. "It wasn't your call. You're too close to the story. That's why you have a producer and editor," she told me bluntly. "But the main point is, that's how you touched people. Most Americans watching the coverage of Hurricane Katrina didn't know anyone affected. But you come into their living rooms every day on CNN. Suddenly, they knew someone impacted by the storm. They saw your pain, and you made them care."

I hoped she was right.

The following day, we made our way back west and stopped in Long Beach at an enormous beachfront condominium complex where my producer, Peter Tedeschi, had shot weeks after Katrina. The buildings still stood wrecked and empty, the entire complex roped off to discourage looters and sightseers. In fact, back along the railroad tracks we'd crossed the day after Katrina, the city had for a time spread razor wire to keep out everyone but homeowners. Though practical, the measure only increased residents' sense of living in a war zone.

While the crew shot, I walked up a side street to look for people to interview. A man wearing a baseball cap and the white-bearded look of a sea captain came out of a FEMA trailer. Dan Sperbeck's home was erased by the hurricane, but neighbors had let him put his FEMA trailer in their yard. For the time being, it was home for him, his wife, and their nineteen-year-old daughter.

I joked that after my short Thanksgiving stay in one, I could appreciate the cramped quarters.

"We like to refer to it as our 'FEMA castle,' " he replied with a smile. "And of course, there's no room. No place for storage. We try and stay outside as much as we can. But we're just grateful to be back in our neighborhood."

As we walked toward our camera, Dan told me how residents had been given daily passes to come in and search through what was left of their homes after Katrina. He found a couple of knives and a few pieces of china. "But the stench. You know, it was the stench and the bodies and the rotten food. That's what made it so difficult down here."

What also made it difficult was fighting the insurance companies. His family had flood insurance. But when it came to the wind policy they'd paid premiums on for years, "you can guess how that scenario pans out," Dan laughed.

"Most people are getting nothing," I replied.

"We're getting nothing. But we're not done with it yet. We're not going to roll over and play dead. This is just going to be a long, drawn-out affair."

Though Dan insisted he didn't want to go on camera, he followed me all the way to our setup at the beach. One of his statements embodied the optimism that still prevailed on the Mississippi Gulf Coast: "You know, you can't kill our spirit. We're still here to stay. And we look out at what it's going to be in another couple years." He squinted, as if trying to block out the rubble with a different vision. "We don't see the devastation you see. We're lookin' two years from now. It'll be the most gorgeous place you've ever seen."

We returned to Bay St. Louis to wrap up our Mardi Gras rubble story. We shot the carnival memorabilia that still covered the walls of Tommy and Linda Kidd's intact second floor. Linda was a long-time member of Nereids, and she and Tommy had collected and framed souvenirs from every Mardi Gras since the Krewe's founding in 1966. One closet overflowed with ornate sequined and feathered costumes.

"You're probably one of the few people in the Krewe who has this," I said.

"I could well be," replied Linda. "I believe what I'll do is probably donate these."

The Mardi Gras room in Cyndi Meyer's house had not fared so well. Ten feet of water had rushed through, turning everything upside down. "It was like a snow globe inside my home, like someone just picked up my house and shook it," she said as she gave us a tour of what was left. The once-brilliant plum-colored feathers on her husband's Mardi Gras hat were matted and shriveled. Cyndi planned to clean it and apply new ones, saving the ruined plumage as a souvenir of what they'd survived. Mud still coated the sequined trim on the bottom of her husband's purple cape. "The mud's the only thing holding them on," she said. "When I tried to wash it, the sequins started coming off in my hands." Cyndi said their insurance adjuster had been taken aback by the tattered costume draped on a stand in the middle of their gutted den. "He couldn't quite figure out what it was or why in the world we were saving it."

Also ruined were boxes of toys they had planned to throw from the floats, including seven-inch "Perfect Man" dolls that when squeezed uttered priceless phrases like, "That diamond is just not big enough for you" and "No, you take the remote. Anything you want to watch is okay with me." "There were Perfect Men floating up and down Waveland Avenue," she recalled with a laugh. "I was hoping no one would find out they were mine!"

As we were packing up, Cyndi pulled me aside and thanked me for the documentary. She had sat and watched it with one of her Nereids friends. "We cried the whole hour. But when it was over, it was as though a weight had been lifted from our shoulders. It was cathartic." She gestured to the bleak structure that used to be her beautiful home. "When you're living in this day after day, you can't step back. You can't fully process what you've been through. Your documentary helped us do that."

I was moved. I had hoped to share Mississippi's untold Katrina story with the nation, but I'd never anticipated the documentary would play a role in the emotional healing of the people of the Gulf Coast themselves.

That point was driven home the next day as I climbed into a convertible for the city's modest children's parade. I was proud that my high school's marching band was participating, performing with new instruments donated by VH1. Also marching were volunteers from the churches and civic groups that had been feeding, sheltering, and providing medical care to local residents for the past six months. Then came children wearing homemade costumes, some riding in mini Mardi Gras floats. One wagon was decorated like a boxy boat, the S.S. *Katrina*. A tow-headed boy in a Batman costume rolled by in a cardboard Batmobile emblazoned with the plea, "Save My City."

Smiles abounded despite the brisk weather. As my car proceeded down the half-mile parade route, I made clumsy attempts to untangle and toss the mass of beads piled next to me. The slow pace enabled residents to walk right up to the car. But they weren't looking for beads.

"Thank you," said one woman, grabbing my hand. "Thank you so much for the report on the Bay."

"Thanks, Kathleen!" called another, waving from the chair on her front lawn. "God bless!"

I threw beads and fought back tears. "We're sticking with you!

~BEADS THROWN BY THE AUTHOR HURTLE DIRECTLY AT THE CAMERA DURING THE BAY ST. LOUIS MARDI GRAS CHILDREN'S PARADE
Photo by Skip Nocciolo/CNN

~Homemade float with a pointed message in the Mardi Gras
Children's Parade
Photo by Skip Nocciolo/CNN

We'll do more," I promised. By the end of the parade, I was emotionally drained. I told people I was just doing my job, but I knew that to
them it was much more.

As grateful as everyone was for the Mardi Gras break from the
ongoing cleanup, harsh reality quickly intruded. Four days later, Lydia, Brooke, and Marie Schultz met with relatives in Utah to spread
Van's ashes in Zion National Park. Just before Katrina struck, he had
visited his sister in Hurricane, Utah, and hiked with her in the park.
"It was more beautiful than I remembered," Van had told his daughter Marie upon his return. "That's where I want my ashes scattered."
That was the first time they'd ever discussed his last wishes.

Nikki Cleveland, her features now even more delicate in contrast to her expanding belly, was adjusting to the fact that her child
would never know her parents. "They loved children. Especially my
father."

"The child would have had a lot of cavities," added Patrick. "Nikki's dad had a sweet tooth. I'm sure he would have passed that on."

"He would have spoiled the baby?" I asked gently.

"He would have spoiled the baby," replied Nikki softly. "But he
would have taught it a lot, too."

I left them sitting silently at the mausoleum on Longfellow Road where the remains of Ralph and JoAnna Dagnall were interred in an unmarked crypt.

While driving out of town, I heard a familiar, reassuring sound—the CSX train whistle echoing in the distance. The railroad bridge was already complete, and traffic had resumed that week.

Pat Kergosien, whose house on Carroll Avenue was less than a third of a mile from the tracks, told me how he used to curse the long, loud warnings from the engines when they broke his sleep in the wee hours of the morning. But the day the inaugural train chugged through town in mid-February, he stood with his seven-year-old son and watched his old nemesis gliding onto the bridge, its freight cars heavy with cargo stretching across the bay for the first time in six months. Pat smiled. The wretched whistle was sweet music.

~15~

Hurricane Season

THE GRAY WINTER SKIES over Bay St. Louis brightened to blue as young leaves sprouted on the crape myrtles and insistent green shoots pushed through the mud and sand deposited by Katrina. But as welcome as the spring signs of rebirth were, they created a gnawing sense of unease. Hurricane season was just around the corner.

Firefighter Monte Strong and his wife, Danielle, were among the many debating whether or not to risk it all again. Their FEMA trailer now sat on Pine Drive next to their one-story brick home, which they were trying to repair on their own.

Even before they began laying the laundry-room tile and nailing down the hardwood floor, they got an offer to buy the house.

"I was born a Bay rat, and I'm gonna die a Bay rat," insisted Monte.

Danielle was more of a gypsy. And she was worried. "It's just scary. It's scary all around. You hate to get back to this point and then, you know, find out that you should have sold your house or you should have left."

Monte could see that the bravado Danielle once exhibited in the face of hurricanes had vanished. And he was concerned because much of the woods and most homes to the north and east between their neighborhood and the St. Louis Bay were now gone. "You know, so there's nothing to stop the water now," he said. "I mean, I'm just thinking we get that type of tidal surge again . . ."

Still, Danielle had a gut feeling that selling wasn't the right thing to do. They had always wanted to raise their children in Bay St. Louis, where they grew up. So they stayed.

The city was getting ready for hurricane season, too. Mike Cuevas, a short spitfire of a woman with a shock of gray hair, had been sending out regular notices for months listing city needs and updating donors around the country on how Bay St. Louis was faring. They sometimes included touchingly personal insights into how citizens and the fifty-six-year-old widow herself were holding up. "People are putting aside the emotional stress, relying on their bodies to get them through the day," read one. "I wake up still dazed and confused, have difficulty focusing on the tasks at hand, have a mind and body exhausted from trying to do way too much."

Mike's latest plea was for a long list of items the city had learned by experience it would need if another hurricane threatened—gas cards, tire plug kits, twelve-volt air compressors, jumper cables, tow straps, sleeping bags, air mattresses, cots, pillows, sheets, and pillowcases, as well as personal-care kits and evacuation kits packed with everything from toiletries, insect repellent, and sunscreen to flashlights and laundry detergent. "It may be the residual effects of the full moon, but my mood is somber, not fatal," ended the missive. "I hope tomorrow some of my normal optimism will return."

It was in fact an ebullient Mike I met in mid-March when we began taping again in Bay St. Louis. Not only had our documentary's success prompted CNN to ask for a sequel, it continued to draw nationwide attention to the town. When I saw her, Mike was directing dozens of spring breakers fresh off the bus from Texas A&M on the niceties of gutting buildings. They swarmed into the city annex, untouched since Katrina, and began hauling out rusted file cabinets and ruined office furniture with an enthusiasm rarely seen in Bay St. Louis these days.

"Every single day, the American public just amazes and overwhelms me," she said as she watched their progress. "I could just sit down and cry. I have goose bumps."

The one area where donations were nonexistent was for city salaries. The town had halted all but essential expenditures in order to avoid laying off any of its 105 employees. "God will provide. He hasn't let us come this far to shut us down. I know Eddie's worrying about it and our comptroller's worrying about it. And that's enough worrying right now." And with a quick handshake, Mike was off to check on another group of volunteers.

Indeed, Americans touched by Bay St. Louis's story were providing. High-school students from Monterey, California, and Pueblo West, Colorado, collected hundreds of prom dresses for girls at Bay High and Our Lady Academy. Firefighters and other New York City volunteers built a fully stocked laundry room for a Waveland woman and repaired the home of a Bay St. Louis woman dying of cancer. Pfizer Inc. donated $100,000 to replace critical medical equipment at Hancock Medical Center. Students from Hoover High School in North Canton, Ohio, raised more than $11,000 to replace books and computers at Bay High. NFL quarterbacks Brett Favre and Steve McNair donated $150,000 to rebuild hurricane-impacted football programs in Hancock County and across South Mississippi. Lime Kiln, the middle school my daughter attended in Fulton, Maryland, raised $800 for football and PE equipment at Bay Middle School. Volunteers with the nonprofit group Persevere were replacing street signs in Bay St. Louis, Waveland, and Pass Christian. And those were just the projects for the month of March.

The "Signs of Hope" effort was the brainchild of a volunteer who noticed that people were wasting precious time and gas trying to find their way in neighborhoods largely devoid of landmarks and street signs. And it wasn't just out-of-towners. Lifelong residents were distressed to find themselves lost in their own hometowns.

Arizona native Suzanne Stahl was determined to rebuild both spirits and structures on the Mississippi Gulf Coast. She'd come down on her own two days after the hurricane, her car packed with supplies. Month after month, she just kept coming back. "The graciousness, the gratitude, the spirit and determination of these people. How can't you?" She worked restoring historic Beauvoir, the last home of Confederate president Jefferson Davis, and repairing a Biloxi cemetery where tombstones had been toppled and bodies disinterred by Katrina's surge. Suzanne regularly passed through Louisiana and saw a vivid difference in hurricane survivors' attitudes. "You know you're in Mississippi when people start telling you what they have instead of what they've lost."

Lydia Schultz was ready to finally confront her loss. Her e-mails to me in March and April as she prepared for her first post-Katrina visit to Bay St. Louis were heart-wrenching.

Subject: Sadness

I have cried all day today and dunno why. I do know why! Kathie, I have no home. I miss knowing that I had that house and that room in the house Van and I still owned. I am at the mercy of others in this house and it is not mine. It would be different if this were my choice, but it was made for me. Sorry. It just seems a tough time.

Subject: going to the Bay

My lot has been cleared. Last week. Van's vehicle hauled off last night. Progress. I *hate* to think about seeing where my precious house was. But I guess I shall have to feel that.

Lots of changes. Lots of things that have to be accepted. I still see the miracles in my life, tho. I have way too much to be grateful for.

Subject: going to the Bay

I am not looking forward to this trip. *Not at all*. It may be better than I am thinking but it is distressing just thinking about a vacant lot. *Seeing* it can't be easier. . . .

Other former residents were making difficult choices as well. OB/GYN Keith Goodfellow had moved his family to Columbus, Mississippi, more than 250 miles north of the Gulf Coast, and joined a practice with seven other doctors. For the first time in more than seven months, Darla and the four children were living in a house. Samantha, the eldest, had been accepted into the University of Mississippi and would start there in the fall.

On May 1, my crew and I arrived back in Bay St. Louis on the heels of the first heavy thunderstorms since Katrina. I stopped by North Bay Elementary School to see the new playground just installed by a group of New Jersey firefighters. I sat with Principal Frances Weiler and watched the children sliding, swinging, and scrambling over the shiny new structure. They could barely contain their glee at finally having a playground after eight long months. "It doesn't get any better than this!" exclaimed one little boy breathlessly.

But the principal told me it had been a different story the previous day, after torrential downpours and howling winds had rattled the town all night. Some children didn't come to school the next morning. Others could barely do their classwork. "I think we're going to have some really good weather forecasters out of this group because they are aware," said Weiler with a wan smile. "They are watchful. But they're also apprehensive."

"What do you tell them?" I asked, wondering how to reassure a school full of frightened children without lying to them.

" 'Your parents are going to do everything they can to keep you safe, just like we will do everything to keep you safe. And that means leaving if there is danger.' That's what children need is that reassurance." Weiler added that principals had also begun to see more frustration and depression among teachers, so the school system had hired a psychologist and a behavioral specialist to help both students and their instructors.

Four-year-old Dawson Strong had been shaken by the thunderstorms. Danielle told me that as the dark clouds rolled in and winds began to whip at the end of baseball practice that night, her blue-eyed son had looked up at her and asked, "Is this another Hurricane Katrina? She's gonna tear our house down again."

"How does that make you feel as a parent?" I asked.

"It's tough that he thinks that this quick we could lose our house again," she said, a hint of sadness in her voice. "And we can't tell him that it won't happen again because you just don't know." Danielle

was chopping a salad in the cramped FEMA trailer while Monte grilled porkchops on the Weber in the driveway.

The firefighter shared some surprising news with me. The next time a Category 3 or higher hurricane threatened Bay St. Louis, the first responders would evacuate. "We told our department heads, you know, we'll go where they want us to go. I mean, we'll pull our Hazmat trailer and load it down with generators and chain saws and bottled water and stuff like that. And you know, then come back once the eye's passed, when it's safe to come back in."

Monte added that they hoped residents would follow suit. "We're hoping that if we get a mandatory evacuation next time, that they'll listen to it and that they will evacuate to where the city is a ghost town and we don't have anybody to have to try to rescue or save or something, you know?"

Most days, the family of five tried not to ponder the what-ifs and just deal with the immediate issues at hand. Like stretching Monte's salary, since Danielle was still out of work. And surviving the near-complete loss of privacy that was a fact of trailer life.

But instead of creating friction, the ordeal had brought Danielle and Monte closer together. "It's made us a lot stronger. We both have a very strong faith," Danielle explained. "We rely on God a lot for what we've been through. And we never really verbalized it to each other prior to the storm. But afterwards, it brought a lot of that up. And it's a connection. It's a whole lot better than what it was before. So it's almost been a blessing, you know, for us to take it as a positive instead of sitting back and saying, 'Poor me.' I don't like the kids to do that, or us. I'd rather we hold our heads up and we just make it through."

Mallorie, Caleb, and Dawson were making it through, though they said little was left for kids to do. Fourteen-year-old Mallorie and her houseless classmates tried to stay out of their trailers as much as possible. "We go to one of our friends who has her house. And we go there on the weekends so we can sleep on a bed."

Though Bay St. Louis was the only home they'd ever known, the kids said when they grew up they wanted to live away from the Gulf Coast and the threat of hurricanes. "I just don't want it to happen again," said Caleb.

When the crew and I arrived to interview Danielle and Monte, I discovered we had something in common. Not only did they know the Schultz family, but Danielle was Brooke's best friend. After the shoot was over, Monte, Danielle, and I sat at the trailer's tiny kitchen table and talked. Our conversation quickly turned to Van Schultz's death. I was stunned to learn that, somehow, the Schultzes had also reached them after the storm and asked them to search for Van. They, too, were plagued by guilt for not getting to the house and locating his body before Brooke did.

"I was her best friend. I should have found a way to get there and look," said Danielle. "But we'd lost our house. And I was trying to take care of the kids, find somewhere for us to stay."

"No, I was with search-and-rescue. I should have found him," Monte said. "We knocked on the doors, yelled out, but if we didn't get any response we moved on. We didn't spend time in every house—diggin', you know, trying to find people."

"I didn't even know where the house was," I said. "We tried to get there, but the roads were blocked. And we just ran out of time."

We looked at one another, recognizing the pain we all felt.

"You know, I think we all did the best we could," concluded Danielle gently.

I hoped the discovery might ease my nightmares, which had taken a disturbing turn since the documentary. In one, I was standing atop a tall dam overlooking a river valley, and a flash flood was expected. Huge machinery was driving enormous pilings in to reinforce the structure. Still, cyclists, joggers, and mothers with children moved nonchalantly down a path on the riverbank. Suddenly, a massive wall of water rushed down the valley. People ran screaming, trying to escape. As some tried to climb the dam, I looked for ropes to throw to them. I watched one man try to hang on, but he was swept away. So I climbed over the railing, locked my arms around it, and dangled my legs for people to grab hold of so I could pull them up. People started clinging to my legs and . . . Then I woke up, not knowing whether I had saved anyone or not.

In another, I was in a building with tall plate-glass windows as floodwaters swelled outside. For a while, the windows held, and I and the other people inside watched transfixed as the murky water rose higher and higher. Suddenly, the glass exploded and water poured in, filling the building almost to the ceiling. It was like the final scene of *Titanic*, people thrashing and screaming and pushing others down to stay afloat. I knew the only way to survive was to get away from them. So I held my breath and dove deep, down to the ground floor, staying under as long as I could. I would pop up for a second and dive again, until finally things grew quiet. I surfaced and clung to the rafters, silently regarding the carnage around me.

I knew the dreams had to do with the e-mails and calls for help, which had only increased since the documentary. I answered and helped those I could, but I couldn't respond to everyone. One angry New Orleanian who'd moved to the Goodfellows' Diamondhead neighborhood and lost her home berated me for not calling her back, though I had answered her first e-mail. She listed stories done by National Public Radio and the local *Sun Herald* newspaper. "I am really disappointed in CNN's response or assistance in this. Could you guys throw us some time? This is real news and really occurring." She apparently missed the dozens of reports I had done during and after the storm, as well as the documentary. My husband told me to shake it off, but it magnified the feeling that whatever I did wasn't enough.

It didn't help that the problems with some insurance companies weren't going away. I met with the residents of a devastated neighborhood, Jordan River Estates, where all but two of the 168 homes had been entirely erased. Meteorological and engineering reports revealed that tornadoes and straight-line winds had lashed the area. Neighbors had banded together and were mapping street by street who was getting paid for wind damage and who wasn't. Some homeowners' wind policies paid in full. Other companies paid half. But some of the largest insurers—like State Farm, which covered more than 30 percent of homes in Mississippi—were paying nothing. Looking at the map, it made no sense. How could one insurer determine wind had destroyed a home and another declare the house right next door had been flattened by water alone? The process seemed illogical and completely arbitrary.

One couple in their sixties, Bob and Kay Wingate, showed me a photo of their Acadian-style home with wraparound porches. Bob was a retired builder, so they had constructed their home higher and stronger than anything in the neighborhood, just to be safe. They had returned to find nothing but eleven-foot pilings reaching toward the sky. State Farm denied their wind-damage claim, insisting water had destroyed the house. But just across the bayou, homes at the very same elevation stood intact. "The same water came right here as came over there. And none of those are destroyed," said Bob, pointing across the water. "To me, that proves that a tornado did touch down."

As I talked with a gathering of the homeowners, they insisted they didn't want help from the government. "We're not asking for a handout," said one woman.

"That's right. We want what we paid for," added a middle-aged man wearing a tan baseball cap.

The group was adamant that it was wrong to saddle the federal government and American taxpayers with a burden that was rightfully the insurance companies'. "I suspect most everybody will be filing suit," said a well-dressed, balding gentleman. "I can assure you I will."

Since the number of lawsuits was mounting, the state of Mississippi was encouraging residents to try mediation. Under the process, a neutral party like a retired judge trained in helping people reach accord would sit down with the homeowner and the insurance company and see if they could reach a settlement.

Nikki and Patrick Cleveland decided it was worth a shot and drove north to Hattiesburg, where mediations were being held in donated space at my alma mater, the University of Southern Mississippi. They arrived on campus armed with documentation to prove that wind had forced their home's collapse before the storm surge arrived. "We have this chart that shows the eye of the storm. We averaged 143 miles per hour," said Patrick, his finger tracing Katrina's path as it came ashore at the state border and then veered into Hancock County.

I went upstairs in McLemore Hall with the Clevelands and waited while the mediation began. Outside, teams of workers swarmed over a large building across the courtyard repairing a roof that had been damaged by Hurricane Katrina more than eight months earlier. I found it ironic that in the room next door the Clevelands' insurance company was arguing that Katrina's winds had no impact on their Gulf Coast home, while I could see with my own eyes the destruction those same winds had wrought seventy-eight miles inland.

After more than an hour, the couple emerged somber and dejected. "Well, we agreed it would be confidential, but let's just say we didn't reach a settlement," said Nikki through pursed lips.

"Was this a waste of time?" I asked.

"Yes," answered Patrick. "Completely."

My producers and I tried to get insurance companies to explain the denials, to come to the Clevelands' or the Wingates' or the Taylors' property and show us the proof that water alone destroyed the homes. We asked if they could provide documentation to support their conclusions. But the companies refused to discuss individual cases, citing privacy issues, and insisted they were investigating claims fairly and covering what was owed under their policies. They pointed out that 71 percent of expected claims in Mississippi had been settled, though they would not reveal for how many pennies on the dollar of the original policies.

Everyone knew court action would be a lengthy process. Still, nearly a thousand Mississippi residents joined two separate lawsuits that spring against State Farm and Nationwide for denying wind claims and blaming the majority of the damage on storm surge. And Congressman Gene Taylor introduced an amendment requiring a federal investigation into whether or not insurance companies wrongly attributed hurricane wind damage to water, thereby defrauding taxpayers by pushing damage payments onto the federal flood program.

As exasperated as homeowners were with the insurance process, an entire category of residents had slipped through the cracks when it came to the recovery: renters. Across the Mississippi Gulf Coast, Hurricane Katrina had damaged twenty-five hundred public housing units and left 80 percent of rental properties unlivable. Displaced while repairs were made, renters were scattered and desperate to get back home.

One of my former classmates, Arlene Dahl Johnson, ran the local senior citizens' center, which before Katrina had served seventy-five people a day. Now, it was down to twenty-five. Many of the elderly had lived in public housing across the street that was inundated during the storm. The one-story brick homes still hadn't been repaired. And the other two low-income housing projects in Bay St. Louis were so badly damaged they had to be demolished. "There's nothing but flat land there now, and we have so many people wanting to come back," said Arlene. "Not just the elderly, but the young, the poor, the single mothers. You know, that's the people we need back in our community to put our community back together. And if they don't have housing, they can't come home."

Arlene told me about ninety-three-year-old Anna May Strong, who had spent her entire life in Bay St. Louis but was now living in Jackson with her daughter and son-in-law. She kept calling and asking when the apartments would be ready. Each time, Arlene had to explain that no one was working on them, to which Miss Anna May would ask, "Well, why aren't they?"

No one had a good answer. Sixty-five of the one hundred public housing units that remained in Bay St. Louis were Housing and Urban Development properties. Arlene said she had been told HUD had no money for the project, so the city was trying to get grants to repair the properties. It was cold comfort for elderly residents who were running out of time. "I actually feel as though some of them want to come home to die," said Arlene. "These are the people who built our community. This is where their roots are, where their families are, their fond memories, right here. They expected to live their life out here in Bay St. Louis and die in Bay St. Louis. And now they're strewn out all over the United States."

I visited one former resident, Tania Reed, and her family in an Atlanta suburb, where they were living while the Bay St. Louis house they rented was repaired. Tania was not a city girl and ached to get back home. "I can't get on the right foot out here in Atlanta. It's so big I can't grasp onto nothin'." She had looked for an apartment on the Gulf Coast, but rental prices were up roughly 30 percent, and those on waiting lists numbered in the hundreds.

Her teenagers were having a hard time fitting in, too. Thirteen-year-old Jenna complained that kids at school thought she and her brother were from New Orleans and kept trying to pick fights. "They wanna fight you for stupid reasons, and that's not called for. I'm just ready to go back home."

Sixteen-year-old Junior had been a wide receiver for the Bay High Tigers. "I missed 'em a lot 'cause I wanted to be there and help 'em out with the season and stuff. I feel like I left my hometown—let them down."

Tania felt the same way. "I have to go back and help them because that's where I'm from. And I feel that I *need* to go back and help. Wouldn't you want somebody to come help you if you was in trouble?"

Some renters gave up. When I tried Shannon Evans's cell phone to see how her efforts to return were going, it had been disconnected. The Greenville, Mississippi, hotel had no forwarding information for her. I never found out what happened to the home health aide and her four daughters. As was so often the case with the poor after Katrina, they were scattered as surely as the fragments of homes the hurricane had strewn for miles in every direction.

Homecomings, though often painful, were possible. I knew Lydia Schultz's would be excruciating. I was glad she wouldn't see her home the way Hurricane Katrina left it. On the trip back three weeks after the storm, I had climbed over a mountain of broken beams, two-by-fours, and mangled appliances to reach the house on Breeden Place. Trees were snapped in half, and a bright yellow buoy lay in the yard not far from one of Van's trademark checkered shirts. Inside, the windows were shattered and the left side of the house had been ripped off, the floor covered with boards and smashed, overturned furniture. Lydia had run a wild bird shop, and she and Van were devoted nature lovers. Broken feeders and birdhouses were sprinkled through the wreckage.

Now, the house was just a concrete foundation. And though people realized they had to start over, at least the debris had an identity. It said something about who had lived there and what was important to them. The empty slabs were so cold and anonymous.

Fortunately, Lydia's visit seemed to have led her toward closure.

Subject: Bay St. Louis

The last two days I spent going around the community. While there is still so much devastation and so many obstacles for the people, there is so much *hope* and progress.

I did go to my house. I couldn't go at first. Saw the street in daylight and could look all the way to the water and decided, can't. So then we were going out at night and I told Sheila, 'Let's go now so I won't get the full effect of the destruction.' I think that was good 'cause then I just could concentrate on the slab and not the surrounding destruction *in addition*!!! It's all so overwhelming. . . . Change is truly the only constant in life and if this hasn't taught us to get that, nothing will or can.

Hugs from here to there!

Lydia

Brooke, too, had been back and seen the slab.

I hate how empty it looks too. One thing I did the last time I was home is went to my dad's and plucked up several of the plants that were in the yard. I brought them back to Georgia and planted them in the back. It is so weird all the sunflowers that are growing in Bay St. Louis. You know it was from the birdseed. I know that was the case in my dad's yard.

I will talk to you soon.

Love,

Brooke

Strange, the traces of lives Katrina left behind. A legacy of sunflowers.

Another sign of resilience appeared on the Bay High football field across town, where as cicadas buzzed young women and men in royal blue caps and gowns took their seats on long rows of folding chairs. Some 125 students of the original senior class of 130 were graduating. That was unimaginable back in November, when school reopened and just a third of the class returned.

"Because of this storm, we now know that we can handle anything that is thrown at us, including flying debris," joked valedictorian Casey Maria Dedeaux to her classmates.

"To see the devastation from day one, I didn't know this would be possible, to be honest with you," said Brian Adam, beaming proudly as his son Trevor crossed the stage and collected his diploma. "Trevor is an even harder worker and more compassionate since the storm."

In fact, the middle linebacker I had met gutting the doctor's office back in November now had plans to become a lawyer and help hurricane survivors on the Mississippi Gulf Coast. "It's something I've always wanted to do. The power to argue for the truth, for the facts, you know. The power to step in when others can't, standing up for common America, helping people."

Trevor and his classmates had acquired wisdom well beyond

their years. "My experience in this storm really made me realize how important the little things in life were, the little aspects of saying 'Hey' to your friends or saying 'I love you' to your family." Trevor looked up at the families in the bleachers, well aware that since Katrina some of the seats that should have been filled would always be empty. "Because at any given moment, you never know when your time is up. Only God knows. You really learn to appreciate the things in life that are given to you every day."

On that day, the graduates savored standing together one last time—the class that wouldn't quit. No hurricane could break their spirits or the bonds they'd forged over the last year. And as they spun in the center of the field, flinging their mortarboards skyward, the cheer that erupted and echoed through the darkening sky was both joyous and defiant.

~16~

One-year Anniversary

THE EIGHT-FOOT-TALL PLYWOOD DOORS on Our Lady of the Gulf Church swung open wide as the beaming bride and her groom exited into the August heat. The crowd followed them next door to the church's community center, transformed temporarily from a rustic volunteer barracks into a reception hall. The evening before, guests had circulated under a tent next to two trailers connected by a wooden deck at what used to be the Bay-Waveland Yacht Club. Not quite the nuptials Gene Taylor had envisioned when his second daughter, Emily, was born. But the congressman joked with friends, "This is going to be the finest wedding ever thrown by a homeless man!"

A mile and a half up the road, twenty-foot pilings now rose from Gene and Margaret's waterfront lot. The new city building requirement was fourteen feet above sea level, but the couple wanted to play it safe. The structure would be half the size of their original home, just 1,350 square feet. "I'm building a throwaway house," said the congressman, who was still sharing his brother's home twenty miles inland.

In fact, forecasts were that the 2006 hurricane season would be even worse than 2005. The dire predictions had frightened many in Bay St. Louis into putting off rebuilding. But Gene wasn't dissuaded. "It's a beautiful place. I love waking up and seeing the dolphins and the pelicans. And I put a pencil to it. Nine thousand eight hundred and eighty days in that house before the storm got it. So if I can get another nine thousand days out of this one, I'll be happy."

But as the anniversary of Katrina approached, I, too, couldn't help thinking, *What if it happens again?* The town was just scraping its way back from the brink. And so many people were living in trailers that were vulnerable to even light winds.

Again, my anxiety manifested itself in my dreams. I was back in Bay St. Louis, and a hurricane was roaring in. Tornadoes were dropping out of the storm clouds. I hit the dirt next to the remaining intact buildings and clung to some exposed pipes to keep from being blown away. After the first tornado passed, I stood and gazed up at the roiling sky with Mayor Eddie Favre. "I feel like I'm looking into the belly of the beast," I told him. Then the vortex opened and a light came from the center. It looked like a mouth, as if the storm were alive and hungry.

Lydia Schultz was going to be in Bay St. Louis for a one-year memorial service for Katrina victims. She hoped to sell her lot to a local builder, the husband of writer Mimi Heitzmann, who back in September had given me copies of her two books. Lydia and I talked and e-mailed often. I told her about my concern that there would be little interest in anniversary coverage, since the rest of the country had moved on.

Subject: We'll all be there

It is just jolting to hear you say that the rest of the country has moved on!!! *I hate that!* . . .

The bureaucracy in rebuilding is also a major problem. Carl Heitzmann is trying to buy my lot and every time I talk to him his voice is an octave higher from frustration over the slab and the building inspectors, yada yada yada. He told me that if he could he would leave because he was soo frustrated just trying to do normal things that *never* took this long before. . . .

Love you big,

Lydia

Lydia's youngest daughter, Marie, found the anniversary was only deepening her sense of loss.

Subject: Follow up BSL special in the works?

Part of me wants to go back for the anniversary, but most of me doesn't. It's just not right . . . my dad not being there. There's no other way to say it. . . . It's not *right*. I get so overwhelmed by it all still. I mean, I got this Edmond-Fahey Funeral Home thing in the mail yesterday about going to the memorial on the 30th . . . and it's just still surreal. . . .

. . . If someone asks me where I'm from originally . . . *that* is when it's the most difficult. . . . Mostly people ask me if I'm "a Yankee." . . . I don't know why. Maybe 'cause of my father's influence? He had wanted to be an English teacher and I try to talk as proper as I can! . . . And then each answer (vague as I try to be in the beginning) ultimately leads back to, "Bay St. Louis, MS" and then I get, "Oh! Were you or your family affected much by the storm? There's not much left there any-more, is there?"

Love to you and your family,

Marie

Volunteers and residents had anniversary anxiety, too. Their greatest worry? That the media would inevitably focus on where the levees broke instead of where the hurricane hit. That Mississippi would be forgotten again.

Subject: Hello Ms. Koch

. . . We are in the midst, as all volunteer groups are, of a dry spell. Katrina is not garnering the attention it once did but the need here is real as you know.

With the Army Corps and FEMA pulling out, residents are

becoming more and more disillusioned. Although I roof, gut, sheetrock, etc., the most crucial part seems to be just talking with the residents (and trust me when I say, I have never done so much physical labor in my life!). I hear more and more onsets of depression, even those who are on the brink of despair and do not want to leave their trailers any longer because it has just become too difficult to comprehend the scope of all that needs to be done still a year after the storm.

. . . We need more help, more volunteers, more funding. In the wake of the largest natural disaster in our nation's history, it is heartbreaking and frustrating to see so many FEMA trailers where homes once stood. They need help. They need for insurance agencies to stop jerking them around, and they need volunteers. I'm a newspaper reporter from Pittsburgh. . . . I'm nothing special. These people are. I hear their pain every day. Please, let their stories come out and don't let them be forgotten.

Laura Halleman

Subject: Waveland

Please use your influence to highlight Waveland's plight. . . . South of the tracks remains devastated, and thousands of residents are still displaced. There is almost *no* progress in this area, and we can't figure out what's going on.

My 81 year old mother moved into a trailer on our ravished property in June. The street is deserted; not one Oak Blvd. neighbor is back. The lots are weed-covered, debris-studded mud flats. The trees are down or dead, and black widow spiders plague the area. There are so many who have not returned because they cannot and still do not know what the future holds. It doesn't make good footage because there is nothing left to film.

I know you care. Please try to do something.

Thanks,

Vicki Sherrouse

And I did care, perhaps too much. When the official entities kept dropping the ball or moving the goal line every five seconds, I couldn't bear standing on the sidelines and watching people suffer.

I was thrilled that CNN had committed to live reports from Bay St. Louis on the anniversary. So I flew down early with a crew to collect material. And just as on every trip, we saw progress—baby steps forward. The debris fields were shrinking and disappearing. Eighty-five percent of the wreckage in Hancock County had been removed. But the deadline for the Corps of Engineers to wrap up was August 29—the one-year anniversary. And as I walked with Mayor Eddie Favre through areas of Cedar Point where roofs, mounds of ruined belongings, and broken two-by-fours still marred the landscape, it was clear the job was not done.

"We were told that if we went with the Corps of Engineers, debris would not be an issue we'd have to deal with," said Eddie.

"They'd take care of everything?" I asked.

"It would be 100 percent paid for and 100 percent complete. I don't even know why we're talking about deadlines," said the mayor in a rare show of frustration. "We have a situation. Deal with the problem! When it's finished, it's finished."

Not only could the cash-strapped city not afford to pay for debris removal, the very sight of the remaining rubble was an impediment to moving forward. At North Bay Elementary, the skeleton of the old school still crouched silently behind the neat rows of portable classrooms. "It's a constant daily reminder of what we've lost, just like driving the streets of our community is a constant daily reminder of what we've lost," said Principal Frances Weiler. "And until those reminders are gone, it's still going to be very, very difficult to have some kind of true belief that things are going to be okay."

Superintendent Kim Stasny said the county was fighting with the federal government to get money to rebuild the schools and might have to close one and consolidate. The process was infuriatingly slow. "Our students may have to attend class in FEMA trailers until they fall apart," she said.

City sales and property tax revenues were inching up, though they were still 25 to 40 percent lower than the previous year. The newly renamed Hollywood Casino, the biggest generator of tax revenue, was about to reopen. But Bay St. Louis was deep in debt. The city calculated it would take $73 million to repair the streets and the gas, water, sewer, and drainage systems decimated by the hurricane. The federal government would cover the majority of the cost. But Mayor Favre said the city first had to come up with 10 percent to get the work going. "We don't have it. We're struggling right now to pay salaries for policemen and firemen and just day-to-day activities of the city. We're not even providing the full services that we provided before the storm." The optimism was fading from the man who'd been such a relentless cheerleader for his town. "We're expecting or projecting that late September, early October, unless something happens, we'll be broke. We'll be out of money. After that, we don't know what we're going to do."

Insurance rates were going up. Premiums in the state's wind pool, considered an insurer of last resort, had increased 90 percent. It meant that even those residents and business owners who could

~THE AUTHOR WITH VIDEOGRAPHER RICH BROOKS AND SOUND TECH
DOUG THOMAS INTERVIEWING MAYOR EDDIE FAVRE NEXT TO
OLD BAY ST. LOUIS CITY HALL
Photo by Brian Rokus/CNN

scrape together the money to rebuild might find they couldn't afford insurance. David and Angelyn Treutel were hoping to soon begin repairs on their home. Almost precisely a year after the hurricane, they had finally gotten the FEMA trailer they'd applied for eleven months earlier. David, whose family had lived in Bay St. Louis for generations, was concerned that if insurance rates remained exorbitant, the very nature of the town could change. "Our coast is made up of a lot of people that work at the shipyards. They work in small businesses. These aren't the wealthy people. These aren't the condominium dwellers. These are the moms and pops. These are the teachers. They just don't have the ability," said David. "Now, we could make it where these become condos and only those people who have a lot of money can afford to live here. But it would surely change the way of life we have down on the coast."

The ongoing court battles were bringing mixed results. A judge upheld the insurance companies' contention that a hurricane storm surge was flooding and was not covered by homeowners' wind policies. Still, United States district judge L. T. Senter, Jr., questioned the clause that appeared to allow companies to refuse to pay for wind damage if any flooding also occurred, calling it "ambiguous" and not "reasonable." The ruling gave homeowners new hope that such "anti-concurrent cause" clauses were not enforceable.

Bob and Kay Wingate had joined the growing list of residents battling their insurance companies in court. "We went to mediation, and they offered us eleven cents on the dollar," said the retired builder, shaking his head in frustration.

"We felt we had no other route but to go ahead and get somebody to take it off our shoulders and give us a rest," explained Kay. "We're tired."

"We are worn out," said Bob, "physically, mentally."

The two had bought a trailer and were determined to live on their slab until the insurance company paid up.

Though Nikki and Patrick Cleveland had not yet had their day in court, they decided it was time to move out of the FEMA camper, which was no place to raise a newborn. Little Emma was now a month old, all smiles and blissfully unaware of the trauma her parents had endured. She slept peacefully in a gleaming crib made by an amateur woodworker who had seen our documentary and been touched by the Clevelands' story. With their permission, he had salvaged wood from Nikki's parents' property and crafted the legs from pieces of the barn, the spindles from the house, and the headboard and footboard from engraved panels on the front door.

Home was now a three-bedroom house thirteen miles inland. Such choices were being made by many who loved the Gulf Coast but hated the hurricane risk. "A lot of things are up in the air. I think you're going to lose a lot of good people," said Patrick. "It's going to be a very different kind of town. It's almost an island right now," he added, pointing out that without the Bay Bridge, Bay St. Louis felt isolated.

Tommy and Linda Kidd had finally gotten some money from their insurance company and were about to start repairing their home. In the interim, they were living in a trailer they had bought and parked in their yard. "It's not as much as we'd like to have or as much as we'd hoped. But the bottom line at this point is, it's somethin' that's getting close enough that we can live with it," said Tommy.

Danielle and Monte Strong and their three children were among the few who on the eve of the one-year anniversary found themselves back in their home. In fact, that was where I was meeting Lydia and Brooke Schultz the night of the anniversary after the crew and I wrapped our reports.

The site for our live coverage on August 29, 2006, was old downtown Bay St. Louis, which except for a few art studios that had reopened was still largely empty. Many had been worried it might stay that way because of a proposal to move the courthouse from Main Street to a safer location nine miles inland near I-10. But the county relented after city leaders like Mayor Eddie Favre argued that the move would kill downtown, since the offices of lawyers, accountants, and title companies would head north, too. On the waterfront, none of the restaurants, bars, and shops had even begun to rebuild. The sea of asphalt chunks had been hauled away, and fill dirt had been brought in to create a rough temporary roadway where Beach Boulevard used to be.

It was in that virtual ghost town, right next to the wreckage of my family's old ice-cream parlor, where I heard church bells toll solemnly at 9:01 A.M., commemorating the hour Hurricane Katrina's thirty-plus-foot storm surge smashed into Bay St. Louis. Later in the day, citizens gathered on the grounds of the old city hall for a candlelight vigil and a reading of the names of Van Schultz, Ralph and JoAnna Dagnall, and the other county residents who died in the hurricane. A ship's bell rang after each name, the reverberations cutting deep as it sounded fifty-six times.

I ran into an old classmate, Tish Haas Williams, who now headed the chamber of commerce. "We're holding up good," she said, drawing a deep breath. "It's just like the feeling I had when my twins turned one year old. I made it! But then I'm like, where have we made it to? But I think we've turned the corner."

Tish and her family had to recover not only from the loss of their home but from the death of her seventy-three-year-old father, Mike Haas, in March after the storm. My classmate Diane Edwards Bourgeois had lost her father, Ed, to lung cancer in late July.

Many older residents, some who were ill but also others who appeared healthy, had died since the hurricane. Some said they gave up. Others suggested that they couldn't bear to face the radically changed Gulf Coast. Speculation also circulated that a toxin in the post-hurricane air, soil, or water had killed them. Tish believed Katrina's wrath had taken a heavy toll on civic leaders like her father, a respected attorney who among other things had helped establish the local airport and the Port and Harbor Commission. "He spent his whole life building Hancock County and building a home and building a business. And then it was just gone. I don't think he could stand it. It killed their spirit and their hopes."

In the months after the hurricane, coroners were overburdened, so the actual cause of death was frequently unclear. Regardless, most considered Mike Haas, Ed Edwards, and many other older citizens who died that year to be uncounted victims of Hurricane Katrina.

As darkness fell, I wrapped my final live shot at the end of Main Street and was packing my things when I saw a group approaching. "Kathleen, is that you?"

"I told you she'd be here!" said another familiar voice.

As they stepped into the pool of light next to the satellite truck,

I recognized the young people who had organized the Second Street Elementary School shelter.

"Come on!" one of them said. "You've got to come down to the Fire Dog with us."

The Fire Dog Saloon had been a popular waterfront bar and restaurant before Katrina reduced it to nothing but a shell. I walked with them, wondering what could be going on, since nothing had reopened. I heard the hum of a generator as we approached and was astonished to see colorful holiday lights strung inside the empty structure and a dozen people drinking and chatting as though they were enjoying just an ordinary night out. The atmosphere was perfect. We laughed and talked and reminisced and wondered what was next for our town. I looked around at the bizarre setting and thought there was nowhere on earth I'd rather be at that moment. There was something inspiring about the audacious insanity of it all.

But others were waiting for me, so I said my goodbyes and drove to Monte and Danielle Strong's house. The trailer was gone. Yet as the door swung open wide, I barely noticed the completed home and was instead drawn in by Lydia's warm, welcoming expression. She wrapped her arms around me. "Hey, Kathie! How are you?"

"Wiped out, Lydia. What a day. How are you doing?" I asked, pulling back and holding her hands in mine. "Are you okay?"

"I'm making it through," she said, cracking her steel magnolia half-smile that dammed back the tears.

Brooke was outside talking with friends. After a while, she popped in for a few minutes and joined me, Lydia, and the others at the kitchen table. She made brief small talk but clearly wasn't interested in discussing what had brought us all there—Katrina and her father's death. When talk turned to frustration over the slow recovery in Bay St. Louis, she cut it short with, "If you're angry, you're living in the past. If you're fearful, you're living in the future. Stay in the present!" And with that, she headed back outside to see her friends.

I was both disappointed and relieved. Our phone conversation back in the fall hadn't settled things. I felt the need to look her in the eye and apologize in person. I wanted to try to read the pain in her face, to understand where she was in her difficult journey. But I was also afraid of what I would see there. What if I found anger instead of absolution?

I left not long after Brooke, since the crew and I had one more shoot in the morning before leaving.

As we drove toward Biloxi the following day, I found my excitement building. So many efforts over the past year had fallen short. So many people had been disillusioned and disappointed. But bright, shining threads were woven into the tapestry of loss. The selfless gestures of Mississippians to their fellow citizens. The compassion and dedication of the thousands of volunteers rebuilding the Mississippi Gulf Coast. The endless generosity of people around the country and the world who opened their hearts and wallets in an effort to do what the government alone couldn't—make an entire region whole again. I was about to meet one of them.

Steve Kessler owned a successful van conversion business in Warsaw, Indiana. Running on his treadmill Mardi Gras morning, the Fox viewer for some reason had switched channels to CNN. He saw our report about Biloxi janitor Lucy Williams. Steve wanted to do something to help Katrina victims but didn't care to simply write a check to the Red Cross. Before becoming a businessman, Steve had been a janitor. He called his wife into the room to see the report. "I'm going to help that lady," he said.

The next day, Steve called Miss Lucy, introduced himself, and asked, "Do you trust me?"

"Well, I don't know you, but I suppose so," she replied.

"I want to build you a house."

And so it began. Steve came to Mississippi to meet Miss Lucy and flew in crews to demolish her home and clear and grade the lot. He had an architect draw up plans. Over the last six months, carpenters had been hard at work constructing a lovely three-bedroom home. It would be finished today.

A radiant Miss Lucy met us at the curb in a turquoise dress, her hair carefully coiffed, beaming with pride. Behind her, a cheerful yellow one-story house with a bay window and a comfortable front porch had taken the place of the wrecked structure left by Katrina. A pole standing in the front yard proudly flew the American flag

~The new home built for Lucy Williams by Warsaw, Indiana,
businessman Steve Kessler
Photo by Lucy Williams

and a yellow banner reading, "Explorer: America's Van." Steve, a tall, lean man with a ready smile, came striding down the driveway. Miss Lucy called him the answer to her prayers. "He just came right down and just went to work. And he just like a angel that the Lord just sent down to bless me."

The interior was still bare of furniture. But the walls of rich crimson and golden pumpkin reflected Miss Lucy's warm personality. Steve explained that she was the interior decorator. The home boasted a chandelier in the dining room, ceiling fans in every room, and gleaming hardwood floors. Price had not entered into the equation. "We tried to do it right," said Steve. "I don't know what the dollars were. I haven't really kept track."

When I had found out months earlier what Steve was doing, he'd insisted he wasn't rich, just successful. He said that if every American of means came down and rebuilt just one home, the Gulf Coast could be put back together in no time. "It's not really that difficult. You just have to jump in and help the best you can. I knew this was what I was supposed to do, and I did it."

Miss Lucy walked us out to our van and gave me a joyous hug. "I got a smile on my face that I just can't take off. I am so happy. I just get up every morning and thank the Lord."

As we headed for the airport, I thought about Miss Lucy's words. Was it divine intervention or pure coincidence that Steve had seen our report back in February? I was still so angry over both the hurricane and Mississippians' continuing struggles that I'd stopped going to church. I'd lost faith in God as well as the institutions that were supposed to protect Americans when things went wrong. It seemed all people could count on was one another.

~17~

Fall 2006

KAY WINGATE OPENED THE DOOR of the trailer and stepped outside with her coffee to check the weather. For a moment, she was startled by the cacophony of hammers and circular saws that bombarded her. Jordan River Estates had been empty for so long as residents fought to get paid by their insurance companies and then struggled to find contractors that she and Bob normally woke to nothing but the cries of sea gulls feeding on schools of shad in the bay. Five homes were now under construction in the neighborhood. Kay took a seat at the picnic table to enjoy the crispness of the late-October weather and the new sounds of progress.

In Washington, Congressman Gene Taylor stepped to the podium in the House Radio-TV Gallery to release the recommendations of the Katrina Task Force. He and other lawmakers had spent months developing proposals to better deal with disasters in the wake of Katrina. "Number one, we have to take the antitrust exemption of the insurance industry away. No one should be above the law. Number two, we have to have all-perils insurance."

The task force had found an obvious conflict of interest existed when adjusters were left to decide whether damage claims would be billed to the federal flood insurance program or the insurance companies that employed them. Lawmakers recommended the federal government be allowed to offer wind as well as flood insurance, so homeowners would truly be covered for "all perils" and would not be caught in disputes over what caused the damage and who should pay for it. Gene admitted that in the Republican-controlled Congress, such a proposal had little chance of succeeding. "I'm a realist. On the insurance thing, we're planting the seed."

As lawmakers looked for a solution, many Bay St. Louis homeowners were still dealing with the problem. Lydia Schultz had sold her house but was still hoping for a settlement from the insurance company so she could start over.

Subject: How are things?

. . . The lawsuit is still in the air and I have my moments of sheer, utter doubt about whether I did the right thing. Should I have gone for the grant and tried to rebuild then sell to recoup? I just don't know. . . . I would *never* have filed suit if they had not denied my claim *before* even seeing the house. Nor did they look at the house until *months* later. And then it was told to the Private Ins. Claims adjuster that, "Yes, it looks tornadic but we are still denying the claim"!!!!!!!!!!!!!! There is that part of my policy that claims they will always be there for us in times of trouble and they will always deal with me fairly. That they have *not* done.

I love you and thanks soooo much for keeping in touch.

Lydia

Our second documentary had been released. Again, positive feedback flowed in. I was particularly touched by an e-mail from a volunteer who had just returned home to Minnesota after helping in the hurricane zone.

Subject: Helping Bay St. Louis, MS

Giving of just one week of blood, sweat and many prayers simply isn't enough to me. It seems that this disaster has grabbed my heart up here in Minnesota where the Hurricane has not been on our front page in over 13 months. When I shared my experience with dozens of people today they all were in shock. . . . They are under the impression that all is well in Mississippi and New Orleans. Nothing could be further from the truth could it?

I want to thank you for the reports, for giving the people down south who do not have anyone in their corner a voice. I am now concentrating on how I can rearrange my schedule in 2007 to allow for more trips south—perhaps to Bay St Louis. . . . They are in my heart thanks in great part to your updates.

Please keep the rest of America updated on your city's struggles—it is a matter of life and death for our fellow Americans who feel so abandoned and forgotten.

Gratefully yours in Minnesota,

Patti Simmet

I had mixed feelings about wrapping the Bay St. Louis documentary project. We were the only network to focus in-depth on Mississippi, showing the nation not only the incredible devastation where the hurricane actually roared ashore but the citizens' bravery and resilience in its aftermath. We exposed the capricious nature of post-hurricane damage claims, in which some residents got paid while neighbors with identically damaged houses got nothing simply because they'd bought insurance from a different company. Journalistically and editorially, we had every reason to be proud. But in the end, I wondered what difference we had made. If laws weren't changed, the very same thing could happen to other coastal residents after the next big hurricane. And volunteers and donations were dropping. Disaster fatigue was setting in.

I was exhausted, too. I had made fifteen trips to Mississippi and done the two documentaries while at the same time covering the White House, the Pentagon, aviation, and any other beat CNN needed. Still, I could never say no, even if every trip back was like ripping open a wound that was just beginning to heal.

I was, though, reluctant about a new request. Our Lady Academy, the school I attended when we first moved to Bay St. Louis, had decided to launch an annual fund-raiser by roasting a local citizen. And at its inaugural dinner dance for four hundred people, it wanted to honor me.

I was flattered but didn't see how I could be the first choice. Congressman Gene Taylor and chamber of commerce director Tish Haas were far more deserving. But the school insisted. And I learned that on the day of the fund-raiser, the KaBOOM! organization would build a playground just north of Bay St. Louis for the students of two nearby elementary schools that were destroyed. I had been anxious to help on a build ever since I met founder Darrell Hammond in November and heard about Ginny Vegas's personal mission to help the youngest hurricane victims. So I said yes.

As I sat on the plane headed south, I realized the dinner would give me the chance to do what I'd been longing to—thank the people of Bay St. Louis. They were the ones this dinner should celebrate, not me. I felt like an imposter because no matter what I did, it seemed to fall short. Yes, I'd spoken at fund-raisers around the country and at my own church. Generous donors pledged $550,000 to my town and the region. But it was a thimbleful of help in an ocean of need. I still felt I'd let the Gulf Coast down.

The next morning, I was up bright and early in my jeans, KaBOOM! T-shirt, and sneakers, ready to get to work. The site was a complex of FEMA portable classrooms near Stennis Airport where five hundred students had been attending class for the last year. In fact, some parents were worried constructing a playground at a temporary location was a waste of money. "They were afraid they were going to go ahead and get stuck with no playground once they moved," explained Lori Jugan, project director for the local Rotary club that came up with the idea and helped fund it. "But we said no. The whole point is, get fun back into the lives of these children now. We promised we would either build another or move the one that we build."

Principal Jan White was thrilled with the idea. "This is a life-saver for all these kids that have lost their homes and their toys." She pointed out the school grounds were so bare that students had been reduced to having PE in the parking lot.

The children designed the play space, and members of the Stennis Space Center Rotary and a Rotary club from Titusville, Florida, joined more than seventy-five volunteers from Gulfview and Charles B. Murphy elementary schools and one eager reporter to build it. We were long on energy but short on experience. Fortunately, the KaBOOM! coordinators were adept at molding green volunteers into smoothly working units. I started on the bridge team. Once we had the bright orange span solidly planted in place, I moved to mixing cement and spreading mulch. It was a chilly morning. But by the time we wrapped up, most had broken quite a sweat—in my case, topped with a fine layer of cement dust.

That was when an old friend from Bay St. Louis, Mark Proulx, showed up and began taunting me. "Look at you!" he laughed, pulling out his camera to capture my disheveled appearance. "I don't

~The author and a volunteer mixing cement for a new playground at Gulfview and Charles B. Murphy elementary schools in Kiln, Mississippi
Courtesy of KaBOOM!

believe this! Anyone else being roasted would be out getting their hair and nails done. You're a mess!"

"Oh, shut up, grab a rake, and make yourself useful," I said with a smile.

Mark had been instrumental over the last year in getting out information about Bay St. Louis in articles he wrote for the website Gulfcoastnews.com. The primary source of detailed news on the Mississippi Gulf Coast after the hurricane, the website provided such an invaluable service to those desperate for information that it had just received the 2006 award for service journalism from the Online News Association.

"Time for the ribbon cutting!" announced KaBOOM! site chief Caleb Marshall. The "ribbon" turned out to be a long strip of construction paper taped across the enormous purple triple slide that was the central feature of the new playground. The paper was covered with little cut-out hands colored and decorated by the schoolchildren. "Children aren't allowed to work on the builds," Caleb ex-

~Children getting their first look at the playground just built for them by volunteers
Photo by Mark Proulx

plained. "The students made this banner so they could do something to contribute." I smiled. Mississippi children, just like their parents, were loath to take something for nothing. I grabbed one side of the banner, and another volunteer took the other. On the count of three, we pulled it in two as the crowd erupted in applause.

"Okay, time for you to go clean up," said Mark. "Can't have you miss your own roast!"

I dashed off, showered, changed, and then with a deep breath headed into the Hollywood Casino ballroom. It was full of old friends, neighbors, and classmates. I didn't know what to expect. But I knew I stood in awe of them and everything they'd survived over the past fourteen months.

David Treutel and Mark Proulx did the roasting. They told funny stories—like the one about the high-school prank when a friend covered himself with a blanket of Spanish moss, twigs, and brush one night and hid in the bayou, only to pop out and convince a carload of us that a swamp monster was on the loose. Everyone else quickly learned it was a hoax, but I told the story for months until finally the guilty party marched into our ice-cream parlor wearing

~THE AUTHOR AND OTHER VOLUNTEERS TEARING THE BANNER
OFFICIALLY OPENING THE PLAYGROUND
Photo by Mark Proulx

the moss monster costume. They also told serious stories about my post-Katrina relief efforts, down to soliciting new boots for local firemen, since they wore out so quickly in the noxious mud that coated Bay St. Louis. "Kathleen is my hero," concluded Mark.

I cringed. I was no one's hero. But at least I had a chance to set things straight.

Though normally I used written notes, that night I just let the words flow from the heart. "I appreciate this wonderful honor and the kind words of praise from Mark and David. It's quite a year we've all been through. But if you're looking for a hero, look at the person to your right and to your left, and look in the mirror. You are the real heroes. Because you stayed. You stuck it out under the worst conditions imaginable. And you refused to give up no matter what anyone else said.

"Like Father Tracey, whose own family in Ireland told him not to come back to Bay St. Louis because there was nothing left. He came back anyway. Or like chamber of commerce director Tish Haas Williams. Tish lost both her home and her father this year but has just kept on going, advocating tirelessly for the county, helping businesses get back on their feet. Or ham radio operator Brice Phillips, who when the hurricane hit, thank God, hauled his equipment to the EOC so local officials had a way to communicate and citizens a way to find out where to get food, water, and shelter. Or Mark Proulx and the folks at Gulfcoastnews.com, who have given people around the country information on the struggling Gulf Coast when there was nowhere else to turn. Or Mayor Eddie Favre, still in his shorts. Eddie, what can I say? You are all heroes. My heroes and my inspiration. Because from that first Thursday when I walked through the rubble of our town, I was overwhelmed. I didn't know where to start. I felt like an ant trying to move a mountain. But then I saw you all helping one another and the volunteers pouring in, and I realized that together a million ants can move a mountain. And that's what you've done."

As the crowd rose in applause, I noticed residents smiling at one another and realized that for perhaps the first time they were celebrating what they'd accomplished together.

Weeks later, I was back at home working out and flipping

~The author, Father Michael Tracey, and Jackie Howard,
president of Our Lady Academy, at the "Hooray for the Bay"
roast to raise money for the school
Photo by Mark Proulx

through the channels. I'd started exercising regularly in January to
relieve stress. It was either that or I was going to explode. I usually
watched Comedy Central, since I found laughter was indeed good
medicine. But I paused on a local station when I saw Sheryl Crow
talking to Oprah about surviving breast cancer. She was one of my
favorite singers, and I appreciated her work to help the Gulf Coast.
The show was on overcoming trauma and also featured designer
Dana Buchman talking about her learning-disabled daughter, Char-
lotte. A montage of famous women who had survived dramatic
challenges in their lives ran at the end of the show, most of them
echoing a point Sheryl Crow had made: To get through crises, you
have to love yourself.

Right. That's a no-brainer, I thought as I worked out. *You've got
to love yourself.* But then I slowed to a stop. All the pain and frustration and despair of the last fifteen months fast-forwarded through
my brain. A light bulb went on. I didn't love myself anymore. It
didn't make sense, but I still believed I'd failed the people of the Gulf
Coast. I was so consumed by guilt that I felt I didn't deserve love. In
fact, I hated myself.

I had been in denial for a long time, but I finally realized I couldn't go on like that. I needed help. I told my husband that evening that I wanted to go into therapy.

"Why? You're fine," Rick said. It was a testament to how well I'd hidden my pain, both at home and at work. I'd been fooling everyone and lying to myself.

"No, I'm not."

I called and scheduled an appointment.

~18~

Winter of
Discontent

IT WAS NOVEMBER 30. Normally, Sue Reed and the workers at the headquarters of the Boys & Girls Clubs of Gulfport would have been busy sorting and distributing carfuls of toys to the temporary club locations up and down the Mississippi Gulf Coast. Hurricane Katrina had leveled nearly all of their facilities, so the one thousand children the clubs served were meeting now in trailers, and the Christmas parties were just two weeks away. The director sat at her desk and stared at an empty warehouse. Toy donations weren't just down. They had stopped. She had reached out to groups like Toys for Tots, but no one had toys to spare.

Then Sue remembered Suzanne Stahl, the tall, sandy-haired woman from Arizona who had sent out-of-town volunteers to help at the clubs, since so many regulars had left the area. She drafted an e-mail.

Subject: Hi from Mississippi

Suzanne,

Things are progressing very slowly here. Obviously since the year anniversary the coast has really dropped off the radar screen. . . .

Last year I could have paved a road from here to the moon with all of the toys that came to the coast from everywhere for all coast kids. This year there is really nothing going on at all. . . .

I didn't know who else to contact and you came to mind. I know it is late but you have a lot of contacts and I thought you might be able to help us find an avenue to find some gifts for our kids.

Thanks Suzanne!

Sue Reed

The next morning, I was at work in the CNN White House booth when I got an e-mail from Suzanne. She shared Sue Reed's appeal and added one of her own.

Subject: Need Your Help in Mississippi

Dear Kathleen,

They service some of the most at risk kids in the region and their membership has increased with the layered issues that now exist. . . . Sue has not made a plea to me like this in the past 15 months. She has only expressed thanks for the funds/resources that I've sent and never pleaded for more. . . .

I am hoping that you can either rally your coworkers over the next two weeks to do a collection for these kids or if you could do a story about the need for support for these children at this time. . . . I know first hand that these kids are having a particularly difficult time right now, so I am hoping that you can find a way to help.

Suzanne Stahl

I couldn't believe what I was reading. It was one thing for the rest of the country to have the mistaken impression that the Katrina-stricken region had recovered. But for people to have forgotten about the neediest of all, the children, was simply unacceptable. Most of these kids now lived in trailers. They had lost their homes, their schools, even the clubs that tried to keep some stability in their lives. Now they were going to lose Christmas, too?

"Elaine, can you cover the briefing today?" I asked Elaine Quijano, the other correspondent on duty. White House press secretary Tony Snow's briefing would begin soon and last about an hour. I needed to act fast if we had any hope of rounding up a thousand toys in two weeks.

"Sure, what's up?" she replied.

"Something important."

Luckily, I was an electronic pack rat and had saved all the e-mails I'd received since the hurricane. I began forwarding the "Need Your Help" e-mail to anyone who had expressed interest in aiding the Gulf Coast—viewers, volunteers, churches, Rotary clubs, even parents at my daughters' schools. I called CNN and arranged to put toy collection boxes on every floor. I also put a box in the White House press break room with a sign explaining the children's plight. Then I held my breath and waited.

In just over an hour, responses began to come in. A volunteer in Minnesota was spreading the word at her church, and a radio station there wanted to interview Sue Reed. Voice of America White House correspondent Paula Wolfson was organizing a toy drive at her office and among extended family. The Rotary club in Jonesboro, Arkansas, that had served the Thanksgiving dinner in Bay St. Louis was starting a collection and passing the e-mail to other clubs and to WBIR, a Knoxville, Tennessee, television station. The Rotary club in Petal, Mississippi, was sending a Wal-Mart gift card. Its members would bring toys to the next meeting for delivery south.

I was particularly heartened at the response from volunteer Bruce Reynolds. After seeing our February documentary, his Jackson, Mississippi, church had decided to adopt Bay St. Louis, Waveland, and Pearlington. Members had been making trips down every month to help with gutting and reconstruction. I knew they were not only committed but organized.

As the next two weeks flew by, the toy drive snowballed beyond everyone's expectations. I didn't know if it was the holiday season or the fact that the poignant e-mail struck a chord as it was forwarded around the country. Not only were toys pouring in, but individuals ranging from investment bankers in New York to a middle-aged couple in Colorado were sending checks. Churches and Rotary clubs were supplementing their toy donations with thousands of dollars in cash. On the December 13 deadline for mailing the toys, I dashed around Washington emptying the collection boxes and carting everything to CNN to pack. In the end, we sent seven huge boxes south to Mississippi, along with a check of contributions from my fellow White House correspondents. To encourage donations, FedEx was picking up the tab for all the shipments.

Bruce Reynolds made two trips south to deliver a truck and then a U-Haul packed with toys collected by Wells Church. A woman from Florida brought a partial truckload. Suzanne Stahl flew in from Arizona to help distribute the toys that had arrived at the Boys & Girls Club headquarters. Between the two hundred boxes that were shipped to Gulfport and the truckloads driven in, some

~THE AUTHOR WITH TOYS COLLECTED IN WASHINGTON FOR THE BOYS & GIRLS CLUBS OF THE MISSISSIPPI GULF COAST
Photo by Tom Bentz

ten thousand toys were given out to children along the Mississippi Gulf Coast. Donations came from Alabama, Arizona, Arkansas, California, Colorado, Florida, Georgia, Illinois, Kansas, Maryland, Minnesota, New York, Nevada, Oklahoma, Oregon, South Carolina, Tennessee, Virginia, and Washington, D.C. A total of three thousand dollars was left, plus a fifteen-thousand-dollar donation for the Boys & Girls Clubs to use for reconstruction and operating expenses. The Jonesboro Rotary had rallied so much support from clubs around the nation that it collected an additional ten thousand dollars, to be used to provide a Christmas for needy families in Bay St. Louis and Waveland.

We had done it! Not just a thousand toys, but ten times that! And it was all through e-mails, phone calls, and word of mouth, since the collection was over by the time any CNN shows expressed interest in the story. Sue Reed sent out thank-you e-mails, but the pictures she attached said it all. The look of glee on a blond-haired girl's face as she showed her friends the doll she'd just received. A beaming girl in red pants patterned with Christmas lights standing with her arm around Santa. The blissful smiles on the faces of boys and girls snacking on sandwiches, fried chicken, and cantaloupe, giant coloring books and shiny new boxes of pencils and markers stacked in the middle of their tables.

Just when I thought it was the best Christmas I could imagine, it got better. A nonprofit called First Book, in partnership with the Department of Education, was donating 200,000 new books to schools and libraries along the Gulf Coast. I could never forget how, after the hurricane, the sight of the muddy, ruined books strewn across the floor of North Bay Elementary's library had brought me to tears. Now, 14,755 pristine books would fill the shelves at North Bay and the Hancock County Library, where Superintendent Kim Stasny joined in a ceremony with Deputy Secretary of Education Raymond Simon to accept the generous gift. "This is a wonderful time," Kim gushed. "These new books open the world to our children."

The superintendent herself had just been recognized for her work in getting the local schools reopened just forty-seven days after the hurricane. Her peers in the Mississippi Association of School

Administrators had named her superintendent of the year. "This is really humbling," said Kim. "I just felt like I was doing what I needed to be doing. My heart was in full mode to get those schools back up and going."

But I knew that when riding the post-Katrina roller coaster, every high was followed by a low, and the holidays proved no exception. In mid-December, State Farm announced it would no longer offer wind coverage for new customers in Mississippi's six southern counties. Many feared that as the lawsuits mounted, insurers would simply start fleeing the state. It was beginning.

Nonetheless, most who were suing were angry and committed. Lydia Schultz had been stunned when State Farm subpoenaed all the bank records for the house she and Van had owned. "What does it show? We paid our bills. The house was almost paid for. Eight thousand dollars left. Van and I owned it," she told me, perplexed. "What does that have to do with a tornado hitting it? Is it just harassment? Who the hell knows?"

Still, she decided to give mediation a try in case she could get a reasonable offer.

Subject: Just an update . . .

I returned for my mediation which turned out to be a complete farce. The deposition was scheduled to take place a couple hours later so I knew that there would be no resolution in mediation if they were planning the deposition ahead of the mediation. Go figure. Anyway, they offered me $25,000. They absolutely refused to believe that there is any wind damage. *Everything* is flood, according to State Farm. In their world, the winds were never above 95 mph in BSL!!!!!!

The attorney for the deposition grilled for one hour on my past. From my first marriage to now. He harped and harped on why we didn't get flood ins. and I told him we were told . . . that we didn't need it and that we were told to take that money and go enjoy it. He had 50 ways of asking the same question and of course tried to put words in my mouth. It was absolutely bizarre to say the least. They are certainly spending a great deal of time and money trying not to spend money. . . .

I am trying to get to a place where I am expecting nothing and am in work mode for another 5–7 years. This loss will be hard to overcome. But I still have blessings and need to concentrate on them.

Well, take care. Love and smiles to the family . . . *all* of them.

Lydia

I wondered when homeowners would finally get some clarity from the courts about what precisely insurance companies owed them. I didn't have to wait long. Shortly after New Year's came another ruling from Judge L. T. Senter, Jr., of the district court. This time, he directly addressed the claim by some insurance companies that they owed nothing if wind and water—instead of wind alone—caused the damage. The judge ruled that because State Farm couldn't prove there was no wind damage and further couldn't prove only water caused all the damage, it would have to pay homeowners the full amount of their wind policies. A jury awarded the couple who sued $2.5 million in punitive damages, which on appeal was reduced to $1 million.

The ruling apparently shook the state's largest insurer. Less than two weeks later, lawyers for homeowners reached a tentative settlement whereby State Farm would reopen and possibly pay the claims of some thirty-five thousand Mississippians it had denied after Hurricane Katrina. While the settlement sounded promising, producer Brian Rokus and I were bombarded with e-mails from residents who believed the deal was tilted heavily in favor of the insurance company. Just four days later, Judge Senter apparently agreed and rejected the proposed settlement, questioning whether it was "fair, just, balanced or reasonable."

Just over two weeks after that, on February 14, State Farm made a stunning announcement. Instead of simply ceasing wind policies in South Mississippi, it would no longer sell any new commercial or homeowner policies in the state. The company blamed in part the wave of lawsuits it had faced since the hurricane.

It seemed a case of homeowners winning the battle but losing the war. Yes, perhaps insurers would have to pay for much of the wind damage. But if residents took that money and rebuilt, who would be left to insure the property?

It was shaping up to be a long, grim winter on the Mississippi Gulf Coast. A Katrina blogger reached out to me asking for help for local families who were going without heat, hot water, and electricity. Suzanne Stahl alerted me that the all-volunteer fire department in western Hancock County was running out of fuel and supplies. The county had no money to fund them, yet the volunteers, who had all lost their homes in Katrina, were trying to rebuild their destroyed station themselves. Parishioners from St. Paul's, a beachfront Catholic church in Pass Christian, wanted support for their drive to save the hurricane-damaged structure from demolition.

Residents, in phone calls and e-mails, kept pouring out their hearts.

Subject: Bay St. Louis needs your help!

Thanks! I'm good and my house work is *slow*. . . . Coping seems harder now than before. I believe right after the storm and last year we all just *did* what we had to do. Now, it seems as though the fatigue and frustration of the *slow* process is causing much more stress than before.

I will tell *all* that you send your best. Thank you sooo very much.

Tammy

Subject: Hi!

. . . Sure, people say everything is fine. It is not! It is like a low to high grade fever. I can't explain it to you. I know the medics told me the order of what was to come when I visited the MASH tents after the storm. . . . They were right. The first was intestinal. The doctors said respiratory next. Yep! It happened. The third event to look forward to was the mental part. Well, it is here. I understand it lasts 2 to 3 years. . . .

I know the time is coming when we will be forgotten by most if not all. I am also afraid of our taxes going up so high that we will have to leave. Do you think this could be a possibility? . . . I am beginning to feel we are losing our town. Could this be possible? I hope not.

Thank you so much for listening and sharing. . . . Yes, it is lonely but I know you know what I am talking about. . . .

I cannot believe I wrote all of this. Maybe this is how God wants me to get well possibly. I am so happy you will let me chip away at understanding my own feelings. . . . I think just writing them down is helping. I used to journal but haven't done this in months. This is the next best thing. Thank you Kathie.

Connie

The e-mails and pleas for help were increasingly difficult to deal with. We were done with the documentaries and so weren't tracking and reporting the day-to-day developments in Bay St. Louis anymore. Unless something rose to the level of a major crisis, it was difficult to get network shows interested in a post-Katrina story. It got to the point where sometimes I didn't even respond because there was nothing I could do. I hated admitting that. It was like giving up, something I *never* did. I felt like a failure. But I was emotionally exhausted.

One cold February night, my mood grew particularly dark. I tried working out, but even the post-exercise endorphins couldn't burn away the gloom. I slipped into the hot tub out back and sat staring at the sky. I thought how the same bright stars shone down on everyone on the Gulf Coast, the few back in their homes and the many still wondering a year and a half after the storm if their lives would ever be normal again. There was so much pain and so little I could do, yet so many depended on me. I just wanted it to stop. I wanted it all to stop. For several entirely selfish moments, I contemplated the unimaginable. Finally, I pulled myself out of the water and went inside to write.

The Hot Tub

The warmth, the water, promise relief.
I slip in and look up.
But the stars are too bright.
They cut like shards of glass.
I turn on the jets—the mist will soften their gleam.
Suddenly, one in the center bursts into flame and shoots
across the sky.
It is heartbreakingly beautiful.
And then it is gone.
I can't stop the tears that rush down my cheeks,
Warm but saltier than the water.
I silence the jets.
My arms float as if disconnected from my body.
I slide lower in the water.
It is so welcoming, like a familiar pillow.
My cheek rests on the surface and my eyes close.
I look up again one last time as the stars blur
And I wonder how it will feel when the pain stops.
I am so tired.
But then the moon like a spotlight pierces my rest.
It is insistent.
The breeze rustles my hair.
I get up.
It is not yet time to sleep.

I woke the next morning to horrible news. I hadn't been the only one enveloped in a smothering mist of despair. The day before, authorities in Bay St. Louis had found the bodies of local builder Carl Heitzmann and his wife, author and photographer Mimi Heitzmann. Police said Carl shot Mimi and then turned the gun on himself.

The murder-suicide of two of its most prominent citizens had the town reeling. Carl, highly regarded as a perfectionist and an honorable businessman, had constructed hundreds of homes on the Gulf Coast and had a steady flow of customers waiting for him to rebuild what Katrina had eviscerated. Mimi was a bright, generous spirit with a large circle of devoted friends, like her husband's cousin's wife, Connie Heitzmann, who was the first to reach out to me with a short, plaintive e-mail.

Subject: Help

Kathie,

   Mimi Heitzmann was murdered by her husband Carl Heitzmann and he then shot himself. We need you all down here. People are having heart attacks, suicides etc. . . .
   Please help us! Thanks so much!

Connie Heitzmann

I recalled how Lydia Schultz had mentioned Carl's stress level when he was buying her property. She was devastated by the news.

Subject: A lot of sadness

   I was truly concerned about Carl from the getgo. He'd been in semi retirement but lost so much that was not covered by insurance. And then had to come out of retirement to build. Being the top builder, so many wanted him to replace the houses he originally built over 25 or 30 years now!!! The stress on him. Each time I talked with him last year, I could hear it. He'd tell me how lucky I was to not be there and if he could get Mimi to leave he would go in a heartbeat. I kept asking everyone if he was ok and they'd just roll their eyes because he was on such a short string and so stressed and "going off" on people. Well, last week he learned his secretary and right hand of all these years had stage 4 colon cancer. I just think he couldn't take any more and snapped. Too much for one person to handle along with his depression. Mimi said he was on meds but I think meds can handle just so much. Just as we can handle just so much. . . .

I have not been able to get past this sadness. I am so lucky that I got to spend time with Mimi in Dec. when home. It was a fantastic visit and upbeat as only Mimi was.

Take care. Love to you and yours.

Lydia

I felt horrible seeing what a toll Carl and Mimi's deaths were taking on the normally upbeat people of Bay St. Louis. It was as though someone had let the air out of the happy balloon. One thought was repeated in virtually every conversation I had with residents about the tragedy: "I can't believe it. How could he do such a thing?" I couldn't respond. I understood what it was like to feel overwhelmed by so many people looking to you for help, depending on you to make their lives better—and to realize you couldn't help them all. I understood how someone could feel pain so deep, so profound that there seemed only one way out.

I focused on therapy, which was helping. I was slowly accepting that it wasn't my responsibility to try to fix everything for my hometown. I had always been a control freak. I was learning that the guilt I felt for not helping more people was my way of trying to impose an artificial sense of control over a completely chaotic situation.

I sought out and clung to any positive news about the Gulf Coast, like the e-mail that came on the Ides of March in the final days of a difficult winter.

Subject: New house

Hi,

I was out photographing some of the new houses being built around the area. I have been watching the attached one since they started it. It is built to the rear of where your house used to be. It appears that they have cleaned and are preparing to landscape both y'all's old lot and the one next door. I'm not sure but that is how it appears. Things still moving slowly. I'm uploading some photos of houses going up to my website. Take care, talk with you soon.

John

The attached photo from my former classmate John Wilkerson showed a tan one-story home elevated on steel girders sitting behind what looked like a field of mud where our old house had been. It was one of the first houses rebuilt on the Bay St. Louis beachfront and a cause for celebration. Just like our home, it was supposed to be hurricane-proof.

~New house rebuilt on the Beach Boulevard site of the Koch family's former home
Photo by John Wilkerson

~19~

Second Anniversary

A LONG, DARK CLOUD bank hung on the horizon as organizers began setting up in the empty field next to the beach in Waveland for the anniversary sunrise service. Residents and volunteers emerged from the early-morning darkness to quietly stand where two years earlier 125-miles-per-hour winds and a crushing storm surge had obliterated everything in their path.

CNN again wanted live coverage of the August 29 anniversary, so I stood alongside the crowd organizing my notes and reflecting on the developments of the past few months. Perhaps the biggest was that two lanes of the bridge over St. Louis Bay had reopened in May, finally reconnecting Bay St. Louis and Waveland to the rest of the Mississippi Gulf Coast. The new $267 million bridge was a sight to behold. Gone was the old draw span that used to back up traffic every time a tall boat passed. This bridge soared eighty-five feet high at the center and had a twelve-foot-wide path for pedestrians and cyclists. Bronze plaques with nature scenes created by local artists dotted its length, marking the distance to the shore on either end. The tedious forty-five-minute trek around the bay that residents had endured for almost two years was now replaced by a seven-minute drive. Just as important was the psychological relief that came with ending the isolation from the rest of the Gulf Coast community. Residents were so excited the day the bridge opened that they lined

up in their cars to be among the first to drive across.

Downtown, the first business had finally reopened on Beach Boulevard. The old Hancock Bank, where I'd opened my first savings account as a teenager, had started welcoming customers back in July. The damaged structure had been the source of much amusement to tourists, who frequently photographed its post-Katrina façade with the few letters remaining—"H__COCK BAN_." Now, the 107-year-old building, the flagship branch of the largest bank in Mississippi, was restored to its former beauty, complete with marble floors and vintage lighting. Even the old airtight vault was preserved, having survived the hurricane intact. The only thing the bank lacked was insurance. Rates were so high that it was self-insuring, betting it wouldn't suffer a serious loss. "It's very risky," admitted bank vice president John Baxter. "You have to take some chances sometimes to start a rebuilding process."

Traditional social events like reunions were resuming. I and other members of my Bay High graduating class met in June to celebrate at a local restaurant, Daniel's, which had recently reopened.

Normally, class reunions are sources of adult angst that people grudgingly attend. This evening had none of that. It was like being back in high school but without the teenage awkwardness, competition, and anxieties. Everyone simply relished being together again. I looked around and realized that nearly two years ago most people there had lost everything. Yet I saw no anger, no bitterness, no complaining—just a roomful of people happy to be alive. Even a classmate whose college-age son had nearly died after being bitten by one of the brown recluse spiders that flourished after Katrina was celebrating the simple fact he was starting to walk again. The evening was so perfect that no one wanted to leave. The fatigued owner finally shooed us out so he could lock up.

Neighborhoods were coming back to life. David and Angelyn Treutel, who lived in the devastated Cedar Point community, had finally moved back into their house the previous week. "It's still under construction. And we only have two beds and two chairs," said David with a laugh. "But we're just thankful to be out of the trailer."

I felt encouraged that CNN was updating Mississippi's status on the second anniversary because many still didn't understand it had even been impacted by the hurricane, much less that it caught the full brunt of Katrina. In fact, in the first Democratic presidential debate in April, I was surprised to hear Senator Barack Obama say the Bush administration had failed to mount an effective emergency response "when we had a hurricane in New Orleans." I had just sat next to the senator's deputy press secretary—a charming, enthusiastic young woman named Jen Psaki—at a black-tie dinner a week earlier. I dashed off an e-mail explaining the massive size of the hurricane and where it had dealt its most severe blow. She responded quickly.

Subject: Last Night/Katrina

Kathleen,

You raise a very good point and one that I am happy to pass along. I certainly don't think it was intentional on Barack's part, but many politicians are guilty of leaving out Mississippi and Alabama as you mentioned and that is not how it should be.

Thanks for your input.

Best,

Jen

I was relieved to see her answer. Only one presidential candidate, Arizona senator John McCain, had visited the Mississippi Gulf Coast, so I felt it was important that those who hadn't should have a clear understanding of what happened. After all, the next president would have to pick up the task of shepherding an entire three-state region through recovery from the greatest natural disaster in the nation's history.

Two young women stepped to the microphone to lead the crowd at the sunrise memorial in song as the sky warmed to a rosy peach. I focused my attention back on the present. Ministers came forward next. One observed that we were gathered "to remember the horror and to remember the hope." I regarded the tranquil scene and found myself nodding as he concluded, "All is not well. But God willing, your faith, your compassion, your sense of justice, all will be well."

Despite the positive developments, I had seen troubling changes on this trip home. Residents were bone tired. The exhaustion was etched into their faces. It had been two long years, and most had expected to be much farther along by now. The town still had no grocery store. Rental properties were scarce. No public housing had been rebuilt or repaired. Construction still hadn't begun on the sea wall or on Beach Boulevard downtown.

That fact frustrated many like Tony Trapani, the owner of Trapani's Eatery, which had operated in the waterfront building that once housed my family's ice-cream parlor. The restaurant was in a temporary location two miles inland, and he was not happy about it. "You know, we miss being on the water. We miss the activities of everybody having a beachfront-type atmosphere where you walk out and look at the water." Tony told me about his hope to someday open a two-story restaurant on the site of the old one. But until Beach Boulevard was complete, he could do nothing.

With the exception of Hancock Bank, the businesses operating in the old downtown were on side streets. Small business owners Joy Parks and Pam Collins had reopened their gift shop, Twin Light Creations, on Main Street in April. Their revenues were actually higher now than in 2005 before Katrina. But that didn't come close to making up for their increased insurance expense. "Before the storm, leasing a business and owning a home, our combined insurance was about eight thousand dollars a year," explained Pam. "Now, for less coverage than we had before, we're at thirty thousand dollars a year." All businesses in the area were in the same fix. Pam said most dealt with it by marking up prices. Others rolled the dice and operated underinsured.

Sales-tax revenues were almost back to pre-Katrina levels, so city finances were improving. Work was about to begin on a multiyear federally funded project to replace the city's crippled infrastructure. But as Bay St. Louis was coming back together structurally, Mayor Eddie Favre, still wearing shorts and living in a trailer, continued to fret about its missing residents. A third of the pre-Katrina population of eighty-two hundred hadn't returned. "Our biggest need is putting people in a position to come back. We're not getting people back home yet," he said. "They're not able to rebuild yet. And if they do, they can't afford the monthly insurance premium." In many cases, residents who had owned beautiful, gracious homes were instead rebuilding smaller houses they could afford to walk away from.

That's what had happened at my family's old property. The neighbors who had bought our beachfront home to use as a weekend getaway for their expanding family decided to rebuild small. They ordered a prefabricated steel house that arrived in sections and was lifted into place by cranes and bolted together like a life-sized Erector Set. It was supposed to withstand 155-miles-per-hour winds. When complete, it resembled the fishing camps raised on stilts that dotted the back roads between New Orleans and Bay St. Louis.

When I first saw the new house in June, I was less troubled by its appearance than by the disappearance of any trace of our old home. Crews had jack-hammered apart and hauled away the foundation, raked out the old shell driveway, and spread a heavy load of grass seed. I stood in the fresh green yard and tried to position myself where my room had been. I looked at the water, then to the west, and finally back toward where the pecan grove had been. Yes, this was the spot. Workers had stripped it so clean that even an archaeologist on a dig would have a hard time finding proof another home had ever stood here. I felt a strange knot in the pit of my stomach. It was like an episode of *The Twilight Zone*. My family had been erased.

As a child whose family moved constantly, I had always embraced change. It was new and exciting. And as a CNN general assignment correspondent, I loved the challenge of bouncing from beat to beat, from one story to the next. But Katrina was different. I started out like many on the Gulf Coast, wanting things rebuilt exactly as they had been, down to the last brick, board, and beam. But then I realized that was not just impractical, it was impossible. Construction costs were up roughly 30 percent, so rebuilding what had been was prohibitively expensive. Just as important was seizing this opportunity to not just rebuild the Mississippi Gulf Coast but to make it better. Still, I sometimes found it difficult to embrace the new, unfamiliar structures that appeared and the changing landscape they created. It meant acknowledging that the Bay St. Louis I grew up with now existed only in the memories of those who'd known and loved the town as I did.

Some people were able to see the charm, beauty, and strength in this new entity that was emerging. Troy Buck, the Marion, Indiana, firefighter who had been Waveland mayor Tommy Longo's right-hand man in the months after the storm, was preparing to move his entire family there. Most astonishing was the fact he'd fallen in love with the place when it was just a battered pile of rubble.

Producer Brian Rokus and I had run into Troy in November 2005 when he was first showing around his wife, Josie.

"You're thinking of moving here now?" I asked, incredulous.

"Well, Troy says the people here are something special," replied Josie. The dark-haired beauty seemed understandably uncertain about the prospect of moving to a disaster zone.

Troy had just finished placing their order with the Sonic waitress. We sat at the outdoor tables munching on the hot dogs and fries that at the time were some of the few food options available outside the church kitchens.

"I told her to just come. She'd see what I mean," Troy said. "I'd move here tomorrow if we could."

"Well, Troy, the little matter of finding a house could be a problem," Brian pointed out with a laugh.

"I know," said Troy. "We're just looking around right now."

True to his word, Troy had e-mailed this summer to announce the move was on.

Subject: It's a small world after all!

. . . After the first of the year you can reach me at this email, call 1411, just ask for Troy Buck in Waveland, or I will be the guy around 5 A.M. sitting between the War Memorial and the City Pier with *two* cups of coffee. See you there!

Troy Buck

The day before the second anniversary, Gene Taylor gave me a tour of his blue clapboard home on North Beach Boulevard. It was finally nearing completion. Though he had initially described it as a "throwaway house," he was not a man to give up easily and had used every engineering innovation available to ensure it would last. Tall cement columns were sunk two yards into the ground and anchored at the base by a foot-thick cement pad. The flooring was set on a diagonal to resist the torque of wind and wave action. Following the suggestion of a boatbuilder, he had run twelve-foot-long three-quarter-inch bolts from under the house up through the roof to hold it in place. "We went back and bolted everything from top to bottom, so it's literally tied to the columns or tied to these twelve-by-twelves," Gene said. The new house sat twenty-five feet above sea level, eleven feet higher than the one destroyed by Katrina. Inside, the two-bedroom home was a modest 1,350 square feet. Instead of sheetrock, the walls were cypress bead board, which was sturdier and more water resistant.

"Have you created an actual hurricane-proof house here?" I asked.

"No. I have made a hurricane-*resistant* house," he said. "I have done everything humanly possible so I don't have to go through this again."

Even the congressman was clearly fatigued by the ordeal of the last two years. "We are now where I wish we had been a year ago. You're starting to see some houses come back. The land really looked like it was hurtin' for a long time. All the trees were stressed. So many of them died. Everything was brown. And so, if you notice, things are starting to get green again. Those trees that made it are startin' to sprout out a little bit." He gestured to the south, where a cement-block foundation was rising from an otherwise vacant lot. "And you see, I'm the third house on this block goin' back up. So that's some good news. But again, here we are two years to the day of the storm and I'm only the third house on this block."

Gene believed the pace of rebuilding would pick up, since homeowners were finally beginning to get paid by their insurance companies. He himself had settled with State Farm earlier in the year. "Four or five lots that you passed, those people only got their checks this week. And that's 'cause they sued. And so that's gonna help. Now, people have some money."

But he echoed what I had heard from so many—building costs were up, and finding affordable insurance was nearly impossible. Before he dropped his policy with State Farm, the company had quadrupled his rates for fire and theft and cut out all wind coverage. Gene was still pushing hard for passage of his all-perils bill, so average people could buy both wind and flood insurance from the government and know they were protected. It had passed committee and would be voted on by the entire House of Representatives in September.

"Doing nothing is absolutely the worst thing. The federal government already did get stuck with the bill. It's not a matter of whether or not they're going to get stuck. The taxpayers already did get stuck with bills that the insurance companies should have paid," Gene said. "Remember, a typical homeowner policy says if you lose everything or if your house is uninhabitable, they put you up. They pay the rent. They find a place for you. And then they fix your house. So when they went on all these properties one at a time and said, 'We're not paying,' that not only meant they weren't paying to rebuild the house, they weren't paying for the cost of putting those people up. Who paid that? The taxpayers paid."

Lydia Schultz was still battling for payment for damage to the home she and Van had owned on Breeden Place. She told me she longed for the day it would be over. I knew the insurance fight made it even harder for her to move past Van's death. I wouldn't be seeing her on this anniversary. She and her daughters, Brooke and Marie, had been invited to be in the Chicago audience for Oprah Winfrey's live show on Katrina. Lydia was a fan. Though she and her daughters had to pay their own way, she called it a "chance of a lifetime." I was glad they would all be together on what for them was an extraordinarily difficult day.

Many found that the wounds from the loss of loved ones were healing slowly. At a memorial service at a tiny Bay St. Louis Baptist church that had been crushed by Hurricane Katrina, I met a short, sturdy woman named Linda Fallon, who wore her brown hair pulled back in a ponytail. She still remembered every detail of the day after the storm, when she had found her mother's lifeless body in the remains of her home after rescue workers relented and let her through. "People told me, 'Don't go back there! Everyone's dead.' And I said, 'Not my mama. She'll be alive.' And a man went back there with me. He wouldn't let me go alone. And I found her covered with mud from the storm surge. Her skin was still soft from the mud," she said quietly.

Linda described how the hurricane was still taking an emotional toll on the town, though many tried to hide it. "You see everybody's pain. You know, you look through people. And sometimes we cry alone. Sometimes we cry together. Sometimes we cry in a group. But we always hang in there."

I dreaded meeting two other women at the service. They were the sister and mother of Edgar Bane, who had died in his Waveland home along with his wife, Chrissy, and their disabled sons, twelve-year-old Carl and fifteen-year-old Edgar Jr. Chrissy's family had learned of their deaths when watching a CNN report showing a search-and-rescue team discovering the bodies. I was mortified that the story hadn't been held until the families were notified. But Rose Shaffer and Dorothy Prestenbach were less concerned about how family members had gotten the news than about how they were still impacted by the deaths.

Rose, Edgar's mother, said her other son, who still lived with her, was despondent over the loss of his brother. "He was thinking about committing suicide here awhile back because he missed his brother so much." She, meanwhile, was tormented by the thought that her son and his family had suffered. She wondered whether or not in the afterlife they were now at peace. "I wonder where they are. If they're okay. It's terrible. Just terrible." Her mouth opened in a silent cry.

Edgar's sister, Dorothy, found the debris, the empty lots, and other ever-present reminders of Katrina obstacles to her emotional recovery. "Everybody says, 'Get on with it.' We really can't get on with it when everything's still messed up around here. We're trying our best."

The pastor of Calvary Independent Baptist Church tried to keep his flock focused on the bright side, like the volunteers who helped repair the church and the pastors who had come to help minister in the weeks and months after the hurricane. But now, two years later, he admitted hope was getting harder to come by. "It's difficult, it is, to try to convince them that things are going to get better," said Pastor David MacDonald. "And they are. But it's the waiting that's the hardest part."

While some grieved together, others mourned privately. Nikki and Patrick Cleveland drove to the mausoleum on Longfellow Road to place flowers on her parents' crypt. Patrick stayed in the car with one-year-old Emma on the brutally hot day. Nikki got out and stood alone next to the still-unmarked crypt, thinking how much she could have used her parents' support right now.

It had been a difficult summer. Patrick found himself increasingly exhausted by his work as a large-animal vet. "I have a pretty demanding job, so I'll ignore a certain amount of fatigue. But I was bone weary all the time." He developed a rash under his right arm that wouldn't go away, and the lymph node there started to swell. After a July x-ray, CAT scan, and biopsy, Patrick was diagnosed with Hodgkin's lymphoma, a cancer of the immune system.

Every other week, Nikki drove him to Mobile for his four-hour chemotherapy treatments. Sometimes the anti-nausea drugs worked, and sometimes they didn't. She dreaded the trips home as Patrick slept, her handsome husband's now-bald head leaning against the window while his face turned shades of green and yellow. *Please stay asleep*, she would pray, hoping to get him home and safely into bed before the powerful concoction killing the cancer turned his stomach inside out.

Little Emma was unfazed by Patrick's odd appearance, though she didn't understand why she no longer had free access to her parents' bedroom. Nikki was determined to keep Emma from seeing how sick her father was and to ensure Patrick got much-needed rest. She found that when she could barely keep going, the energetic blue-eyed toddler would stretch her arms up for a hug and smile her gummy smile, and problems would melt away.

In the car waiting while Nikki paid her respects on the anniversary, Patrick, too, was grateful for their daughter's bright spirit. The nonstop motion machine motivated him to fight the disease that he suspected was somehow connected to all the water he had inhaled while fighting Katrina's storm surge.

I was relieved to see that fighting spirit on display at a morning ceremony at the beachfront Veterans Memorial in Waveland. A crowd of roughly a hundred gathered on the bulkhead jutting into the Mississippi Sound, sleeves rolled up, downing bottled water and swapping stories of where they had each been two years earlier.

Judee English, a twenty-year resident of Waveland, told me how after the storm subsided she'd walked from Highway 90 down to Coleman Avenue, where she owned a business. "When I walked over the railroad tracks and saw everything leveled, I was just shocked. And it's somethin' I'll never forget, you know, when you just see everything crumbled."

She tucked her curly strawberry blond hair under her visor and said she wasn't troubled by the fact that most of America had moved on and didn't know about Mississippi's long slog back to normalcy. "I guess it's understandable. That's the way I look at it. People have their own lives. We're strong down here. We're dealing with it every day, and we're progressing forward. And it just takes time. Like they say, Rome wasn't built in a day, you know."

Judee proudly pointed out that it had taken her just four months to get her business up and running again, though she was still in a FEMA trailer and fighting her insurance carrier to pay for wind damage to her home. She refused to complain, instead offering advice she had learned the hard way: "You honestly need to live every day and enjoy every day. You can lose it all. Anybody can lose it all anywhere. It doesn't have to be a hurricane. So I just tell people, 'Appreciate what you have. Go see the people you need to see. Don't put it off.' "

Waveland assistant fire chief Mike Smith had eight feet of water in his home. "It seems like it's been forever. But it seems like

~Only the top floor remained of this Waveland house overlooking Judee English's tarp-covered slab.
Photo by Mark Proulx

only yesterday, if that makes sense," he said, struggling to express his thoughts on the anniversary. "Probably the most frustrating part is the slow recovery. But it was an unprecedented event." Mike praised the dedication of volunteers like those who had rebuilt his parents' home in the tiny Shoreline Park community. "That part of it is wonderful. The nation needs to know that even though this is two years, there's still a need for volunteers down here. Because there are people that fell through the cracks totally, that's after two years still living in a FEMA trailer. I can't hardly fathom that."

In fact, a second-anniversary review by the Gulf Coast Business Council reported that, while twenty-seven thousand trailer recipients had found other shelter, sixteen thousand Mississippians still had nowhere else to live. The report blamed not only a lack of affordable housing but also the shortage of affordable and available insurance. Still, the roughly half-million volunteers who had poured into the area over the last two years were making a difference. FEMA had managed to remove more than 46 million cubic yards of debris, more than three times the amount left behind by Hurricane Andrew in Florida in 1992. But a logjam remained in federal funds for repairing hospitals, schools, infrastructure, and public buildings. Only 43 percent of the money had been spent.

The crowd buzzed over news that the man to talk to about those issues, President George W. Bush, would be back in Waveland and Bay St. Louis that very day to meet with local politicians and business leaders. Mayor Tommy Longo stepped to the podium to give a taste of what they would tell the president. "We're not complaining. We're fighting every day. We get up and the first question is not, you know, 'What's the state giving us today?' or 'What is the federal government going to give us today?' We get up and we go to work. And each day, we end up a little better than we started. And we're just asking for the federal government to remember us and help our citizens make their lives whole again."

An hour after the ceremony ended, the presidential motorcade zipped past the Veterans Memorial. I was glad that, just as on his first visit, the president was being driven down the beach and would see the area where recovery was the slowest. Weeds had by now grown waist-high on most of the former homesites, obscuring the empty slabs. Sprouting almost as fast were For Sale signs, many of them tacked to the empty columns protruding from the brush.

A few residents came out of their FEMA trailers to watch Bush's black limousine, its American flags waving. And just a few dozen were on hand to hear the president's remarks after his meeting in Our Lady of the Gulf Church's community center. The president said he was impressed with the "can-do attitude" of people at what he called "Ground Zero." "We've got a lot of work to do. These two mayors brought their problems to us. People are worried about insurance here. They're worried about bureaucracy. . . . And obviously we've got some more issues that we're trying to work through." Bush promised more federal help and vowed the region would be better than before.

One report suggested it was just a carefully scripted photo op. But most people I knew were buoyed that the president had remembered Mississippi. These days, they relished any encouragement they could get and avoided the negative, even down to the routes they drove through town. "You know, you can drive down certain streets and never see anything destroyed. Everything looks just fine," explained my high-school classmate John Wilkerson. "So you can arrange your routes so it appears the storm never struck."

"But then he says, 'Let's go driving down the beach or to Cedar Point,' " said his wife, Mary Ann. "And I ask, 'Are you trying to depress me?' "

Linda Kidd was ready to move on. She and Tommy were back in their vinyl-sided home on the bayou, the new main floor and open kitchen decorated in calming tones of antique beige and white. The night of the anniversary, the two proudly prepared a seafood feast for me and my producer, Brian Rokus. The scene was a sharp contrast to the mangled, muddy mess we'd both seen on our first visit to their home.

We were about to sit down to dinner when Linda got a call from their son.

"Mama, remember where we were and what we were doing two years ago?"

"I don't want to," said Linda. "I don't want to look back. It's too hard. It's over."

As we returned to Washington, I wondered when it would really be over. How long would it take Mississippians to rebuild and find peace?

Peace, it turned out, would remain elusive. Less than a month after President Bush praised the resilience of local citizens and committed to helping the region rebuild, the Corps of Engineers announced a massive voluntary federal buyout to convert flood-prone Mississippi Gulf Coast neighborhoods into public wetlands or recreation areas. The plan targeted seventeen thousand homes, more than ten thousand of them in Hancock County. It would encompass more than half the landmass in Bay St. Louis.

The news stunned the town. Residents and businesses in the buyout zone who had rebuilt worried they'd wasted valuable time and money. Those in the safe areas wondered if the town could survive such a huge loss of tax dollars. Those who hadn't yet rebuilt—from homeowners to businesses to developers—were suddenly in limbo.

"It's kind of got everything on hold right now," a frustrated Eddie Favre observed. "It's a bad situation."

The federal government had used buyouts to remove tens of thousands of homes from danger after floods in the Midwest in 1993, in some cases moving entire cities. But buyouts normally were offered soon after a disaster, before people started to rebuild. Some Mississippi residents said they would have considered the offer earlier, but not now. I myself had asked the mayor right after the storm if some hard-hit areas shouldn't be rebuilt. He had said possible changes might include limitations on certain types of development in certain areas. But as months turned into years and no buyout option was even mentioned, the focus instead turned to the alternative—rebuilding higher, stronger, and smarter.

I was furious at the mixed signals being sent by the federal government. The president came, patted everyone on the back, and said, "Keep up the good work," and before the motorcade's dust settled the Corps of Engineers followed with, "Please leave"? It was ludicrous!

The sucker punch from the federal government was followed by a body blow from the courts. In September and November, the Fifth

Circuit Court of Appeals overturned Judge L. T. Senter, Jr.'s ruling striking down insurance companies' "anti-concurrent cause" clauses. The ruling meant that in homeowner policies that included such clauses, residents could collect payment only for hurricane damage they could prove was caused by wind alone. Many homeowners on the Gulf Coast gave up and decided to settle.

Fortunately, Lydia Schultz's attorney had come to terms with her insurance company before the rulings. Lydia was ecstatic.

Subject: Smile!

. . . They are sending the checks out next week. They have even lowered their fee!!!!!! Unheard of in this day. I keep sending them good, positive blessings. I see and know that angels have been with me always. Sometimes their work is more evident than at other times. It's fun when you can feel and see it.

Smiles,

Lydia

Nikki and Patrick Cleveland had given up their struggle with Nationwide Insurance shortly after Patrick was diagnosed with cancer. Their settlement was far less than what their coverage had promised, but it gave them closure. "He got all upset that he would leave me and Emma with all this stuff hanging," said Nikki. "We did it to give Patrick peace."

Many Gulf Coast residents clung to the hope that such battles could become a thing of the past. On September 27, the House of Representatives passed by a vote of 263–146 Congressman Gene Taylor's all-perils bill, which would allow residents to buy both wind and flood coverage in a single policy from the federal government. The fiscally conservative Blue Dog Democrat thanked his colleagues for taking a step to give some security to the 52 percent of Americans who lived in coastal regions. "This is creating a program where the nation won't have to ride to the rescue next time," said Gene. "Because people will have bought the insurance ahead of time in a program that pays for itself, in a program that says, 'If you built it right, you pay your premiums, and an act of God destroys your house, you're gonna get paid.' I can't think of anything that's more fiscally responsible. I can't think of anything that's more right for the citizens."

Now, all the congressman and his supporters needed was for the bill to be passed by the Senate and signed by the president.

They would have a long wait.

~20~

Third Anniversary

AT SIX-THIRTY IN THE MORNING, courier Nelson Archer dropped the thick stack of newspapers dated August 29, 2008, on the chair next to me in the cramped CNN booth in the basement of the White House. "There you go!"

"Thanks," I replied, staring intently at the tropical weather report on the computer screen in front of me.

"Where's the smile? What's got you so down this early in the morning?"

"Sorry, Nelson." I turned and forced a brief smile for the ever-amiable gentleman who daily lugged papers, mail, tapes, and more between the various D.C. beats and the main bureau. "I'd just rather not be here today."

I cut the plastic band and started sorting through the newspapers, noting that not a single front page mentioned this was the third anniversary of Hurricane Katrina.

It wasn't that I didn't enjoy being assigned to the White House. After all, it was the most prestigious beat in the network. But I didn't like covering it to the exclusion of all else, and that's precisely what I had been doing since November 2007. I was asked to fill in for three months while White House correspondent Suzanne Malveaux went on the road to cover the presidential campaign. But three months turned into six months, and now it was clear I wouldn't be free until after the election in November.

Today, Republican presidential candidate John McCain announced he had chosen Alaska governor Sarah Palin as his running mate. On the political front, that was the story of the day. Meanwhile, on the Mississippi Gulf Coast, a flurry of preparations was under way as the first hurricane since 2005 threatened the area. Gustav had already strafed Haiti with seventy-five-miles-per-hour winds, killing fifty-nine people. The hurricane was headed toward Cuba and the warm waters of the Gulf of Mexico, where it was expected to strengthen.

Rather than marking Katrina's third anniversary, people in Bay St. Louis were packing and leaving. David and Angelyn Treutel were heading to his sister Missy's house near Mobile, Alabama. They had established a backup location for their independent insurance office there on high ground, where they could handle phone calls, process claims, and access their computer files if their new Bay St. Louis office was damaged.

Linda Kidd had driven to Long Beach to stay with Tommy's brother and sister-in-law. Their neighborhood, located at a high elevation, was one of the few that hadn't flooded in Katrina, so she felt safe there. "I got Linda out of here quick as I could," said Tommy, who planned to stay at their house and keep an eye out for looters. "She was ready to go. She's not quite as adaptable as I am. I can deal with it."

Nikki and Patrick Cleveland and my high-school classmate Diane Bourgeois and her husband, Gene, all lived in the county more than sixteen miles north of the water. Though not out of reach of tornadoes, they all felt reassured now that their difficult decision to leave Bay St. Louis had been the right one.

Since the threat Gustav presented was still unclear, firefighter Monte Strong had to work. Danielle and their three children planned to seek refuge with friends in the northern part of the county. The husband had shown up with a huge trailer, and they were busy packing everything they could carry, down to the barbecue grill and patio furniture. Danielle walked through each room, digging in closets and drawers to make certain she wasn't leaving behind something

important. "Anything that was sentimental that was in the house, we packed up, unlike the last time. Every framed picture, I went throughout the whole house and took 'em all down," she said when I called to check on the family. Next to the death of their dogs, Danielle found the loss of irreplaceable family mementos the hardest to bear. "I have zero. I have no childhood pictures of me. Nothing. I lost everything I had, all my high-school stuff. The kids lost everything. I don't want to do that again."

As my friends in Bay St. Louis prepared to leave, I managed to negotiate my way back to the Gulf Coast. The Republican National Convention would be under way in St. Paul, Minnesota, all week. After his speech there Monday night, President Bush would follow tradition and make no further public appearances until it was over. So I persuaded CNN that I would be of more value to the network covering Hurricane Gustav than sitting at the White House doing nothing. I would be one of two CNN reporters in Mississippi, while twenty would be positioned in Louisiana.

Everyone was taking this hurricane seriously. By Saturday, Mississippi officials were already announcing evacuations, school closings, and shelter locations for Monday, when Gustav was expected to make landfall. The Bush administration, wary of repeating its Katrina missteps, not only pre-positioned resources and emergency teams up and down the Gulf Coast but sent Homeland Security secretary Michael Chertoff and FEMA director David Paulison to meet with officials in the threatened region. The president declared a state of emergency from Alabama to Texas. By Sunday, Republican presidential candidate John McCain suspended most activities at the GOP convention for the following day because of Hurricane Gustav, now a dangerous Category 3 storm.

As I sat Sunday on the near-empty plane to Gulfport, I was relieved that so many people were leaving. Some three million residents were expected to flee the Gulf Coast, making this the largest evacuation in United States history. An easy camaraderie prevailed among the passengers on the flight, everyone eagerly sharing why they were flying toward, and not away from, the storm.

"We're trying to get there, babe!" I heard a middle-aged couple behind me assuring their daughter on the phone before takeoff. Mark and Julie Kael had cut short their trip to Europe to race back to be with their daughter and newborn grandchild, who had evacuated to Lacombe, Louisiana. The Kaels had lost their home in St. Bernard Parish in Hurricane Katrina. The trip back would be tough, now that the highways out of the Louisiana coastal parishes were on contraflow, all lanes carrying traffic north. But the cheerful couple told me they knew the back roads. "We'll make it," they said. "After what we've been through, this is nothing."

Another group of vacationers, best friends Joy, Starr, and Marsha, chatted about their game plan. Hurricane Gustav had interrupted the young women's "girls' weekend" in Fort Lauderdale, Florida. The ground-floor apartment Joy and Starr shared in the small Mississippi town of D'Iberville had flooded in Katrina. This time, they weren't taking any chances. They'd retrieve their cats, Simba and Oreo, and ride out the hurricane at Marsha's house away from the water north of I-10.

As I listened to their stories, I could tell the spirit on the flight was different from what I'd encountered three years earlier in flying south to cover Katrina. Then, I had noted a distinct sense of foreboding. This was a plane of survivors.

I realized I was a different person, too. I'd let go of the guilt. I was starting to embrace the change Katrina had forced on the Gulf Coast. I was still working on making peace with God, trusting, and having faith again. But I was stronger and wiser. After what I'd been through with Katrina, I knew I could face anything. I also had a new respect for even a "small" Category 3 storm, since that had been Hurricane Katrina's classification just before it blasted ashore near the Louisiana/Mississippi border.

I felt sorry for the other journalist on the flight, Weather Channel meteorologist Mike Seidel. Passengers continually prodded him for details on where Gustav was headed. Would it strengthen or weaken? How bad would conditions get on the Mississippi Gulf Coast?

Just in case, the military was beefing up its numbers. Our flight included plenty of men and women in uniform. They were a reassuring presence, since the United States military had been the star performers after Hurricane Katrina, rescuing residents, clearing roads, airlifting in food and water, and maintaining order.

When we deplaned, the flight attendant replaced her usual scripted farewell with a simple, "Be safe."

As I waited at the luggage carousel for my bags, I noticed Joy standing alone, pensive. "Joy, is everything okay?" I asked. She and her friends had been so upbeat when I talked to them earlier.

She shook her head. "I sat in the back of the plane crying my eyes out," she said, though in true Mississippi style she insisted she wasn't complaining. "We're blessed. But I don't want to do this again."

Her plaintive reply echoed the sentiments of most along the Gulf Coast. They had come so far. People were finally moving back into their homes. The nonprofit organization KaBOOM! had just completed its one hundredth playground in the hurricane zone, returning to Bay St. Louis, where its initiative began back in 2005. The week before, the generous Jackson volunteers from Wells Church had made their twenty-second trip to Hancock County. In total, they had helped rebuild more than fifty houses. Even Lydia Schultz had finally made the decision to move back to the Gulf Coast, though to Picayune, a town well inland. No one wanted to contemplate losing it all again.

As my crew and I pulled out of the airport in our rental cars, I glanced at my watch. *Damn!* It was five o'clock. We'd be scrambling to find any supplies at this hour on a Sunday afternoon. We drove north, but storefronts on both sides of Highway 49 were already boarded up. Mississippi National Guard forces in Humvees rolled down the streets. Lines snaked around the few filling stations still open, people stocking up on gas and ice in case the power went out. I was worried because we had to find our own food and water, enough to last three or four days. Finally, we located a pharmacy and a convenience store that still had some food on the shelves. We snapped up the canned goods, peanut butter, bread, juice, and water that remained and headed for the hotel as Gustav's first rain bands began pummeling the coast.

We woke early to a torrential downpour, fierce winds at times whipping the rain sideways. The hurricane was moving northwest and was now expected to hit the Louisiana coast southwest of New Orleans by midmorning. Some areas there were already report-ing ninety-one-miles-per-hour winds and a nine-foot storm surge. Though most attention was focused to the west, CNN's evening show, *AC 360°*, still wanted a story on damage in Mississippi. Nor-mally during a hurricane, I was tethered to a camera doing live reports in one spot. This time, we'd head out into the storm and record what was happening.

All eight of Biloxi's casinos had closed—and for good reason, as we found when we arrived at the beach. The sound had disappeared under the surf. Highway 90 was submerged under at least two feet of water. We videotaped the flooded casino row and proceeded west to see how much of the highway was inundated. The water quickly deepened to the point I could no longer see a trace of pavement anywhere ahead. Highway 90 looked like a raging river, waves tum-bling across the surface. I slowed the SUV to a stop and called our sound technician, Barry Schlegal, who was driving behind us.

"Barry, this looks pretty deep. I can't tell if the road's washed out or not."

"Well, Burke's going to get out and get some shots here. He'll check it out," he replied.

Cameraman Burke Buckhorn stepped out into the driving rain

in his blue vinyl slicker to videotape the crashing waves and the stop sign on the corner that flapped stiffly back and forth in the wind. Then, camera in hand, he slogged into the swirling water in front of us. I held my breath, praying he wouldn't step into a hole or be swept off his feet. Burke swayed slightly as the surge tugged at his legs, then waved us forward.

We turned off the highway and into a neighborhood where the winds had toppled a massive tree onto a one-story white-brick house. Fortunately, no one was hurt, since the owners had evacuated. Neighbor Missy Massey told me she was relieved the hurricane was headed west. "They can have it," the redhead said, waving her hand as if pushing the storm along. "That's ugly, but we can send it somewhere else. I don't mind."

We headed toward north Biloxi, where police reported some neighborhoods had been cut off by the rising water. A twenty-four-hour curfew was in effect, leaving emergency vehicles our only company on the deserted roadways. As we approached, I thought nothing of the police car sitting at the base of the Popps Ferry Bridge over Biloxi's Back Bay. If crossing was dangerous, the vehicle would have blocked the drawbridge, I reasoned. But as we started creeping across, gale-force winds buffeted the SUV, pushing it from side to side. I struggled to stay not just in my lane but on the bridge. As the road arched higher, I swore I could feel the bridge shaking. I remembered reading a local emergency alert about some bridges being closed due to high winds. Why hadn't the police stopped us? I was shaking when we finally reached the other side.

My producer, Beth Hall, slowly exhaled. "Whew!"

"We won't go back that way," I assured her.

Unable to find the flooded neighborhoods, we turned west to Gulfport. Downtown, the entire brick façade of a building vacant since Katrina had collapsed into the street. Several businesses, including a filling station, had lost their roofs. Signs were ripped from buildings and poles, and flying debris had smashed the windows of several businesses, leaving the interiors exposed to wind and rain.

We continued west into Long Beach, where we found utility crews already out disentangling tree limbs from lines and starting to restore power to the sixty-four thousand Mississippi households without electricity. Just as in Katrina, the damage worsened the farther west we drove. At the height of the storm, conditions from Long Beach to Waveland were so bad that police were pulled in off the streets. As we drove, Burke and Barry listened nervously to the emergency radio transmitter's warnings about tornadoes hopscotching the area and about the potential for loss of life if anyone left shelter. The wind occasionally sent pieces of sheet metal and other debris hurtling down the road. We sometimes had to replot our course when streets were blocked by downed trees or water. But for the most part, Beth and I didn't think we were taking unnecessary risks.

I was, though, worried about Hancock County. Fifty-miles-per-hour sustained winds had been reported, along with an eleven-foot storm surge. Emergency teams had already rescued three people from the inundated Jordan River Shores neighborhood. And just like in Biloxi, several feet of water covered the beach road.

Phones were working, so I was able to reach both Bay St. Louis mayor Eddie Favre and Waveland mayor Tommy Longo.

"It's a whole lot better than it could have been," said Eddie, relieved. Though numerous trees, branches, and power lines were down, leaving twenty-six thousand county residents in the dark, city hall still had electricity. And no lives had been lost.

"Everything's going fine. Everything's come through okay," Tommy assured me. Both cities had some flooded homes and wind damage, but nothing that couldn't be repaired.

However, when we tried to reach Bay St. Louis, we discovered it was cut off. Winds were much too strong for anyone to use the new eighty-five-foot-high Bay Bridge. And Route 603, which ran from I-10 to Bay St. Louis, was covered with several feet of water from the swollen Jordan River. Highway patrol officers blocking traffic from heading south said the surge had also swept debris left over from Hurricane Katrina out of nearby woods and onto the roadway. "It's a mess down there," said one officer as he waved traffic to turn around.

We shot the closed roadway and headed back east to Pass Christian, where we'd be doing our live report for *AC360°*. Police there had plucked the occupants from a swamped car that was now floating down Highway 90. The town's small-craft harbor was severely damaged. We arrived to find a sailboat, three massive fishing boats, pilings, and other debris shoved ashore by Gustav's storm surge blocking the harbor access road. Harbor master Willie Davis was almost in tears as he described how $2 million in federal, state, and local funds had been spent repairing the port after Katrina. The work was nearly complete, and the fleet was due to sail out for the start of oyster season that very day. "This thing here's really going to affect a lot of jobs for a lot of people, 'cause all the seafood dealers and all the shrimpers and, you know, oyster people and stuff like that, they're not going to be able to go back to work right now, when they should be going to work today. So there's a lot of people gonna be affected by it just right here in the seafood industry."

The overhauled harbor had been built to withstand storms. Officials said much of the damage was due to boats left behind by owners who ignored evacuation orders. The vessels became battering rams, bashing apart piers and smashing into one another. Three sank and now clogged the harbor, along with several temporary trailers swept into the water by the high winds. The harbor master predicted it could take weeks, if not months, to dredge and reopen the port to boat traffic.

We did our live report that night with a fishing boat, *Garrett's Dream*, beached precariously on the road behind me. It was now a symbol of dreams delayed. I repeated Mississippi governor Haley Barbour's warning to citizens not to try to return until Wednesday morning, in order to give crews time to clear blocked roads and restore power. In fact, so much debris covered the harbor area that our satellite truck had to park on a nearby hill, forcing Burke and Barry to run power and camera cables across the closed four-lane highway. The scene brought back memories of the morning after Katrina, when we had wandered the same highway in Gulfport, empty of traffic and blocked by mangled truck trailers.

Exhausted after our fourteen-hour day, we returned to the hotel. As it turned out, most CNN reporters in Louisiana were positioned far from where Gustav had dealt its heaviest blow. That night, we were the only team with significant hurricane damage to show. Envious colleagues in Louisiana e-mailed.

Subject: Great story!!

You showed way more damage than we've seen all day! And your love for the gulf coast always shines through. . . .

Susy

Subject: Nice Piece on Gustav!

Wish I had been with you guys. . . . I didn't get much storm action! Good piece!

Mark L. Walz

It was great to be back on the Gulf Coast and able to tell Mississippi's story again. I had resigned myself to the fact that one facet of that story would always be the struggle for survival. But with each storm here—just as after every mud slide and earthquake in California, every forest fire in the West, every punishing nor'easter in New England—people learned. They found new, creative ways to protect lives and property. And if they couldn't bear the risk, they left.

The crew departed for Washington the next day, while I headed to the Carolinas to chase Tropical Storm Hanna. It was invigorating to be on the road again. I was counting down the days until I would be free from the White House, able to pursue a variety of stories again and find new ways to cover Mississippi's post-Katrina journey.

Less than four months later, I got my wish—sort of. Networks and local stations that had busted their budgets covering the long, dramatic presidential campaign were cutting back. In the news business, the pink slips often come at the holidays. So, as the year ended, I was free of the White House—and the news network that had been my home since 1991.

~21~

Fourth Anniversary and Beyond

THE NEW BELL TOWER AND STEEPLE on Main Street United Methodist Church stretched into the bright blue sky as if trying to pierce the billowing clouds that drifted overhead. The copper was still a pristine brown, unlike its weathered predecessor that Hurricane Katrina had flung into the street four years earlier. The long, black tapered structure with its green patina lay on the ground in front of the church for more than a year, a hand-painted sign cautioning cleanup crews, "Do Not Remove Steeple."

The placard was to ensure against a repeat of the "Great Steeple Rescue." Everyone in town knew the story. Days after the hurricane, a bulldozer was about to push the tower aside and dispose of it along with other debris blocking the roadway. Harold Carver, a church elder who owned a clothing store on the corner opposite the church, sprang from his seat there and begged the man operating the bulldozer to stop. The worker, bent on clearing the street, waved him off. But Harold wasn't about to give up. He stepped into his store and returned brandishing a pistol. That got the dozer operator's attention. "Where do you want it?" he asked, chastened. The determined shopkeeper had then watched as the machine carefully lifted the steeple out of the road and onto the grass in front of the church.

~A 2005 PHOTO OF MAIN STREET UNITED METHODIST CHURCH'S MISSING
STEEPLE
Photo by Mark Proulx

"He was looking out for the church and all the history that was being swept away," said then-pastor Rick Brooks.

At the August dedication of the new spire, held on the weekend of the hurricane's fourth anniversary, the eighty-two-year-old shopkeeper was first in line to receive a print of the church framed in wood from the original steeple. Unfortunately, the spire couldn't be repaired. But the church had it re-created in every detail, down to the small, unassuming cross on top. The new structure was carefully engineered to withstand future storms. "We didn't just recover what we had, we recovered something even better," explained current pastor Heather Hensarling. "From an engineering perspective. Better, too, because of the story. The story has been enriched even more."

For almost four years, the church's truncated roofline, like the plywood covering the doors and windows of the county courthouse next door, were visible reminders of what Katrina had taken away.

Now, as I squinted up at the new steeple, I saw the old, familiar downtown skyline returning. The historic ninety-eight-year-old courthouse, where I covered my first trial as a novice reporter, had finally reopened after extensive renovations to repair the damage from the hurricane's winds and storm surge.

I was there to explore both the town's progress toward recovery and my own. I wanted to discover some meaning in what we'd been through. Maybe by putting it all down on paper, I would find healing, even closure.

Now that I was no longer at CNN, I was able to focus on this new project. I hated leaving but realized that, given the long hours that were the norm at the network, I would never have had time to write a book. So far, though, no publisher wanted to gamble on the little town's story. I decided that if Bay St. Louis hadn't quit in the face of Katrina, how could I after a few rejections?

I found a building boom under way. A new firehouse was springing up on Main Street not far from the new city hall on Highway 90. Ground had just been broken for a forty-two-home Habitat for Humanity project to provide housing for seniors, low-income families, and people with disabilities. Work was due to start soon on a

~THE NEWLY RENOVATED HANCOCK COUNTY COURTHOUSE
Photo by Kathleen Koch

new community hall, a plan spearheaded by Rotary clubs in Mississippi, Arkansas, and Louisiana. All around town, crews were busy replacing the broken infrastructure. The work turned the roads into muddy obstacle courses, but it was progress.

Across the Mississippi Gulf Coast, construction crews were erecting or renovating libraries, city halls, senior citizen centers, police and fire stations, piers, marinas, and more. Cities were racing to meet a September 1, 2009, start deadline for any Katrina projects paid for with federal Community Development Block Grants.

I was relieved to finally see such momentum. At the same time, I knew much remained undone. I drove around Bay St. Louis during the fourth anniversary week noting the contrasts.

Highway 90 was packed again with bustling restaurants and businesses. But the town still had no grocery store. The Winn-Dixie shopping center sat largely empty. Stubborn weeds sprouting through the cement foundation were the only signs of life at the boarded-up Pump and Save gas station. Students at North Bay Elementary were still attending classes in portable trailers as the school district fought to get FEMA to fund repairs to city schools.

The arts community in the old downtown was coming back,

~THE WATERFRONT SITE OF TRAPANI'S EATERY AND THE KOCH FAMILY'S OLD ICE-CREAM PARLOR
Photo by Kathleen Koch

hoping to help Bay St. Louis regain its 2001 ranking as one of *USA Today*'s "top ten best small art towns in America." But walk down Main Street to the water and the Hancock Bank was still the lone business open. Only a plucky placard with a broadly smiling stick figure flipping burgers marked Trapani's old waterfront location. Since Beach Boulevard was still under construction, a sign directed visitors inland to shop Main Street and "relive the memories of Old Town."

Tommy Kidd's daughter, Kelyn, had reopened the restaurant with a new name—The West End. The walls were covered with years of Mardi Gras photos donated by the Krewe of Nereids, something customers who'd lost all their personal photos appreciated. But business was slow, since the storm-damaged shopping center next door was still completely vacant.

I found that one house my family had mucked out during our 2005 Thanksgiving volunteer trip had been turned into a realty office. Painted a soft sand tone, the walls inside were now covered not with mold and crumbling sheetrock but the work of local artists. But across town in Cedar Point, I was stunned to discover Gayle Jordan's brick home sitting just as we'd left it. Plywood still covered

~THE EMPTY BEACH BOULEVARD STILL UNDER CONSTRUCTION FOUR YEARS
AFTER HURRICANE KATRINA
Photo by Kathleen Koch

the front door and window. Old toilets, sinks, and wiring collected dust next to a blue dumpster outside. I peeked in and saw bare sub-floor and walls that were still just two-by-fours. I wondered what happened. We had worked so hard, and the interfaith minister had been so determined to repair her hurricane-ravaged home.

Around the corner on Boardman Avenue, a wide concrete walk-way leading up to a rectangular stoop was the only remaining trace of the Bay St. Louis Little Theatre. The otherwise empty lot was now enveloped in waist-high weeds.

The acting troupe had relocated across town, buying a long-vacant century-old building that had been the backdrop of director Sydney Pollack's *This Property Is Condemned*. The 1966 movie star-ring Robert Redford and Natalie Wood was shot in Bay St. Louis, where Tennessee Williams had written the one-act play. The local actors were determined to save the ivy-choked structure, one of the last historic buildings left in town after Katrina. But they had all lost everything, so raising money for the renovation was a challenge. "We had to somehow, through our tragedy and our grief and our time spent rebuilding our lives, we had to make sure the theater came back as well," said Cheryl Grace, president of the theater's board of directors. "We had to! We could not disappoint. It's part of the fabric of the community."

I asked Cheryl about the ceramic comedy and tragedy masks and the banner with the 1946 founding date that I'd seen in the rub-ble of the theater. "We found it!" she assured me. "It's underneath my guest bed. We're going to put it back into the theater once the theater's built."

I drove to another important place, Nicholson Avenue. Like other main thoroughfares to the water, it had been repaved. I was in-spired to see the resilient live oaks heavy with leaves, their branches again reaching toward one another across the allée. A few homes had been rebuilt. But vacant, overgrown lots prevailed. Owners had posted stern No Trespassing and Private Property signs on the sur-viving trees, steps, and broken bits of foundation.

In the residential areas of Beach Boulevard north and south of downtown, more homes were popping up. Most, like Congressman Gene Taylor's house and the one on my family's old property, were

~Nicholson Avenue in Waveland
Photo by Kathleen Koch

~One of the hundreds of still-empty homesites
in Bay St. Louis
Photo by Kathleen Koch

raised fifteen to twenty feet on columns. In between, the former homesites and residual debris were nearly completely obscured by vegetation.

As I drove around town, I noticed several homes that appeared vacant, some with bits of blue FEMA tarp still covering the wind-damaged roofs and cars with flattened tires rusting in the driveways. New Bay St. Louis mayor Les Filingame explained that they were among the roughly 250 abandoned properties homeowners had simply walked away from, temporarily or permanently. "It's a really big problem," he said.

Half were salvageable, so the city boarded them up in hopes the owners would eventually return and fix them. The rest needed to be torn down. But that was costly for a city still missing 20 percent of its population. And Bay St. Louis wasn't alone. Governor Haley Barbour's fourth-anniversary report on Katrina recovery found that a fifth of the 52,512 homes damaged or destroyed on the Mississippi Gulf Coast hadn't been repaired or rebuilt.

The house at 928 South Beach Boulevard where Nikki and Patrick Cleveland had ridden out the storm and where her parents had died was among those that looked much as they had after Katrina

~An abandoned hurricane-damaged house in Bay St. Louis
Photo by Kathleen Koch

hit. The garage and the arched breezeway to the now-missing front door protruded from the sea of weeds and vines that swamped the property. The sturdy river-rock fireplace remained, a beam near the top marking where the roofline had once been. Around the perimeter, the rusted steel rebar was bent like strands of metal spaghetti in the direction the hurricane had torn the fourteen-inch-thick concrete walls. The physical evidence of the storm's force still took my breath away.

I visited Nikki and Patrick at their home in the north of the county to find out how they were doing and what was happening with her parents' property. Patrick had fully recovered from Hodgkin's lymphoma. Little Emma, a rambunctious three-year-old, dashed through the house, chattering and curious. Nikki was pregnant again, her slight, graceful frame accentuated by her growing belly.

Her parents' house was still owned by the estate because the three siblings couldn't decide how to dispose of it. "It's difficult to divide evenly three ways without selling it," said Patrick. "And I don't know that anybody's quite ready to sell."

Nikki thought often about her parents, Ralph and JoAnna Dagnall, and admitted she had trouble imagining someone else living

~WEEDS SLOWLY OVERGROWING THE DESTROYED REMAINS OF THE DAGNALL HOME ON SOUTH BEACH BOULEVARD
Photo by Kathleen Koch

on the land where she'd grown up. "I still don't want to accept that. But I'm beginning to realize that's probably what's going to have to happen." She spoke wistfully of her girlhood on the water and how she would like the same for their children. But Nikki couldn't consider living there again or rebuilding on the lot in Jordan River Isles anytime soon. "It would still be too difficult," she said with a sigh.

"Once you've lost everything once, it's hard to build back on the same spot," agreed Patrick. "It's really hard."

"Maybe if we hadn't been in there when it all happened, maybe I'd feel differently," she said.

Still, Nikki and Patrick were settled and happy in their new life. They'd both grown and matured as a result of the ordeal they survived. All-day shopping trips or recreational outings now had less appeal than a quiet day at home with the family. "For me, it's more about not sweating the small stuff anymore. Things don't matter," Nikki said. "I used to love my wedding china. Don't have it anymore. Don't really need it. It's just, all the stuff that I loved and I wanted, I don't need that anymore. Family time is more important."

Nikki had recovered from surgery she had the year before to

~PATRICK, NIKKI, AND EMMA CLEVELAND AT THEIR HANCOCK COUNTY HOME THIRTEEN MILES INLAND
Photo by Kathleen Koch

rebuild her sinuses. "I had no openings in my sinus tracts. The normal drainage was gone. It was very painful." She worried it may have been caused by the months they lived in the FEMA trailer. The federal government in 2008 had found that in hot, humid climates the trailers emitted high levels of the gas formaldehyde, which could lead to an increased risk of cancer and respiratory illness. Hundreds of residents who claimed they were sickened were suing as a result. "I don't know if it had anything to do with it," said Nikki. "I was so grateful for the camper, I would never join the lawsuits."

Patrick had been deeply affected by having a close brush with death not just once but twice. "Sitting in a tree naked facing the storm, it's sort of hard to live a bad life after that. I wouldn't feel right. If I was kept here, there must be a reason, so I better get to it. I should accomplish something, whatever that may be."

The belief that God had allowed him a second chance gave the veterinarian faith he would beat cancer. "The whole time during that, I thought to myself, *Why would I be spared and then die two years later?* I felt like I would get through it, that there was more to come in my life."

As we said goodbye, our conversation turned to the nearby town. As content as the couple was, Bay St. Louis would always be home. "The town was so great. It was so peaceful," Nikki said. She smiled gently and hinted at an eventual return. "Maybe our family could get that back. Maybe one day."

My high-school classmate Diane Bourgeois, who had also moved into a home in northern Hancock County, had found a way.

~VIEW OVER THE MARSH AND CANALS FROM DIANE AND GENE BOURGEOIS'S FISHING CAMP
Photo by Kathleen Koch

She and her husband, Gene, bought a fishing camp in Bay St. Louis on a canal off the Jordan River to use on weekends. Her entire life, Diane had lived within a block of the bay, and she realized it was something she needed. "There's just something about living near the water. It gets in your soul," she said as we stood on her porch overlooking the marsh and the canal beyond. The sun was rising, and a soft mist drifted off the water. Diane insisted she had no emotional ties to her temporary home. "It's a place to come kind of be a part of the Bay again without having to live here full-time. Because I couldn't, I couldn't do that. I couldn't take it physically, emotionally, take the pain. And I will run fast when the next storm comes. If I lose it, I lose it. There's not that attachment."

Though many areas looked normal again, Diane noted that the once-lush forests still bore testimony to Katrina's destructive force. "There are spots, you know, that break your heart—the devastated tree lines and the broken sticks that used to be gorgeous trees. That's the part that's hard," she said. "You look at the trees that are broken in two. That's gonna take twenty, thirty, forty years for that to recover. That doesn't happen overnight."

In fact, a 2007 study found an estimated 320 million trees had been destroyed by Hurricane Katrina. The brutally amputated trunks were everywhere. Climbing vines covered many of them, as though the forest itself was trying to hide their naked ugliness.

As surprised as I was to see Diane back in Bay St. Louis, I was stunned to find the Goodfellow family had also returned to the Gulf

~Hurricane-damaged woods in Bay St. Louis
Photo by Kathleen Koch

Coast. Darla had been adamant that she and the children wouldn't risk losing everything again. But they'd never felt like they fit in up in Columbus. "We were outsiders, and it was very evident that we were never going be accepted," said Darla. "It wasn't home. We missed family. We missed friends."

Keith had joined a group OB/GYN practice in Gulfport, and the family had bought a home there in a high-elevation neighborhood that suffered no water damage during Katrina. The kids were back in school and making new friends. Keith relished fishing the waters of the Mississippi Sound again and kept his boat in Bay St. Louis. "We get over there quite a bit. To me, it's just like a different neighborhood."

They still owned their property in Diamondhead, where only three of their fifteen neighbors had rebuilt. The Goodfellows were waiting to see if the federal government would include the area in the new, scaled-back buyout program announced in February. The Corps of Engineers now planned to offer voluntary buyouts to just two thousand coastal residents, instead of the seventeen thousand proposed in 2007. That plan had been scrapped over concerns it would destroy the Mississippi Gulf Coast economy.

Keith was glad to see a growing number of friends and patients moving back to the area as well. He'd recently run into the elderly woman who had needed the gynecological procedure just days after the hurricane. "She told me that she had told a friend who was in touch with one of these relief agencies what I did. And that woman was the one who sent the three guys over to help me clear out my office. I didn't know where they came from, how they got there. I finally found out!"

Secret gestures of kindness. Strangers helping strangers. As countless and inspiring as such stories were, Keith said Katrina also taught him a hard lesson: "Take nothing for granted. I know at this point in one day I could be a homeless person and struggling to support my family. You just never know. No matter how well you plan, you never know."

Darla still struggled with anything that smacked of putting down roots, from buying furniture to hanging pictures on the wall. "I wonder, am I going to have to take it down again? Am I going to lose it?" She laughed when sharing the story of how after nine months of sleeping on an air mattress, she had finally relented and let Keith buy a bed. "Finally, he walked into a store and said, 'What about that one?' And I said okay. So he bought the biggest, most obnoxious, tallest bed that you've ever seen in your life."

"I was ready to sleep in a real bed," chuckled Keith.

I was relieved to see the healing that both Diane and the Goodfellows had experienced. But I was saddened to learn that some longtime residents who'd stuck it out and repaired their homes were now, four years later, considering leaving.

"I would like to move now. If houses would sell, I'd want to move away from the water," stated Danielle Strong, her blue eyes flashing. The back-to-back evacuations in 2008 for Hurricanes Gustav and Ike had been too much for her. "I want to be able to, when there's a hurricane, not worry. Not have to be out of my house. I want to be able to stay at my house and not have to pack everything up. I'm just wore out."

That was a difficult admission because the Strongs had redecorated and expanded their one-story house on Pine Drive. It looked like a model home inside and out, the river birch they planted in the front yard after the storm now double its original size.

Monte said that if they moved, they'd stay nearby. After all, he still had his job as a firefighter in Bay St. Louis and also now occasionally helped out at the firehouse north of I-10 in Diamondhead. At both stations, Monte nervously noted the lack of all-terrain vehicles and Jet Skis, airboats, and other emergency watercraft. "I still feel like today that the city is not where they need to be as far as preparations for another storm like Katrina."

The father of three acknowledged he took things more seriously since the hurricane. The family also spent more time in church. His relationship with Danielle remained strong to the point that he even helped her teach Bible school once a month. "It's just something, you know, I didn't think I would ever do." As we talked, I realized the tension I used to see in his face had vanished. Monte, like many of my friends in Bay St. Louis, now seemed relaxed and happy.

Danielle agreed her faith had helped get her through. Still, she didn't want to be tested again. "I remember that feeling of not being able to process anything. Being mush. I couldn't be rational." Gone was the defiant young woman who was never bothered by hurricanes.

Sixty-nine-year-old Linda Kidd had lived in Bay St. Louis since she was in high school. But the one-two punch of Hurricanes Gustav and Ike had her reeling, too. Both storms had damaged the lower level of Linda and Tommy's freshly repaired home on the bayou. "It just scared Linda to the point where she was ready to leave. The effect four years down the road is as bad as the immediate shock after," said Tommy. "If we have anything else like that again, I'm hopin' the real-estate market will be back, 'cause I don't think I can keep her there."

The couple now had a granddaughter living with her parents outside Atlanta. "Linda would move to Roswell to be near that baby girl in a minute," Tommy said.

"And leave the Bay?" I asked.

"I wouldn't. But she would."

I met up with Tommy on Main Street, where he was helping a resident figure out how to remove the remains of a massive hurricane-damaged tree that had finally toppled. Tommy was leading Bay St. Louis's final cleanup after Katrina, targeting everything from abandoned homes to forests and local waterways. He was disappointed it wasn't progressing more quickly and that the economic downturn had slowed the town's recovery. Still, he was a firm believer Bay St. Louis would eventually get there. "It's fun to me to see the changes and the improvements and see what the future's gonna hold. There's potential for this to be the happy, fun place it was eight or ten years ago," Tommy said. "I think we're still not fully discovered yet. I've always said Bay St. Louis was one of the best-kept secrets in the country."

My friends David and Angelyn Treutel still operated their independent insurance business out of rental space on Highway 90. Though the yellow Acadian-style building they owned downtown had been repaired, it was difficult for customers to access until Beach Boulevard was complete.

But business was going well, and the couple had developed side careers as speakers on dealing with disaster. "We're perceived by

our industry as the poster children for the right way independent agents are supposed to handle and serve their clients," said David. "There's very few people that have the experience we have. Katrina gave us a national forum that we never would have gotten." Since the 2005 hurricane, the two had spoken to audiences in more than twenty states and testified twice before Congress on the need for insurance reform.

Though repairs on their one-story white-brick home had been done for more than a year, the empty nesters had furnished only the master bedroom and the living room. "We're okay with that. We just got tired of buying stuff. It makes it easier to circulate," David said with a grin.

As much as the town had suffered and lost, David remained excited about what it was becoming. "We've had—the city, the officials, the leaders—the chance to reshape this town unlike we would ever have had the opportunity were it not for a disaster of this magnitude. We've been able to do things from the grass roots up. When all the dust settles, there'll be a lot of positive things that will outlive most of us here today. It'll show that there were resilient people that built the city back, and built it back in a better way than it might've evolved on its own."

Congressman Gene Taylor welcomed the progress along the

Mississippi Gulf Coast that he and others had fought for long and hard. But insurance rates had gotten so high and so many insurance companies had pulled out that the number of residents turning to the insurer of last resort—the state wind pool—had nearly tripled. "Until insurance gets affordable again, you will have communities with virtually brand-new utilities, and people can't afford to live there. You got water lines, sewer lines, nice streets going to vacant lots that people can't afford to live on," he said.

Gene was disappointed that the Obama administration would not support his proposal to allow homeowners to buy both wind and flood insurance from the federal government. "I remain convinced that the nation can do it and charge less than what the private sector is charging," he said. The bill that passed the House overwhelmingly in 2007 was never acted on by the Senate and died. So Gene was pushing for a new House vote, though the Senate still had little interest in tackling insurance reform, particularly in an election year.

Gene and his wife, Margaret, were happy in their new, small two-bedroom home. It rose a full twenty-five feet above sea level, so high that standing on the front veranda was like being perched in a tree house. The interior had the bright, fresh feel of a beach cottage, and the décor was crisp and spare. "I just don't have a desire to own as many things as we did before," Gene said. "I don't want to lose it again. I really do still look at things and imagine what they would look like under three or four inches of mud and all beat up."

Two of their most precious possessions sat on a coffee table in front of the couch. One was a carved mahogany sea turtle Gene had been given by a Panamanian Indian chief during an Armed Services Committee trip to Central America. He'd unearthed it while clearing debris from their property with a backhoe. But even more astounding was a Waterford Crystal Capitol dome his parents had given him the day he was elected to Congress in 1989. Gene struck it with a shovel months after the hurricane as he dug a trench for a water line. "I thought it was an old brick. I just couldn't believe it. It was unscathed! How in the heck that thing did not get destroyed is just beyond comprehension."

I asked Margaret if it was a challenge to maintain their scaled-back lifestyle. After all, Gene was a congressman and Washington was a city that revolved around wealth and power. "There's got to be pressure, right? Certain expectations?"

"I kind of feel free of those worries. You kind of feel like you know something," she said. "It is hard sometimes when people don't get it. And you don't expect them to, in a way. It's kind of sad that a lot of people spend their lives chasing things that don't really have a lot of meaning."

I didn't have to be a reporter to see the pattern. People had been deeply changed by their Katrina journey—the majority for the better, amazing as it seemed. And it wasn't just adrenaline-driven optimism. Along with the pain and suffering while surviving, digging out, and rebuilding had come profound personal growth.

That applied to even those fortunate few whose homes were undamaged. My middle-school friend Pat Kergosien said that rather than be paralyzed by survivor's guilt, he got busy helping those who had lost it all. "My line is, I think the Lord saved our house so we could be out helpin' doing other stuff." That included rebuilding his office in Gulfport and Our Lady Academy, the small private school his three daughters attended. It was not the sort of thing Pat was normally into. "I was not someone who volunteered and joined things and got all involved," he said. "That's totally against my nature. I was put in the position where I needed to be at the time."

~GENE AND MARGARET
TAYLOR'S NEW HOME ON
NORTH BEACH BOULEVARD
Photo by Kathleen Koch

In fact, Hurricane Katrina seemed to reveal people's true natures. "Some you thought would do very, very well and you would go into battle with fell apart. Other people that you didn't give the time of day to were just straight and steady and strong," said Pat. "It didn't have to do with how much money they had, where they lived, if they were native to Bay St. Louis or just moved here recently. It was the character of the person."

As much as the people were tested, the leaders of the towns bore the heaviest burden. I met Waveland mayor Tommy Longo in his temporary office. Construction of a new city hall at the site of the old one on Coleman Avenue wasn't due to begin until 2010. On the wall hung a tattered flag that had flown over Waveland four years earlier when Katrina barreled ashore.

Tommy joked that he had taken a beating, too. "I'm certainly weathered and worn. I didn't have a gray hair there," he laughed, pulling off his trademark baseball cap and showing me the gray that speckled his dark locks. It dominated his beard, too. "I've been through the experiences of ten lifetimes in the last four years—and the city has, too."

Tommy seemed now to be at peace with the deaths of the half-dozen residents who had refused to heed his warning to evacuate. He told me how their families had come to him asking about their states of mind, since he had been the last person to see them alive. "I told them that they were very happy and they were in a great space and, you know, made a decision that turned out to be bad." He shook his head. It was something he never wanted to experience again. "I wish there was a way that legally we could force people to leave when they're in harm's way. We just can't. Thank God the majority did."

The man who at the tender age of twelve had watched his then-mayor father organize the post-Camille rebuilding of Waveland was proud of how his staff and citizens had rallied this time. "We have come so far. There's never been a road map for what we've had to do here. We've had to replace an entire city. It has been a real test of our fortitude. It's been a real slog. It's draining. And it still goes on today. People don't realize, you know, Katrina's not over for a lot of people."

~Jan and Eddie Favre in front of their home on Main Street
Photo by Kathleen Koch

I found it hard to believe that for the jovial captain at the helm of Bay St. Louis's recovery, it was over. Mayor Eddie Favre had decided after twenty years not to run for reelection. He and his wife, Jan, were out of the trailer and nearly done refurbishing a house on Main Street that used to belong to his aunt. "The last four years have taken a toll. I just needed a break," he said. Eddie, still wearing shorts, said he had always told residents he never intended to be mayor for life. "I would tell 'em, 'If it ever comes to the point I don't have everything to give, I don't have the right to ask you to put me back in office.' "

Looking back over the last four years, the ever-upbeat Eddie insisted on counting his blessings. First was his city staff. "From the very beginnin', these folks, they lost everything, too. But they put it all aside and were committed to puttin' the city first. And that's what they did." Then came the resourceful citizens who after the hurricane opened impromptu shelters and started taking care of one another. "Those people just jumped in and did the job that needed to be done 'cause there wasn't any Red Cross, MEMA, FEMA, Salvation Army for days and days and weeks in some cases. They jumped in and did what they needed to do."

Eddie said he wished the town had been better prepared to coordinate the aid that came pouring in from individuals, organizations, and cities across the country. "In the early stages, we had no control over it. We didn't have anything set up for 'em to bring it to." Some donations ended up ruined by the elements or pilfered by looters until enormous tents and a reliable distribution system were set up. Most of that was organized by volunteer groups including CityTeam, which had recently pulled out after three and a half years helping feed, clothe, and rebuild homes for thousands of county residents. "It was amazing, the help. And it's still coming, that's the thing," said the former mayor.

His only disappointment was how long it had taken to fix things like the still-unfinished Beach Boulevard. "Four years later, it's still not done. It's not like you're building a space rocket," he said with frustration. "We did everything we could to coordinate matters. It's like everything under the sun happened to delay the project." Perhaps the biggest hurdle was that the city, the county, and five state and federal agencies involved in reconstructing the road and the sea wall had to sign off on every decision. Still, Eddie was gratified to see the many municipal projects now under way. "It's just the satisfaction of knowing that so much good came from such a horrible disaster."

Eddie, like most people I talked to, believed he, too, had been changed for the better. "You really learn how to put things in perspective. Anything that we ever had, we lost. But we still have the most important thing. And that's each other." He smiled at Jan, whom he'd married a year and a half after the storm.

Then they did something astonishing—waxed nostalgic about the early months after Katrina. "It was amazing. It really was," Eddie said of the spirit that prevailed, everyone sharing what they had, taking care of neighbors, and living simply, just getting through one day at a time. "It would be nice to reclaim some of that patience and understanding. I wish we could go back to it."

"I feel bad saying it, but I really miss it," agreed Jan. "We were all so close. I miss it."

As I left the two, I marveled at their ability to focus on the upside. Cynics might call them Pollyannas, but it was their way of dealing with what the town had suffered. Everyone seemed to have found their own coping mechanisms.

Lydia Schultz, too, had made it through to a better place. She was now married to a wonderful man from Waveland. They were refurbishing an Acadian shotgun-style home in Picayune that they jokingly called "the shack." "For someone who wanted nothing after the storm, nesting feels good," she admitted when we met for coffee. "I walk in the house every day and I'm so grateful."

She didn't come back to Bay St. Louis often. It was still too hard. "We drove down a couple weeks ago, and I still drive with my mouth open. Four years and I'm still shocked. It's still amazing. It's a horrible amazing. People away from here have no clue." Bay St. Louis was no longer the town she knew. Still, Lydia set her jaw determinedly and suggested maybe one day she would make peace with what was left. "I know that the only constant in life is change. That's the only truth."

As we said goodbye, I studied her face. I noted a strength and resolve that were new, yet somehow familiar. Then I realized I'd seen them all week. This was the new Katrina face.

I pulled up at Our Lady of the Gulf Church. I hadn't attended mass there since it was repaired. In fact, other than holidays, I hadn't been to church in years. I was glad Father Tracey was in Ireland on his annual visit to his family. I was afraid his wise, gentle eyes would settle on me and see the void and doubt that still remained.

I went in and knelt in a side pew. And I began to reflect on how so many had managed to find a silver lining in Katrina. Perhaps I could, too.

~Lydia Schultz and Dennis White
Photo by Kathleen Koch

Like the people of Bay St. Louis, I was stronger and more resilient. I'd forged new bonds with old friends and formed countless
new relationships with many either impacted by the storm or motivated to help. The thousands of volunteers had given me new faith
in the generosity of mankind. Lydia and I had become extremely
close. I now jokingly called her my "second mom." After seeing pov-
erty and deprivation inflicted on people I knew, I had become active
in helping the poor in ways I never had before. I now understood
that no matter how insurmountable a problem may seem, determined individuals coming together could begin to set things right.

But perhaps most of all, Hurricane Katrina brought me home.
When I moved from Mississippi to Washington, D.C., I had revert-
ed to the familiar pattern of my childhood—pack up and never look
back. Though I had made a handful of visits to the Gulf Coast, I
became immersed in my family and job. Now, I truly saw how this
remarkable town had shaped who I was. I had reconnected. I appreciated Bay St. Louis as never before, the innate goodness of the
people surpassed only by their fortitude and determination in the
face of overwhelming odds.

Maybe I had something to be thankful for. Maybe I could trust
again. Perhaps, as the residents so often said, I was blessed. At that
moment, I let go of the anger and resentment and the conviction
that I had been toiling alone, forgotten and betrayed by a once-mer-
ciful God. I felt a rare calm. And as I left the church, I wondered if
this was the end of my Katrina journey.

Three days later, a publisher contacted me asking to see more
of the manuscript I'd started writing about Bay St. Louis. Nine days
after that, I had an offer to publish it.

As I typed away at my keyboard, Mississippi's Katrina story
continued playing out with drama and consequence. On October 8,
the Mississippi Supreme Court handed down a landmark decision
that validated Judge L. T. Senter, Jr's early rulings that hurricane
wind damage was a covered loss for which insurers must compen-
sate homeowners, even when storm surge contributed to the damage. No longer would homeowners be told that they would not be
compensated for the destruction wrought by hours of devastating
winds simply because water washed over their property afterward.

But more than four years after the hurricane, it was unclear how many residents would act on the ruling, since most had already settled with their insurance companies.

Then, a week later, President Barack Obama made good on his campaign promise to visit the areas ravaged by Hurricane Katrina. His only stop? New Orleans. I was shocked and disappointed. While the previous administration had certainly mishandled the hurricane response, President Bush made a point of visiting Mississippi on every trip to New Orleans. Bush regularly referred to the Mississippi Gulf Coast as "Ground Zero," since it was in Katrina's deadly northeast quadrant and had taken the brunt of the hurricane. Meanwhile, everything from an independent 2006 investigation to recent court rulings had concluded that the Louisiana levee breaches were a preventable failure of human engineering, and that New Orleans' main levees were never overtopped by Katrina's floodwaters.

Editors of the Biloxi-Gulfport *Sun Herald* and advocacy groups involved in the Mississippi recovery effort asked the president to reconsider and encouraged residents to call, e-mail, and write the White House, senators, and congressmen expressing their dismay. Congressman Gene Taylor sent President Obama a sharp five-page letter that began by pointing out he had yet to visit the Mississippi Gulf Coast since the hurricane.

The White House responded that the Obama administration had invested critical resources in Mississippi's rebuilding and recovery efforts. "I don't think this is about rhetoric. I think this is about results and action," said Press Secretary Robert Gibbs. Press officials added that by cutting through red tape and improving coordination between federal and local agencies, the Obama administration had cleared at least seventy-five projects that were in dispute in Louisiana and Mississippi.

But I noted that the White House never explained *why* President Obama hadn't gone to Mississippi. As a reporter who had covered the White House, I knew that myriad factors came into play, among them a tight schedule. The president was due to speak at a Democratic fund-raiser in California after his New Orleans stops. And the administration may have had political concerns. The debate over health care reform was turning nasty, so savvy presidential handlers would wisely avoid any venue where protestors might appear.

On the Mississippi Gulf Coast, residents were less stung by the presidential rebuff than worried about its consequences. President Obama's actions reinforced the prevailing national misperception that only New Orleans had been hit by Hurricane Katrina. The growing fear was that the history books would eventually reflect that fallacy and that Mississippi's courageous struggle to rebuild would be forgotten.

On my most recent flight south, my seatmate had been from New Orleans. I asked the well-dressed African American woman in her early fifties if residents were aware how Mississippians resented all the attention that went to the flooded city.

With a sad chuckle, she responded, "Well, did you know we sat here saddled with this mayor and governor who couldn't do anything right and looked over at Mississippi, wondering how you were putting things back together so fast? We were jealous of you!"

I was floored. I had never considered how things looked from the other side of the state line. Both areas were bruised and battered. Maybe it was time to lose the envy and simply celebrate our mutual progress down the long road to recovery.

I found increasing inspiration as I chronicled Bay St. Louis's story. When I flew to Mississippi in mid-November, my seatmate was a resident who had known my family and run a local debris removal operation after the hurricane. Brian Logan smiled knowingly when I shared my astonishment at the statues of Jesus and Mary throughout town that survived the storm. "We saw a lot of that," he responded.

Brian described how, time after time, teams went onto property to demolish homes and found religious pictures and artifacts intact. "We'd go inside, the rest of the house was trashed, just debris all over the place. And the statues would still be standing. They were just clean, sittin' there. It was amazing. And it wasn't just one or two. It was probably fifty to a hundred that we would see that were like this. It was pretty overwhelming."

Brian said he and the others talked about their miraculous finds every morning before they went out on the day's job. "I think it touched a lot of people. It was pretty powerful. It shows you that

~ONE OF THE MANY UNDAMAGED RELIGIOUS STATUES SPOTTED AT
MISSISSIPPI HOMES RUINED BY HURRICANE KATRINA
Photo by Mark Proulx

there really is a God. There was no other explanation."

I was on the Gulf Coast to watch my brother's three youngest children. Mark and his family had recently moved back to Mississippi and were thrilled to be home. But his mother-in-law had just passed away, so he, his wife, and his oldest daughter were flying to Wisconsin for the funeral. While I was back, I also hoped to talk with two Bay St. Louis friends I had missed on my last visit.

Diane Frederick was waiting for me in the yard of her brick rancher when I pulled up. Ironically, the hardworking housekeeper had moved back into her hurricane-damaged home faster than anyone I knew. Volunteers had completed the repairs in ten months, expanding the home by eight hundred square feet to accommodate the wheelchair of her husband, Allan. Unfortunately, he never saw it. Allan died just two days before Katrina's first anniversary.

"I am doing good. I am blessed," said Diane, giving me a hug and showing me into the house. It was spotless, of course, the décor warm and welcoming. Because she had the room, she'd taken in her five-year-old granddaughter and her twenty-eight-year-old daughter, Nikki, who had diabetes and was on dialysis. She had given them the master suite while she slept in the tiny guest room across from her teenage daughter, Cookie.

"I believe that for a reason the storm came through here. It made us see, look at things differently," Diane said. "It made us know that God is still here." The waves of volunteers, she insisted, were proof. "They came with open hearts and open minds and left their families and came here to help us. And to me, that is true, true brotherly love."

Diane wasn't afraid of losing it all again. "If I have to start all over with a matchbox, I will stay right here in Bay St. Louis. There is no place like it. This is a place you can raise your children in. If you want to leave your door open, you can leave your door open. If somebody is in need, everybody comes through with a helping hand. This is home."

I could think of no better definition.

My next stop was the newly rebuilt rectory. I barely opened my mouth before Father Tracey remarked on the transformative effect of the hurricane. "It brought things out in people—gifts, strengths that they never realized they had. I know it did in me personally."

"Like what?"

"A courage. A faith. A hope. God putting you in a place that you were meant to be."

~FATHER MICHAEL TRACEY
OUTSIDE THE NEWLY
CONSTRUCTED RECTORY AT
OUR LADY OF THE GULF CHURCH
Photo by Kathleen Koch

As we talked, I wondered if this was all meant to be. The hurricane. The losses and deaths. The struggles and suffering. The doubt. And finally, the acceptance and spiritual rebirth.

I had promised to take my nephews to the beach while their sister was at swim practice, so I left to pick them up, and we headed toward the water. So many No Trespassing signs dotted Beach Boulevard that I took a chance and steered the SUV up my old driveway. We climbed the steps to the house and knocked. A teenage boy answered.

"Hi! I used to live here, and I was wondering if I could park in your driveway while I take my nephews down to the beach."

"Sure," he said "Hang on a sec. My mom's been wanting to meet you."

A brunette in her forties appeared behind him and ushered us in. "I'm Robin Riviere. And this is my husband, George. You already met our son, George Jr."

The boys wandered back to the teenager's room to play video games while Robin and George showed me the house. "You'll like this," said George, pointing to a plaque hanging next to the wet bar. "If you're lucky enough to live in Bay St. Louis, you're lucky enough," it read.

They told me how they'd both grown up in Louisiana but always loved vacationing in the Bay. Robin's father had bought our old brick house for his children and grandchildren to use on weekends. He later rented it out to a friend. But after the hurricane when he erected the modest steel home in its place, the others stopped coming. So Robin and George bought the house. At first, Robin and their son lived here, returning to Louisiana on weekends. The past summer, they had finally sold their home in Covington and moved in full-time.

"This sounds really hokey, but this is the first place that I just feel like it's where I'm supposed to be," said Robin. "This is home. This is my heart."

She described being so awed by the incredible panoply of colors as the sun rose over the bay that she snapped a photo of it every morning. "You wake up and get to look at that every day! It's too beautiful. I had to start taking pictures."

"We might make a collage out of all the different sunrises," suggested George with a smile.

Over Robin's shoulder, I saw the sturdy branches of the live oaks silhouetted against the brilliant slices of crimson clouds cutting across the afternoon sky. It was the view I used to have from my bedroom window. It felt so good to be back.

I'd promised my nephews time on the beach, so I collected the boys. As we walked down the stairs with Robin and George, I noticed the barbecue pit my dad and brother had built from the brick remains of the house destroyed by Hurricane Camille. Stacked neatly next to it were bricks from our old home.

"Robin, you saved all those! What are you going to do with them?"

"Do a walkway. Or put 'em in a fireplace or something," she said, eyeing the stack. "I'm not getting rid of them. That's what's left. So I'm going to do something."

I felt reassured. For the first time since my family left, this wasn't just a weekend getaway or a simple beach rental. A family owned it, lived here, and cherished the property as we had. It felt right, like it was meant to be.

George spoke up. "You know, the next time you're here, you come stay with us. This is your home, too."

The unexpected offer was like dropping anchor. I was no longer adrift. "Thank you," I replied, hugging him tightly. "Now I don't feel so much like I've lost something, but that I've gained."

My fair-haired nephews and I walked across the long front yard toward the beach. I told Joshua and Jeremy that their daddy and I had grown up in a brick house that used to be right here before Katrina knocked it down.

Seven-year-old Jeremy looked up at me with his enormous blue eyes and asked, "Why did God make the Hurricane Katrina come?"

It was the question I had been asking since August 29, 2005. It was the question that had given me nightmares. It was the question that had shattered my faith. It was the question that had propelled me on a quest to understand how the hurricane affected the people of my town, how it changed them and those who came to

~Jeremy and Joshua Koch on the beach in Bay St. Louis
Photo by Kathleen Koch

Mississippi to help them. If I could find the elusive answer, maybe I could find peace.

But walking down the "steps to nowhere" left after the storm, I knew I needed an answer a child could understand. And as I tried to explain, it dawned on me that maybe the answer was simple. "I don't think God made the hurricane come. God doesn't want to hurt people or their pets or destroy their houses and ruin their things, all their toys. And some people did die in the storm—people I knew. I think God let the hurricane come, let nature follow its course. And then we were supposed to learn from it. Learn how to help each other. Learn what was important."

We held hands and dashed across the street to the beach. The answer seemed to satisfy him. And in that place where it all started, it finally satisfied me. We walked up and down the beach for hours collecting shells, seaweed, and driftwood as the sun slipped below the horizon and the aqua sky faded to a golden amber.

Author's Note

    While the majority of this book is based on events I witnessed and experienced, some occurred when I wasn't present. My accounts of those events and the quotations included are based on the memories of those who were present. They may not be perfect, just as my own memories may not. But it is our best effort to get as close to the truth as possible.

    I make liberal use of e-mails throughout the book. Occasionally, they have been edited for length as well as style and grammar.

A portion of the proceeds from this book will be donated to
Pneuma Winds of Hope and LESM Coast Recovery Camps,
two nonprofit groups working on the
Katrina recovery effort in Bay St. Louis.

Acknowledgments

Thanks to Kevin Corke and Greg Kelly for telling me I needed to write a book. Thanks to Cliff Hackel for noting my early floundering attempts and steering me to his wife, Kerry Hannon, to whom I am indebted for patiently guiding me through the book-proposal process. Thanks to Linda Konner, my agent, for being a relentless advocate and skilled negotiator. Thanks to John F. Blair, Publisher, for believing in this project as much as I do. Thanks to my producers Beth Hall, Emily Probst, Janet Rodriguez, Brian Rokus, and Peter Tedeschi for joining me on this journey and for their help as I wrote the book. Thanks to CNN, whose generous support throughout the process made this book possible. Thanks to Anderson Cooper for finding time during his heroic coverage of the Haiti earthquake to write the foreword. Thanks to Kim Abbott, Nancy Lamberton, and Martha Townes for reading the early versions and giving sage critiques. Thanks to Margaret Balliet, Tom Bentz, Chuck Carr, Ken Cedeno, Mimi Heitzmann, Larry Keith, Carolyn Kergosien, Gerri Koch, Mary Lou Koch, Alec Miran, Skip Nocciolo, Mark Proulx, Janet Rodriguez, Brian Rokus, Chris Stasny, and John Wilkerson for their invaluable contributions to the photography. Thanks to Kim Abbott, Mark Elliott, and Beth Lewandowski for their help managing publicity and designing my website. Thanks to Rich Lippmann for his wise insights into the publishing world. Thanks to my parents, siblings, and friends, whose enthusiastic support and encouragement kept me going. But most of all, thanks to my husband, Rick McNaney, and my daughters, Kaitlyn and Kara, for their help, understanding, and patience as I undertook the hardest thing I've ever done.

Index

Cuevas, Connie, 176
Cuevas, Mike, 238, 239
Cuevas, Savannah, 176
Currie, Sheila, 73, 77

D'Angelo, Mia Belle, 209
D'Angelo, Steve, 209
D'Iberville, Miss., 308
Da Beach House, 54
Daddy O's, 37, 171, 201
Dagnall, Jennifer (Nikki's sister), 113
Dagnall, JoAnna, 25, 26, 30, 31, 49, 113, 143, 199, 236, 260, 323
Dagnall, Ralph, 25, 26, 30, 31, 49, 113, 143, 199, 236, 260, 323
Dagnalls, The, 153, 163
Daniel's Restaurant, 289
Dantagnan house, 47
Davis, Geena, 128
Davis, Jefferson, 239
Davis, Willie, 313
De La Rosa, Gil, 17, 63, 72, 72, 73, 86, 87, 93
De Montluzin home, 8
Dedeaux, Casey Maria, 250
Department of Education, 279
Diamondhead, Miss., 79, 80, 118, 119, 213, 244, 327, 328
Dijon, France, 164
Disaster Corps, 186, 187, 189, 196
Doctor Zhivago, 86
Drackett, Peter, 126
Dunbar Avenue, 57, 187, 330

Eckerd, 69
Edmond-Fahey Funeral Home, 254
Education Department, 161
Edwards, Debra, 89
Edwards, Ed, 260
Egan compound, 44
Emergency Operations Center (EOC), 68, 69, 113, 149, 203, 272
English, Judee, 298, 299
Eppert, Crystal, 61
Eppert, Paul, 61
Erector Set, 292
Escambia County, 213
Espy Street, 65
Esters Boulevard, 228
Europe, 308
Evans, Janelle, 140
Evans, Mariah, 33

Evans, Shanell, 33
Evans, Shannon, 24, 33, 34, 139, 140, 157, 248

Fahey, Edmund, 112, 113
Fallon, Linda, 296
Fantastic Stranger, 169
FastTrac, 226
Favre, Brett, 239
Favre, Eddie: author's dream, 253; before Katrina, 19, 20; during Katrina, 35; Government buyouts, 302; Hurricane Gustav, 312; insurance claim, 200; living conditions, 114, 158, 174; looting, 68, 69; mayoral duties after Katrina, 175; new home, 259, 334; President Bush's speech, 210; rebuilding, 146, 147, 203, 239, 257, 335; returning residents, 292; shorts, 209, 272; spirit of citizens, 148; surveying damage, 47, 49, 256; Thanksgiving, 192, 194
Favre, Jan, 334, 335
Favre, Karen, 47
Favre, Mike, 35
Federal Courthouse, 73
Federal Emergency Management Agency (FEMA): applying for trailers, 140; blue tarps, 208, 322; David Paulison, 308; debris rule, 190, 191; flood maps, 199; food deliveries, 112; identifying properties, 127; leaving, 254; lines, 155; mistakes, 158; moving out of trailer, 258; rebuilding schools, 161; school portables, 160, 256, 268, 318; sickness caused by trailers, 325; slow response, 87, 101, 151, 334; trailers arriving, 156, 157; trailer Christmas decorations, 198; trailer life, 183, 186, 195, 211, 232, 237, 242, 299, 300, 301; Troy Buck (aide to Mayor Farve), 150; waiting for trailers, 138, 166, 174, 203, 214
FedEx, 278
Fiddler on the Roof, 218
5th Avenue, 73
Fifth Circuit Court of Appeals, 303
Filingame, 322
Fire Dog Saloon, 144, 261
First Baptist Church (Long Beach, Miss.), 65, 66
First Book, 279

is, 213; second anniversary, 290, 300; 228 area code, 79; volunteers, 195, 195; weather conditions, 166; writing book, 337, 339
Missy (David Treutel's sister) 78, 130, 306
Mobile Bay, 38
Mobile, Ala., 16, 17, 28, 29, 38, 40, 57, 101, 107, 130, 135, 157, 165, 169, 214, 298, 306
Monica (Mick's cousin), 77
Monie, Rickie, 217
Monroeville, Ala., 163
Monterey, Calif., 239
Montgomery County Police Department, 132
Morrell Foundation, 203
Morris, Teddy, 168
Mother Nature, 223
Mother Teresa, 197
Mount Pleasant, S.C., 184
Murphy, Jim, 76
Murphy, Nancy Belle, 55
Murray, Kenny, 11, 16, 17, 38, 39

Nagasaki, 97
NASA, 8, 22, 55
Nashville, Tenn., 175
National Guard, 78, 112, 140, 146, 156, 179
National Guardsmen, 92, 175
National Hurricane Center, 15
National Public Radio, 244
Nationwide Insurance, 247, 303
NBC Nightly News, 14
Neiswenter, Charlie, 39, 107
Nereids Parade, 221
Nevada, 279
New England, 314
New Hampshire, 226, 227
New Jersey, 241
New Orleans: author's drive through, 218; Barack Obama, 290, 338, 339; Bay St. Louis in relation to, 9; broken levees, 40, 41; Bush's visit, 208; CNN Gulf Coast bureau, 164; evacuees, 123, 124, 248; fishing camps, 292; founding of, 11; forgetting, 267; Hurricane Gustav, 310; Katrina landfall, 28, 39; Kenny Murray, 16, 17; looting, 60; Mardi Gras, 227; media focus on, 125, 126, 207, 244; reporters in, 102

New Orleans' Ninth Ward, 216
New Waveland Café and Clinic, 156
New Year's Eve, 209
New York, 222, 278, 279
New York City, 239
Nicholson Avenue, 89, 97, 98, 130, 208, 320, 321
Nick (dog), 71
No More Tears in Heaven, 169
NOAA, 101
Nocciolo, Skip, 223
North Bay Elementary School, 141, 177, 178, 180, 183, 241, 256, 279, 318
North Beach Boulevard, 19, 44, 45, 48, 114, 161, 201, 294, 332
North Canton, Ohio, 239
North Carolina, 227
North Second Street, 75, 104, 105
Notter, Richard, 65, 66, 68

Oak Boulevard, 255
Obama Administration, 331, 338
Obama, Barack, 290, 338, 339
Ocean Springs, Miss., 40, 74, 78, 80, 107, 109, 132, 194, 195
Ogdens, The, 88
Ogden house, 99
Oklahoma, 279
Old Spanish Trail, 70, 168
129th Army Band, 175
Online News Association, 270
Oregon, 187, 279
Oreo (cat), 308
Orlando, Fla., 126
Our Lady Academy, 10, 186, 239, 268, 332
Our Lady of the Gulf Catholic Church, 10, 95, 144, 152, 182, 186, 204, 205, 252, 301, 336, 341

Palin, Sarah, 206
Panama City, Fla., 15, 22, 138
Panama, 122
Parks, Joy, 292
Parton, Dolly, 158
Pascagoula, Miss., 8
Pass Christian, Miss., 22, 62, 63, 64, 74, 77, 89, 126, 127, 157, 211, 239, 282, 312
Pasternak, Boris, 86
Paulison, David, 308

Waffle House, 66, 82

Wal-Mart, 61, 62, 68, 69, 77, 87, 96, 107, 108, 112, 117, 277

Walz, Mark L., 314

War Memorial, 294

War of the Worlds, 216

Warner, Bob, 192

Warsaw Rising, 222

Warsaw, Ind., 262

Washington D.C.: asking for volunteers, 195; author's move from Miss. to, 337; Brian Rokus, 159; CNN bureau, 164; Christmas toy drive, 278, 279; e-mails, 74; Education Department, 161; evacuees, 123, 124; Gene Taylor, 265, 331; Hurricane Rita, 154; leaving Miss., 102, 111, 302, 314;

Washington Post, 21

Washington Street, 24, 49, 139

Water Street, 17

Waterford Crystal Capitol dome, 331

Waveland Avenue, 233

Waveland Police Department, 171, 201

Waveland, Miss.: Bay Bridge, 288; Bay High Tigers, 175; Bush's visit, 208, 300; Daddy O's, 172; damage, 97, 117, 131, 149, 151; during Katrina, 38; Edgar Bane, 296, 297; evacuees, 57; Hurricane Gustav, 312; Killer Sharks band, 193; Krewe of Nereids, 221; lack of food, 164; lack of media coverage, 255; Lydia Schultz, 335; Mike Smith, 299; Mimi Heitzmann, 169; Tommy Longo, 26, 68, 148, 150; Troy Buck, 293, 294; relief efforts and donations, 116, 156, 203, 239, 277, 279, 333; residents, 85, 165; second anniversary, 298; Sonic, 213; Waddy LeBourgeois, 143; Wal-Mart, 96, 112

WBIR, Knoxville, Tenn., 277

Weather Channel, 309

Weiler, Frances, 141, 178, 179, 241, 256

Wells Church, 278, 309

West End restaurant, 319

Whispering Pines, 212

White House: beat, 13, 268, 276, 305; Bush's Mississippi visit, 207; Christmas toy drive, 278; Hurricane Gustav, 307; leaving CNN, 314; Lockhart, Joe, 164; Obama administration, 338; press briefing, 160, 161, 277; response to documentary, 231; staffers touring Katrina destruction, 211, 212

White, C.C., 185

White, Dennis, 336

White, Jan, 269

Wilkerson, John, 287, 301

Wilkerson, Mary Ann, 301

Williams, Bobby, 230

Williams, Bryan, 14

Williams, Lucy, 229, 230, 231, 262, 263, 264

Williams, Tennessee, 320

Williams, Tish Haas, 260, 268, 272

Willow (dog), 63, 64

Winfrey, Oprah, 273, 296

Wingate, Bob 258, 245, 265

Wingate, Kay, 245, 258, 265

Wingates, The, 246

Winn-Dixie, 69, 318

Wisconsin, 155, 340

WLOX-TV, Biloxi, Miss., 29, 83

Wolfson, Paula, 277

Wood, Natalie, 320

World War II, 97

wunderground.com, 15

Yarborough, David, 68

Young, Tom, 78

Zehner, Jane, 27

Zion National Park, 235